Choices and Change
Reflections on the Caribbean

Winston C. Dookeran
Editor

Inter-American Development Bank

The views and opinions expressed in this publication are those of the authors and do not necessarily reflect the official position of the Inter-American Development Bank.

Choices and Change: Reflections on the Caribbean

© Copyright 1996 by the Inter-American Development Bank
1300 New York Avenue, N.W.
Washington, D.C. 20577

Distributed by
The Johns Hopkins University Press
2715 North Charles Street
Baltimore, Maryland 21218-4319

Library of Congress Catalog Card Number: 96-77118
ISBN: 1-886938-07-5

*To the memory of my parents,
Sumintra and Mewalal*

Editorial Board for This Volume

Winston C. Dookeran, Editor
Steven B. Bloomfield
Alan K. Henrikson
Donald D. Halstead

Foreword

This book had its genesis in a conference, "The Caribbean: Identity, Politics, and Economy," held at Harvard University in the spring of 1994. This conference covered a wide range of research and policy issues in the political economy and international relations of the Caribbean region. Within the context of rapid and constant changes in global relations, scholarship is continually faced with new challenges, one of which is to bridge the gap between theory and practice in public policy. By meeting this challenge, the conference has enriched the current dialogue on Caribbean affairs.

The Center for International Affairs was pleased to work with the conference co-sponsors: The Fletcher School of Law and Diplomacy of Tufts University; the Inter-American Development Bank; and the North-South Center of the University of Miami. We particularly wish to acknowledge the Inter-American Development Bank for supporting these efforts from the very beginning and for contributing notable expertise and helpful advice all along the way. We hope this study will be useful to citizens of the Caribbean, as well as to policymakers, researchers, and students of the region.

> Robert D. Putnam
> Clarence Dillon Professor of International Affairs
> Director, Center for International Affairs
> Harvard University

Contents

Preface
   Steven B. Bloomfield ix

Introduction
   Winston C. Dookeran xiii

Chapter One
   Crosscurrents in Caribbean Policy Analysis
   Winston C. Dookeran 1

Chapter Two
   Adjustment and Growth in the Caribbean: The Missing Ingredient
   Nancy Birdsall 15

Chapter Three
   Caribbean Identity and Survival in a Global Economy
   Charles A.T. Skeete 25

Chapter Four
   The Future of the Caribbean Community
   Havelock R.H. Ross-Brewster 35

Chapter Five
   Caribbean Regional Cooperation and Strategic Alliances
   David E. Lewis 41

Chapter Six
   Adjustment, Reform, and Growth in the Caribbean
   Bertus J. Meins 63

Chapter Seven
   The East Asian Experience and Its Relevance to the Caribbean
   Sarath Rajapatirana 97

Chapter Eight
    The Caribbean in Economic Transition
    Elena M. Suárez 125

Chapter Nine
    Political Management of Conflict in a Multicultural Society
    Ramesh Deosaran 137

Chapter Ten
    In Search of Caribbean Basin Sociocentric Self-Interest
    Karen S. Walch 151

Chapter Eleven
    The United States, Democracy, and the Caribbean
    Richard J. Bloomfield 163

Chapter Twelve
    The Group of Three: Political Concertation, Trade Liberalization,
       and Regionalism in the Caribbean Basin
    Andrés Serbin 173

Chapter Thirteen
    The European Union and the Caribbean: Challenges Ahead
    Amos Tincani 187

Chapter Fourteen
    The United States, the Caribbean Basin, and
       the Post–Cold War International Order
    Alan K. Henrikson 197

Contributors 229

Preface

The events leading to this book's publication began in fall 1993, when Winston Dookeran came to Harvard's Center for International Affairs as a Fellow. After discussing some current political and economic issues affecting Caribbean countries, we agreed to place the Caribbean region on the Center's agenda. To examine issues of Caribbean political economy and international relations, the CFIA planned and co-sponsored this conference, "The Caribbean: Identity, Politics, and Economy," in May 1994.

The Caribbean has entered a very unsettled period. As the conference brochure stated:

> The Caribbean, now in turbulent times, is redefining its place in the world. Frontiers are being challenged. New economic borders are emerging. Political options are widening and the international agenda is being reshaped. The call is for a "new insertion" and different terms in a changed global economy, and for a renewal of democracy, where the impatient urgings of a new generation of English-, Spanish-, French- and Dutch-speaking Caribbeans must not be ignored.

Coming soon after the West Indian Commission's report, *Time for Action*, the conference addressed a wide range of political and economic issues that will influence the region's future development. The week before the conference, two events occurred that underscored the Caribbean's changing scene. First, Dominica was placed under a state of emergency after police put down a riot triggered by increases in license plate fees, and American medical students—sound familiar? —expressed concern for their own safety. A State Department official in Washington was quoted as saying that the government of Dominica seemed to have the situation under control, and that despite certain similarities to the situation in Grenada eleven years before, "history would probably not repeat itself"—and it did not.

Then, a few days later, *The New York Times* reported that the State Department would close its embassy in Grenada "in response to budgetary pressures." The State Department had decided that Grenada, which had recently resumed diplomatic relations with Cuba, "[was] of little strategic importance." According to the story, embassy functions would be transferred to Barbados, as part of a shift of State Department resources to Eastern Europe and the former Soviet Union. These events pointed to the changing politics of the region: not even Cuba could be viewed in the same terms as before.

Clearly, 'political options were widening and the international agenda was being reshaped,' but, in the United States there is a tendency to view the Caribbean region almost exclusively in terms of U.S. focus and concerns. "What will the U.S. *do* about Haiti?" or "What will the U.S. *do* in post-Castro Cuba?" we ask, as though the Caribbean existed purely in terms of global security strategies. It is of course far more: a complex, even baffling multiethnic region with deep historical ties to Europe, Asia, Africa, and the Americas. To encourage a more meaningful dialogue, the conference brought together persons with different experiences and backgrounds from the United States, Canada, Latin America, the Caribbean and Europe.

The Caribbean region is now experiencing a tremendous convergence of forces for change, both from within and without. We hope that the research and policy perspectives expressed in the various chapters will promote more insights and studies, and that this book will make an important contribution to Caribbean studies.

* * *

We would like to acknowledge the support and encouragement of Professor Robert Putnam, Director of the Center. The Inter-American Development Bank played a most important role, and we wish to thank Director of External Relations Ms. Muni Figueres for her decisive support, and Executive Director Rogelio Novey for his continuous advice. We also thank other members of the IDB, including former Executive Director for the Caribbean, Jagdish Siewrattan, for their contributions. Professor Alan Henrikson, Director of The Fletcher Roundtable for the New World Order at The Fletcher School of Law and Diplomacy of Tufts University, and Professor Anthony Bryan, Director of Caribbean Affairs at the North-South Center of the University of Miami, made significant contributions which we gratefully acknowledge.

We were pleased to have the participation of individuals from the following institutions:

- Inter-American Development Bank
- The World Bank
- The University of the West Indies
- The Caribbean Policy Group, Antigua

- The Center on American Studies, Havana
- The Venezuelan Institute of Social and Political Studies
- The Delegation of the Commission of the European Communities in Washington, D.C.
- Caribbean/Latin American Action
- The Graduate Institute of International Studies, Geneva
- U.S. universities, including the American Graduate School of International Management (Thunderbird), Brandeis University, Brown University, Florida International University, Harvard University, the Massachusetts Institute of Technology, the University of Miami, Stanford University, and Tufts University.

At the Center for International Affairs, my colleagues Yong-Joo Kim, Caílin Gallagher, and Thomas Murphy were ever patient and creative in managing the affairs of the conference. We also thank Harvard undergraduates Allison Guagliardo, Thao Ngo, and John Patterson for their willing assistance.

Steven B. Bloomfield
Director, Fellows Program
Center for International Affairs
Harvard University

Introduction

The Caribbean littoral contains scores of different states, dependencies, and territories. However, before attempting to come to grips with this extraordinarily heterogenous region, it might be worthwhile to consider which Caribbean we generally employ as our personal frame of reference. For instance, do we usually think of the English-speaking Caribbean, of the Caribbean Commonwealth? But then what of Bermuda, Florida, and the other Gulf states: are they too part of this Caribbean? Or do we think of the French-speaking Caribbean that includes Haiti and numerous other islands, as well as three of France's overseas *departements*? Perhaps it is the Dutch-speaking Caribbean that forms part of the Kingdom of the Netherlands; or the Hispanic Caribbean of Cuba, the Dominican Republic, Miami, and the North and South American nations that form the region's western boundaries. But what of the indigenous Caribbean of the Caribs and Arawaks? And what of the Caribbean diaspora, and the immigrant Caribbean, with its historical ties and cultural affinities with Africa, Europe, Asia and the East Indies, and its educational and economic links to the United States?

The point here is that, as a crossroads of world history in which East meets West along North-South economic fault lines, the Caribbean is all of these and more. It is a region that presents profound contradictions, as well as a far too often overlooked cultural, ethnic, linguistic, and religious pluralism. At the same time, despite conditions that have long divided the region and turned it inward, a greater and more unified sense of Caribbean identity is now being born. One encounters this everywhere, particularly in our music and literature; it is a yearning also expressed in the preface to the West Indian Commission's report, *Time for Action:*

> We the diverse people of scattered islands and mainland countries plucked from far continents by cruel history, draw strength from our variety of race and culture and place of origin...Historical forces and the Caribbean Sea have divided us; yet unfolding history and the same Sea, through long centuries of struggle against uneven odds, have been steadily making us one.

Yet how will the Caribbean fit into a world which, after a half-century of East-West polarization, is now undergoing profound change? More specifically, one could ask, How will the Caribbean secure a new space for itself in an emerging global order where economic geographies are transcending traditional geographical boundaries, and new international regimes are erasing not only the region's preferential terms of trade, but the ties that have historically bound it to the rest of the world?

In response to similar questions and uncertainties, the heads of government of the Commonwealth Caribbean established the West Indian Commission in 1989. Its report (quoted above) speaks to the issue of identity in the Caribbean, the dialectics of political rearrangements in the region, and the work that needs to be undertaken to prepare the region for participation in the new global economy. "Let all ideas contend" was the Commission's watchword, as it attempted "to stimulate a public forum on the future." However, as income levels continue to fall and poverty and inequality rise, public confidence in our institutions is being eroded, and a growing impatience is setting in.

Thirty years ago, when many countries in the English-speaking Caribbean "gained" their political independence, public confidence was high, as these new nations took their seats in the UN General Assembly and embarked on programs of social and economic transformation at home. This is no longer the case. Much work was carried out during those years, but prescriptions for the future must be based on a new set of realities. The somewhat belated recognition of this fact has now led to an anxious search within the region for twenty-first century paradigms of development, new notions of nationhood, workable institutions of governance, and viable pathways for entering the mainstream of the global economy.

Accordingly, this volume is broadly concerned with the search for new Caribbean economic and political platforms. The issues covered include the international agenda, economic policy and performance, the implications of the new global economy for the region, conflict management in multiethnic societies, governance, regional integration, identity, and problem-solving initiatives. Some chapters present new theoretical approaches, while others deal with practical issues of policy. They share common concerns, however, and all represent considerable research and thought on new premises for the region's most persistent problems.

In chapter one, this writer traces old and new paradigms that are now engaging the attention of the region's policymakers. Critical challenges are explored surrounding the issues of sovereignty, regionalism, the creation of Caribbean negotiating space, the notion of a regional state, and the beginnings of the post-structural adjustment debate. The chapter concludes with some thoughts on Caribbean politics and identity.

Nancy Birdsall, drawing on extensive experience as a development economist, focuses in chapter two on the major issues of adjustment and growth in the Caribbean and identifies three key ingredients for Caribbean development. She argues for greater exports, more investment in human resource development, and a policy framework for governments that will enable a more dynamic growth for the private sector. In so doing, she presents a provoking and clearly articulated paper on the missing ingredient for the next challenge for the post-structural adjustment strategy of Caribbean development.

Charles Skeete, in chapter three, makes the distinction between the policies required for economic survival and the requirements for Caribbean unity. He skillfully identifies the trade-offs between economic issues and political aspirations, and suggests that the question of identity would perhaps be better served if more emphasis were placed on the political goals of Caribbean unity.

Havelock Ross-Brewster, who follows up these arguments in chapter four, argues forcefully that neither traditional concepts of political unification, nor the proposed approaches to economic integration, are likely to succeed. Instead, he contends that political unification should be achieved in ways that do not necessitate the amalgamation of power in a single center, or in a federation. In this approach, West Indian unity might be better secured through cultural-historical identity, rather than through traditional regimes for regional economic integration, whose feasibility has become questionable.

David Lewis, broadening these arguments both geographically and programmatically in chapter five, looks at the prospects of regional cooperation in an environment in which economic boundaries and national borders are in conflict. He proposes a series of opportunities for developing strategic alliances for cooperation and competition across the Caribbean that include Florida, Central America, Puerto Rico, the Dominican Republic and Cuba. He argues strongly that the Caribbean community should move beyond the subregional CARICOM grouping, and identifies the costs of failing to do so.

Bertus Meins, in chapter six, presents a comprehensive assessment of the structural adjustment process in the region. Meins looks carefully at the interrelationship between fiscal deficits, monetary expansion, inflation and exchange rate pressures, and establishes why some countries have made more successful transitions than others. Meins's analysis leads him to look at the impact of the structural adjustment process and the region's integration in the world economy. This rigorous study suggests the region's medium-term socioeconomic outlook for high-quality growth, as well as improvement in the standard of living.

In the search for comparative strategies, Sarath Rajapatirana examines in chapter seven the conditions that led to the success of the East Asian Tigers. He concludes that "the Caribbean countries have many of the factors that are commonly associated with the success of the East Asian countries, but they have much less to show in terms of performance." Rajapatirana identifies the different institutional settings as a key factor that must be explored further, and argues that NAFTA might provide an opportunity for domestic reforms that will establish the fundamentals of the reform process.

Elena Suárez, in chapter eight, gives an insider's analysis of the economics of transition, and reviews some of the external challenges that will strongly influence the region's economic future. She explores in some depth the erosion of preferential treatments, the revision of European Union policies on bananas, the impact of the Uruguay Round and NAFTA, changes in financial flows, the effects of regional integration, and the possible consequences of a post-embargo Cuba. Outlining some of the key issues in Washington circles, Suárez then focuses on the requirements for establishing a more dynamic private sector development strategy for the region.

Ramesh Deosaran, in chapter nine, takes a refreshing approach to a vexing issue of political management, and examines the relationship between politics and culture in multiethnic societies in the Caribbean. Using the case of Trinidad and Tobago to illustrate his point, he confronts issues of governance and the persistence of formal and informal dimensions of political cultures. Deosaran analyzes the specific issue of cultural policy and patronage in the Caribbean political system, and suggests reforms to improve the legitimacy of the state in the context of ethnic conflict.

Karen Walch, in chapter ten, deals with a little-explored area: the Washington negotiating environment for Caribbean issues. Examining dialogues, lobbying, and consultations with the U.S. legislative and executive branches, she focuses on the negotiating agenda and the resolution of conflict situations. In this regard, she reviews the dialogues for Caribbean Basin Initiative I and II and NAFTA parity, and notes the emergence of more sociocentric definitions of national self-interest, as nation-states realize they form part of a greater political and economic whole.

Richard Bloomfield, in chapter eleven, examines the resilience of democracy in the hemisphere, looking closely at coups in Guatemala, Haiti and Peru, where the political system has been tested. He argues that the outcomes have been mixed, ranging from success in Guatemala to failure in Peru, and reviews the lessons that have been learned. His analysis of the Haiti situation provides genuine insight into the background of events that are still unfolding.

Andrés Serbin, in chapter twelve, examines Latin American–Caribbean relations in a new geopolitical and geo-economic situation. Serbin's assessment of the relationship between the Group of Three (the G-3, made up of Colombia, Venezuela and Mexico) and the Caribbean, and his identification of issues for the 1990s, may well set the beginnings of an agenda for the newly formed Association of Caribbean States.

Amos Tincani, in chapter thirteen, reviews relations between the European Union and the Caribbean against a variety of perspectives, including the evolution of the EU, its relation with the developing countries of the South and the East, and changes in the external environment that face the Caribbean.

Lastly, in chapter fourteen, Alan Henrikson focuses on contemporary U.S. foreign policy towards the Caribbean, exploring the notion that the United States is a Caribbean nation. In this context he examines the development of foreign policy through the Reagan, Bush, and Clinton presidencies, and focuses on some of the key ingredients for the formulation of foreign policy in a new hemispheric and global world.

These are trying times for the Caribbean. Old certainties and models are falling away, but new, sustainable ones have yet to take their place. As a consequence, we are embarked upon a quest for a new identity for the Caribbean, an identity that will allow it to realize wider international economic and political space and greater autonomy. The defining moment for the Caribbean has not yet arrived; in the meantime, much work remains to be done, and many challenges to be met. What is at stake is no less than the region's viability in the new economic and political order of the twenty-first century.

* * *

I wish to thank Steven Bloomfield, Alan Henrikson, Robert Putnam, Richard Cooper, Sarath Rajapatirana and John Coatsworth for their support and encouragement. In particular, I would like to note the hard work, dedication and editorial insight of Donald Halstead, who made a significant contribution to this book. Others who have played important roles include Ann Emerson, Thomas Murphy, Yong-Joo Kim, Caílin Gallagher, Anthony Bryan, Rogelio Novey and T. Gatcliffe. I also wish to thank my wife Shirley for her help and understanding.

Winston C. Dookeran

Chapter 1

Crosscurrents in Caribbean Policy Analysis

Winston C. Dookeran

The Caribbean is a complex, even enigmatic region, characterized by great disparities in size, population, geography, history, language, religion, race, and politics. Notwithstanding these important differences, the economic parameters of the countries in the region are largely symmetrical: they are primarily small economies with narrow resource bases and high trade-to-output ratios, whose GDP is largely related to the export of primary resource and agricultural commodities. Despite persistent efforts, most Caribbean nations still depend on preferential export markets, among other factors. Compared with other developing countries, the standard of living is relatively high, though this is due more to periodic windfalls and protected markets than to the region's productivity or international competitiveness.

The platforms defining Caribbean economic and political space over the last forty years include the triangular trade of the pre-independence period, the era of multinational corporations and U.S. hegemony, and the more recent IMF–World Bank structural adjustment programs. Out of this framework came theories of exploitation, neocolonialism and marginalization, and the export of protest diplomacy. There followed heavy moral and political overtures for protection, special consideration, aid, trade, and investment support from the developed world. Given their history of colonialism, the mandates of nation-building, and conditions at the time of independence, Caribbean nations pursued inward paths toward development that included a high degree of state involvement in the economy.

This approach may have been feasible in the 1960s and 1970s, given the state of development-thinking and the geopolitical structure of the world economy in that period, but it is no longer sustainable. For decades, the plantation economy of the hinterland has adjusted only to a persistent low-level equilibrium, resulting in lower incomes. Although the region's resource-based industries were integrated into the global economy, this resulted in economic enclaves within the domestic economy, without sufficient development benefits. Caribbean countries remain highly sensitive to exogenous forces, such as shocks, exchange-rate manipulation and crises, all of which can adversely affect their critical foreign exchange, their largely export-derived public revenues, and their competitiveness.

The liberalization of the global economic system and other conditions are now eroding the preferential terms of trade on which the Caribbean standard of living is built. Faced with adverse terms of trade, the need for technological advancement, stresses in the political system, and changing political and economic ties with the rest of the world, the Caribbean is confronting its most severe challenges since many of its nations became independent a generation ago.

Political and Economic Imperatives

The premise of any future economic strategy for the Caribbean must be the creation of a dynamic export sector that is sustainable without trade preferences. While push-started by negotiated treaties, this sustainability must be founded on market forces. Yet what meaningful steps have been taken to address this crisis and to create a new generation of exports? How will these new exports relate to the region's domestic capacity, to the unit cost of production and to technology requirements, and how will this transformation be financed? How will the region respond to the worldwide liberalization of financial markets, so as not to place its entire foreign exchange in jeopardy?[1] What new policy framework will meet the looming crisis faced by the region's smaller islands, in particular, many of which are almost totally dependent on the exchange they receive from their sugar, bananas, citrus, cocoa and coffee? Furthermore, are the steps now being taken sufficient to push-start the economy into an integrated world economy, so that it can gain a more equitable share of world commerce?

For these questions there have been only partial answers. Despite a great deal of rhetoric and debate, the region has not yet found ways to change its industrial structure, so that transnational Caribbean enterprises could perform on a more competitive basis in the world economy. The growing gap in the Caribbean between expectations and performance, and the rising tension

---

[1] This scenario is of particular concern, for "despite the rhetoric of the new age of global economy, there are plenty of signs today that we are repeating the dangerous game of competitive devaluation of the interwar period: the worldwide currency chaos in mid-September 1992 and the U.S. effort to undercut the competitive advantage of foreign producers through exchange rate manipulation...are just two recent startling examples of this sort. Furthermore many developing countries are too small to be optimal currency areas, as the costs of floating their exchange rate exceeds the benefits" (Cui 1994, 4).

between intention and reality, has widened the space between the art of politics and the discharge of governance. Political rhetoric tends to base new promises on old premises. In this politics of illusion, yesterday's hopes remain unfulfilled, and new hopes emerge with little expectation that they will lead to action.[2]

In the face of seriously deteriorating conditions and the abandonment of many social goals, the sense that the Caribbean is not preparing for the future is a deep source of anguish for its people. Not only has this resulted in a deep disillusionment with institutions and politicians, but the role of the state and its ability to govern have come into question.

The Caribbean must determine its capacity for entering the mainstream of income-generating activities and reposition itself in world markets by expanding the range of its economy. Accomplishing this task will require new theoretical models to address the practical issues of policy, implementation, and international relations; outward- and forward-looking strategies to design paradigms for development; new approaches to the region's persistent problems; and a plan for integration based on contemporary realities that will increase the region's political space.[3]

To be effective, any new integration paradigm for the Caribbean must go beyond matters of trade and respond to the international situation. This paradigm should link productive structures, promote interaction between the private sectors of different countries, and create technological advances that will reduce the costs of doing business, increase institutional flexibility, and promote social capital among the peoples of the region. The alternative is further economic marginalization and political peripheralization. But what the specific targets and methods will be, and how development will be secured by new integration paradigms, remain uncertain.

Sovereignty and Regionalism

The forces transforming the global environment are propelling the international system in two seemingly contradictory directions.[4] On the one hand, the world is moving towards multilateralism and global integration, with a strong commitment to open markets and international institutions; on the other, it is

---

[2] See Bernal (1993).

[3] For a more comprehensive view of these issues, see Dookeran (1995).

[4] These include the collapse of the Cold War; the worldwide lowering of trade barriers and the integration of markets; the globalization of capital, production, distribution and exchange; technological advances; and the convergence of common interests and concerns.

entering a new era of regionalism, as nations seek to guarantee their markets. Strategies, policies, and institutions that are not in harmony with international regimes and regional common interests are dangerously short-sighted and increasingly untenable. It is not simply that national interests have now inseparably merged with foreign policy; rather, the parameters of the nation-state and sovereignty, of internal and external, domestic and international, must now be understood in terms of a complicated "two-level framework." These developments not only challenge our understanding, but also raise fundamental questions as to economic and political philosophy.[5]

Governments in both the developing and developed world are facing the increasingly difficult task of managing their national economies in order to improve macroeconomic performance, to provide increased levels of public investment for job creation, education and health care, and to develop policies and institutions that will address the issues of poverty and inequity, in an increasingly laissez-faire global environment. Political systems are undergoing stress, as the economic forces for integration outstrip their capacity to make the requisite political adjustments. They are likely to endure only insofar as they are able to adapt.[6] In the Caribbean and other developing regions, this scenario is further complicated by structural adjustment policies, which many argue are undermining the conditions for development. Others fear that building the requisite regional institutions for addressing these problems will result in a loss of national identity and sovereignty. Furthermore, as regionalism is by definition discriminatory, economists and decision makers are concerned about the possible trade-diverting effects of the future regional landscape.[7]

---

[5] For an analysis of the two-level game of international relations and domestic economic and political policies, see Putnam (1988); see also Evans, Jacobson, and Putnam (1993).

[6] On this and related issues see Galbraith (1994).

[7] Examples of the confusion surrounding these issues are readily apparent. The MERCOSUR trade bloc (Argentina, Brazil, Uruguay and Paraguay), for instance, which formed the world's second largest customs union in January 1995, will not establish a supranational court to settle trade disputes, as some members felt that it would reduce their sovereignty (see Foster 1994). Many in the U.S. Congress—even those considered free-traders—were reluctant to pass the Uruguay Round (UR) legislation in late November-December 1994; they feared that the World Trade Organization (WTO), by eliminating the one-country veto and establishing tribunals to rule on trade disputes, would dilute U.S. sovereignty and force changes in a wide range of U.S. environmental and labor laws (see Zuchoff 1994). In a recent nationwide referendum, Norway voted not to join the EU, feeling, at least in part, that its resource base was strong enough to keep foreign bureaucrats from interfering in its "internal" affairs. And the Caribbean Community Common Market (CARICOM) heads of state were determined to keep its expansion under the ambit of elected governments, in part because they feared a devolvement of their sovereignty. In each case there were serious debates as to what constituted the national interests and how integration would affect national sovereignty.

In this, two points should be considered. First, as Bhagwati (1992) indicates, what we are seeing now is a resurgent regionalism. The first round essentially collapsed in the 1960s, primarily because the United States was still intent upon following a multilateral course.[8] The lowering of trade barriers worldwide, however, has extended the "new integrationist" agenda far beyond matters of security, trade and markets, toward convergence on such matters as common regulatory systems, environmental and labor standards, and institution-building. This is leading toward a type of interdependency that can be seen in the new financial geography, where cross-border trading and capital flows make it increasing difficult to distinguish international banks from domestic ones. Furthermore, the removal of strict capital controls in many countries has placed an emphasis on further integration, with the establishment of global safety nets for international trading, external policy coordination, and common fiscal and monetary policies.

The second point to consider is that regionalism need not necessarily be a stumbling block towards a multilateral trading system. The European Community, for instance, furthered the GATT negotiations, and it may very well be that the Western Hemispheric, European, and Asian trading blocs will be better able to carry out the negotiations leading to global free trade than the 120-odd nations that are signatories under the GATT.[9] The danger, of course, is that this will not happen and that, by turning inward, they will fracture the global system. Regardless of the outcome, however, governments and other actors can no longer define their interests primarily in terms of their geopolitical boundaries, but must increasingly do so in regional and even global terms.

Regional integration is a necessary step for solving the Caribbean's problems, but its countries resist taking the next step, that of building institutional and private sector linkages. The goal has been to reduce tariffs and to maximize internal trade—but without establishing external linkages that would increase the Caribbean's international and regional trade. The result has been an integration with no convergence, whose premises are outdated, and institutions that may be efficient, but, in terms of achieving the real goals of integration, are certainly ineffective. This is due, at least in part, to the region's insularity: divisiveness remains a prominent, even an institutionalized feature of

---

[8] The most notable exception to this, of course, was the European Common Market, now the EU, which the United States supported primarily out of regional security concerns. The same can also be said for the U.S.S.R. and COMECON.

[9] The Free Trade Area of the Americas (FTAA), formed in December 1994, seeks hemisphere-wide free trade by 2005. The EU is currently expanding its borders into Eastern Europe and the southern Mediterranean; and the eighteen members of APEC (Asia Pacific Economic Cooperation forum) have just signed an agreement to establish a free trade zone among developed nations by 2010, while developing nations in the region will meet these requirements by 2020.

the domestic political scene. The cultural basis for a new integration process must address matters of Caribbean identity and social capital, so that it will be more durable, and be premised on the integration of peoples, not just policies. In this, integration should also be less anxious about trade, investment, and the creation of human and physical capital, and place a greater emphasis on what Robert Putnam terms "social capital," a vital ingredient in the mix for economic development.[10]

This psychology also extends to the construct of sovereignty in the context of the region's nations that are still engaged in the task of nation-building. But as difficult and painful as integration might be, collaboration on agreed-upon agendas and shared responsibility for the promotion of common interests do not mean that the nation-state will disappear, or that national sovereignty will be lessened; in fact, the outcome may well be the reverse. Sovereignty is often confused with notions of size and unilateralism, but its essence—the capacity to make effective, intelligent, and timely decisions that promote a nation's welfare and autonomy—is altogether different.

In Keohane's analysis, sovereignty is twofold, formal and operational. In terms of formal sovereignty, "a state has a legal supremacy over all other authorities within a given territory, and is legally independent...except where it has accepted obligations under international law" (Keohane 1993). In this, all legally recognized states, regardless of size, are "*égaux en droit*" (Etienne 1993, 3). Nations sacrifice some operational sovereignty, or "legal freedom of action" (Keohane 1993, 91), when they enter into international agreements, but they do so in return for reciprocal limits on other states. If entered into wisely, such agreements will increase economic wellbeing at home and enhance government's options and its ability to govern. Far from limiting the state's power, therefore, the establishment of regional common interests and joint problem-solving processes where the grounds for interdependence exist may heighten national autonomy, particularly when these agreements are entered into with a view as to how one can benefit from a greater integration with the external world, while at the same time supporting the multilateral process.

---

[10] Distinct from human capital and social expenditures, social capital, as defined by Putnam, "...refers to features of social organization, such as networks, norms and trust, that facilitate coordination and cooperation for mutual benefit. Social capital enhances the benefits of investment in physical and human capital...and seems to be a precondition for economic development, as well as for effective government. Development economists take note: Civics matters." (Putnam 1993, 35-37; Putnam 1994, ch. 6). While social capital is specifically concerned with the grounds for public policy and institution building, on another level it is reflected internationally in the emerging norms for cooperation, multilateralism, and shared concerns and responsibilities, as opposed to traditional opportunistic, unilateral models of international relations.

Building Negotiating Space

We in the Caribbean have rationalized that our smallness constrains development, but in fact, size is not in itself an issue. The city-states of Hong Kong and Singapore have achieved high levels of prosperity and growth without significant natural resources, preferential trade accords, or proximity to the U.S and European markets. They did so by linking their economies with the world economy and achieving external economies of scale, rather than relying on internal forces. They determined their cultural strengths and built on them, developing policies and strategies that unleashed the microeconomic forces for growth, and complementing these with the macroeconomic framework. This was a matter of clear goals, skillful strategies, and sound policymaking, not market size. China, on the other hand, with its authoritarian government, large internal market and substantial resources, was unable to modernize its economy outside the global framework; nor have other large nations, including India, Indonesia, Brazil, Russia, Pakistan, Bangladesh, Nigeria, and Mexico, been able to do so, though many have excellent resource bases.[11] The point, then, is that the political and sociological legitimacy of the nation-state are not threatened by changes in operational sovereignty per se; rather, today's world requires that the nation-state cede more of its operational sovereignty, in order to uphold its legitimacy and viability.

Historically, the U.S. attitude towards the Caribbean has been conditioned by the geopolitical significance of the region's proximity, and this is still true, despite the end of the Cold War. The regional agenda has decisively widened, however, and there is now a convergence of interests on such issues as drug trafficking, money laundering, immigration, the management of common resources, environmental degradation, and the strengthening of democracy. The Caribbean must seek to establish a new relationship with Washington in the light of these circumstances, and since resources and attention have shifted from the region, it will be taken seriously only if it negotiates as a unified entity.

Furthermore, if the Caribbean is to strengthen its negotiating position at a time when both the United States and the European Union are preoccupied with matters unrelated to Caribbean development, it must speak with a greater voice. The Caribbean and its neighbors in South and Central America need to work together in greater harmony, if not always in total agreement. Regionalism is an inescapable feature of the landscape, and the asymmetrical integration of the Caribbean nations with its larger neighbors does not, as many fear, present a bona fide threat to Caribbean identity. On the contrary, it will enable

---

[11] See Wolf (1994).

the Caribbean to distinguish what is uniquely its own, while at the same time facilitating the emergence of a trans-Caribbean identity that encompasses the Caribbean littoral.

The Association of Caribbean States (ACS), created soon after the West Indian Commission report had recommended that CARICOM achieve greater cooperation and economic integration within the Caribbean Basin, was an effort to respond to global conditions.[12] But without an explicit agenda or clearly identified targets, the precise function of ACS is unclear, and it is in danger of becoming an expansion of outdated and ineffective structures that cannot deal with the present crisis.[13]

Open Regionalism and the Regional State

The best model that the Caribbean can consider at this juncture is a form of open regionalism, which encompasses a number of the above issues and trends.[14] In a time of great uncertainty regarding the eventual outcome of the multilateral and minilateral trading systems, open regionalism encourages nations to form subregional trading blocs in ways that facilitate linkages with others, thus synthesizing the globalization and regionalization trends. While an open regionalism includes some preferential elements, import barriers are low, and it allows for the open-ended participation of its members in other trade agreements and regional schemes, so that these various groupings will function as building blocks towards global accords and an open and more transparent international economy.

The first round of regionalism led to a form of integration that widened the production base, erected trade fortresses and began to build on policy convergences. This cycle is now over, and the integration process being pur-

---

[12] Prime Minister A.N.R. Robinson of Trinidad and Tobago took the initiative in establishing the West Indian Commission in the late 1980s, in order to examine the issues facing the future of the Caribbean. Its 600-page report, Time for Action, contained more than two hundred specific recommendations (West Indian Commission 1992).

[13] Twenty-four states signed the convention establishing the ACS on 24 July 1994 in Cartagena, Colombia. Those who became full members are: Antigua and Barbuda, the Bahamas, Barbados, Belize, Colombia, Costa Rica, Cuba, Dominica, the Dominican Republic, El Salvador, Grenada, Guatemala, Guyana, Haiti, Honduras, Jamaica, Mexico, Nicaragua, Panama, St. Kitts and Nevis, St. Vincent and the Grenadines, Suriname, Trinidad and Tobago, and Venezuela. The non-independent territories and countries eligible for associate membership are: Anguilla, Bermuda, the British Virgin Islands, Cayman Islands, Montserrat, Puerto Rico, Turks and Caicos Islands, the U.S. Virgin Islands, France (for Guadeloupe, Guyana, and Martinique), and the Netherlands (on behalf of the Netherlands Antilles and Aruba).

[14] For a discussion on how Caribbean open regionalism might be built, see Dookeran (1994). For a comprehensive treatment of this subject, see ECLAC (1994).

sued by CARICOM, despite the recent inclusion of Suriname, has reached its limits. The current round of regionalism, however, which combines the integration of production with open markets, is representative of an intermediate position in a global move towards a more open multilateral trading system. The Caribbean must accept the realities of the new global economy, and a policy environment must emerge to provide a development buffer zone, as we strive to emerge on a higher international platform. In this context, the establishment of the ACS can be seen, not as an integration process per se, but as an attempt to strengthen the region's negotiating position in international diplomacy. This poses an opportunity for the Caribbean to move away from its traditional posture of protest diplomacy towards a more affirmative stance, in which its vital interests are identified and promoted in anticipation of changing balances in world politics. Furthermore, it lends credence to the notion that a non-sovereign "regional state"—one which could exhibit the same sort of cooperation in world affairs that the Scandinavian countries often demonstrate, and perhaps move towards regional cooperation on economic policy matters, the funding policies of the international financial organizations, as well as cooperation in the UN and other multilateral organizations—may well be more appropriate to the conduct of international relations than the nation-state.

Post-Structural Adjustment

Since the oil crisis of the 1970s, the path towards development in many of the world's poorer countries has been hindered by deteriorating terms of trade for export commodities and inappropriate development policies. These difficulties culminated in the debt crisis of the 1980s, following which many developing countries had to restructure their economies along the lines of structural adjustment policies. These programs consist of both short- and medium-term measures for improving the overall economic situation by such means as cuts in public spending, contraction of the money supply, changes in import restrictions, devaluation of the currency, and the privatization of state enterprises. In general, this new orthodoxy views the market as the major instrument of reform, while the state is seen as the key obstacle to development.[15]

The structural adjustment policy debate in the Caribbean has centered around the sequencing of measures and a time period for these policies to

---

[15] The five basic strategies of structural adjustment programs include the reduction of domestic demand, resource reallocation, the increase of foreign and domestic savings, and increased economic efficiency in the use of resources. (See Norton 1987; for specific economic measures, see IMF 1986.)

work, when it should have focused on substance. After a decade of adjustment, development still remains an elusive goal. This is largely a static model, based on two-dimensional premises that cannot be supported. The neoclassical policy prescriptions for "getting the prices right," such as reducing costs, getting the right technology, flexible exchange rates, and removing price controls and subsidies, are all well and good in themselves, but competition is a complex, dynamic phenomenon in which price is only a single element. Moreover, while strict fiscal and monetarist measures may promote stabilization, they will not unleash the internal forces for change that will result in growth; and while the divestiture of state enterprises, for instance, may be necessary to balance the books, unless privatization takes place within a post-structural adjustment framework *for* development, it will not result in a new platform from which output, income, and well-being can be increased. Furthermore, such a framework must engender the dynamics for endogenous growth, so that the industrial structure of production may be transformed, creating new vehicles for the empowerment of peoples which will yield a high-level equilibrium and momentum for sustainable development.

Similarly, the measures for "getting the state out of the way" ignore the need for an enhanced state role in building meaningful regional institutions that will create and promote an environment of growth. The state is needed to enforce regulations, formulate and implement policy, build international linkages, forge collective public and private sector initiatives, and promote human resource development that will bring the disadvantaged into the development process. The world that we now inhabit will likely call for constant economic adjustment; but if the foundations of social life are not to be further eroded, this process must be countered with a "high-energy politics...capable of...repeated basic reform," involving intensified public participation and democracy (Cui and Unger 1994, 85). Correcting economic accounts regardless of social costs can only destroy any basis for future growth.

The state must be redesigned, but not eliminated. Callaghy points out that "contrary to free-market mythology, the state has always played a central role in economic development...[and] economic adjustment in the Third World today requires a balanced tension...between state and market forces" (1989, 33). While the international financial institutions are slowly coming around to this view, this is the formula in the developed world. Interventionist strategies, such as incentives and subsidies, are at the core of East Asian development. Furthermore, while the structural adjustment paradigm depends on externally propelled growth, these movements are cyclical, as W. Arthur Lewis has pointed out, and there is nothing inevitable about the process.[16]

---

[16] Sir W. Arthur Lewis, a leading West Indian economist, won a Nobel Prize for Economics in 1979.

Political Economy

Development in the Caribbean entails a comprehensive political economy of change, including the development of endogenous growth capacity to drive the economy. Only then can the region benefit from the new and flexible world economy, in which ends and means are readily adjusted to changing opportunities in different countries. This will require an integration model that transcends trade and converges at the institutional level, and facilitates backward and forward, macro- and microeconomic linkages. Eventually a virtuous circle should be created, in which the region can expand its political space and gain greater negotiating strength in the international arena. Merging into a greater political-economic whole should help to free individual states from rent-seeking power bases, bring about greater economic efficiencies, and allow governments to concentrate on governance.

Sustainable development is an affirmative political-economic process, linking economic logic—the measures needed to pursue economic efficiency in both the international and domestic spheres—with political logic, in a synergism that allows them to reinforce one another. Merely opening the economy to the outside will not induce sustainable growth; to the contrary, it will result in further social and economic destabilization. As integration progresses and the state reduces its direct role in the economy, public policy will have an even greater impact on society. There will be winners and losers; to address this situation, government must be strong enough to manage the transition and alter the opportunity structure, so that lower- and middle-income groups will not bear disproportionate burdens. The government must also ensure that poverty issues are systematically addressed with visible effect.

A society is largely defined by citizens who possess a common notion of their identity and a common loyalty to shared ideals. As we move into the next millennium, Caribbean society must create a new sense of civic identity in which people feel free to express themselves, speak their own languages, practice their cultural traditions and transmit these to their children, as they embrace common goals with the larger society. The agenda before us is enormous, but we can neither succumb to the forces of history, nor surrender to the new vulnerabilities that will surface in the path ahead. Our resilience must be founded in our own sense of Caribbean identity, with an enduring commitment to confidence in our future.

Bibliography

Bhagwati, Jagdish. 1992. Regionalism and Multilateralism: An Overview. Discussion Paper Series No. 603 (April). Washington, D.C.: World Bank.

Bernal, Richard L. 1993. CARICOM: Externally Vulnerable Regional Economic Integration. Paper presented at workshop, Economic Integration in the Western Hemisphere: Prospects for Latin America, at the Institute for International Studies, University of Notre Dame, 17-18 April.

Callaghy, Thomas M. 1989. "Toward State Capability and Embedded Liberalism in the Third World: Lessons for Adjustment." In *Fragile Coalitions: The Politics of Economic Adjustment*, ed. Joan M. Nelson. New Brunswick and Oxford: Transaction Books.

Cui, Zhiyuan. 1994. International Chapter 11 and SDR. Outline of presentation to The Reinventing Bretton Woods Committee, New York, 20 September.

Cui, Zhiyuan and Roberto Mangabeira Unger. 1994. "China in the Russian Mirror." *New Left Review* 208: 78-87.

De Melo, Jaime and Arvind Panagariya, eds. 1993. *New Dimensions in Regional Integration*. Cambridge: Cambridge Univ. Press.

Dookeran, Winston. 1994. "Caribbean Integration: An Agenda for Open Regionalism." *The Round Table: The Commonwealth Journal of International Affairs* 330: 205–211.

———. 1995. "Preferential Trade Arrangements in the Caribbean: Issues and Approaches." In *Trade Liberalization in the Western Hemisphere*, 437-470. Washington, D.C.: Inter-American Development Bank and United Nations Economic Commission for Latin America and the Caribbean (ECLAC).

ECLAC. 1994. *Open Regionalism in Latin America and the Caribbean*. Santiago, Chile: United Nations.

Etienne, Henri. 1993. "The Limits of Integration?" Charles Francis Adams Lecture Series, The Fletcher School of Law and Diplomacy, Tufts University, Medford, MA, 14 October.

Evans, Peter B., Harold K. Jacobson, and Robert D. Putnam, eds. 1993. *Double-Edged Diplomacy: International Bargaining and Domestic Politics*. Berkeley: Univ. of California Press.

Foster, Angus. 1994. "Difficult Choices Ahead for Mercosur." *Financial Times*, 19 December.

Galbraith, John Kenneth. 1994. "The New Dialectic." *The American Prospect* 18: 9-11.

Ghai, Dharam. 1992. "Structural Adjustment, Global Integration, and Social Democracy." Discussion Paper No. 37. United Nations Research Institute for Social Development.

IMF (International Monetary Fund). 1986. "Fund-Supported Programs, Fiscal Policy, and Income Distribution." Occasional Paper No. 46. Washington, D.C.: IMF.

Keohane, Robert O. 1993. "Sovereignty, Interdependence, and International Institutions." In *Ideas and Ideals: Essays on Politics in Honor of Stanley Hoffman*, ed. Linda B. Miller and Michael Joseph Smith. Boulder, CO: Westview Press.

Norton, Roger D. 1987. "Agricultural Issues in Structural Adjustment Programs." FAO (Food and Agricultural Organization) Economic and Social Development Paper No. 66, Rome, Italy: FAO.

Putnam, Robert D. 1988. "Diplomacy and Domestic Politics: The Logic of Two-level Games." *International Organization* 42(3): 427–460.

———. 1993. "The Prosperous Community: Social Capital and Public Life." *The American Prospect* 13: 35-42.

———. 1994. *Making Democracy Work: Civic Traditions in Modern Italy*. Princeton: Princeton Univ. Press.

Ramsaran, Ramesh. 1992. *The Challenge of Structural Adjustment in the Commonwealth Caribbean*. New York: Praeger Publishers.

West Indian Commission. 1992. *Time for Action: The Report of the West Indian Commission*. St. Michael, Barbados: West Indian Commission Secretariat.

Wolf, Martin. 1994. "Myth of Empty Sovereignty." *Financial Times*, 5 December.

Zuchoff, Mitchell. 1994. "At GATT's Core: A Debate about Money, Sovereignty." *The Boston Globe*, 27 November.

Chapter 2

Adjustment and Growth in the Caribbean: The Missing Ingredient

Nancy Birdsall

My impressions of the Caribbean region are those of a touring development economist. I emphasize the words "impressions" and "touring," because the Caribbean is not my base of knowledge. As a development economist, however, I hope to bring a comparative perspective to my remarks and to take a relatively long-term view.

I will first consider another part of the world, East Asia, and make some general comparisons to the situation in the Caribbean. I will then come to the missing ingredient for the next stage of adjustment and growth—or perhaps, the next big challenge—in the Caribbean.

Three Ingredients of East Asian Success

First, why is East Asia considered a success? Figure 2.1 shows both the average rate of growth in per capita income from 1965 to 1990 and the degree of income inequality in the early to mid-1980s.

The East Asian economies achieved annual rates of growth above 4 percent, and as high as 8 percent, with very low degrees of income inequality. Over the same period, Latin America had not only much lower rates of growth, but also much higher levels of inequality. While Caribbean countries have somewhat more equitable income distributions than most of Latin America, their rates of growth have also been very low: the Caribbean region as a whole grew roughly 2 percent per year during the 1970s and 1980s.

What were the ingredients for this success in East Asia? Consider three E's: exports, education, and enabling government.

Exports grew rapidly in the region: Korea's exports, for example, grew at an annual rate of more than 20 percent a year from 1965 to 1990. Other countries of East Asia had export growth rates of more than 10 percent a year. Significantly, much of this growth came in nontraditional export sectors such as manufacturing.

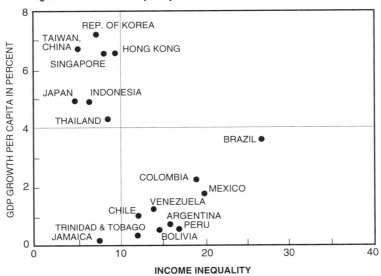

Figure 2.1 Income Inequality and Growth of GDP, 1965-90

Note: Income inequality is the average ratio of the income shares of the richest 20 percent and the poorest 20 percent of the population.
Source: World Bank, 1993.

The benefits of this rapid export growth in East Asia were considerable. First, the resulting rapid growth of employment, and eventually of wages, raised the demand for labor, which contributed to the relative equality of incomes reflected in the figure. Second, exports forced countries to learn from the market and to be globally competitive, resulting in rapid productivity gains. Third, the emphasis on exports provided fewer opportunities for rent-seeking by the private sector with government. Rent-seeking has been more likely to occur in countries that followed import substitution policies. In East Asia, especially in the northern tier countries, government handouts such as directed credit were tied to export performance, and hence to competitiveness in the world market.

What were the inputs to this export success in East Asia? The first was a stable macroeconomic environment. While Indonesia and Korea experienced some periods of double-digit inflation in the 1970s, inflation was essentially under control in East Asia by the 1980s. This in part reflected the fiscal discipline of these countries: their governments were relatively conservative and sensible in spending behavior. They were also able to borrow internationally, in part because of the export growth that made them credible borrowers. A virtuous circle was created: emphasis on exports enabled countries to borrow and to finance debt, a basis for a stable macroeconomic environment, which in turn supported export growth by supporting private investment.

Second, and particularly interesting for the Caribbean, is that most East Asian countries concentrated, either implicitly or explicitly, on using the exchange rate as a commercial tool and not as a nominal anchor to reduce inflation. Again, they were able to do this in part because of their fiscal discipline.

The second E in East Asia is education, a central aspect of a policy stance of shared or equitable growth. East Asia's policy approach to education was first, to achieve saturation at the basic levels, that is, universal enrollment at the primary and (eventually) secondary levels. Second, governments allowed the private sector to enter, at the secondary and later at the tertiary level, to respond to demand that the public sector could not satisfy because of its focus on basic schooling. Finally, in part because of the significant allocation of public spending to basic education, quality was not neglected. The emphasis on quality came not only from the public sector, but also from households that were willing to contribute indirectly to adequate education, because they saw high returns in the labor market. Another virtuous circle was realized, as high returns in the labor market were in part due to the emphasis on exports that had increased labor demand.

Education contributed not only to wage and productivity growth, but also to fertility decline, which made possible higher investments per child in education. Many Caribbean countries benefited similarly from fertility decline; this was much less the case in Latin America.

The third E, the most interesting in terms of the Caribbean states, is what might be called "enabling government." This is the idea of government, not as the engine of growth, but as an enabler or catalyst of private sector growth. In East Asia, government sets clear rules of the game, creating a predictable and reliable environment for investors, and thus an environment friendly to the business sector.

One outcome of enabling government is illustrated in Figure 2.2. The top line, which represents the high-performing economies of East Asia, shows that private investment rates from 1970 to 1990 were around 20 percent or higher. With public investment rates on the order of 10 percent, gross investment rates were 30 percent or more in these countries for very long periods of time, a factor that certainly distinguishes them from most other developing countries. Enabling government to encourage private investment is precisely the point illustrated here.

The third line in this figure represents Latin America, including the Caribbean. The Dominican Republic has a good record of private investment with a spike in the later period, but the situation in Guyana is even grimmer than the average for Latin America. Private investment rates in Latin America averaged a bit above 10 percent until the 1980s, when the debt crisis hit the region. In 1990 they were still below 10 percent.

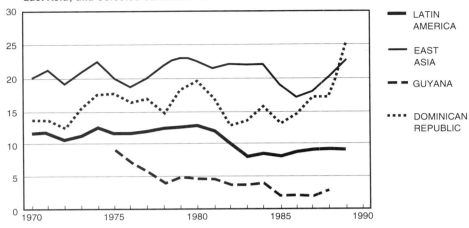

Figure 2.2 Private Investment as Percent of GDP: Latin America, East Asia, and Selected Caribbean Countries

Source: Pfeffermann and Madarrassy 1992.

The Caribbean Situation

But how do these three E's fare in the Caribbean? Export performance is not bad in the aggregate. Caribbean economies are very open economies and have a tradition of substantial exports. Macroeconomic management of the economies has been good, and on the fiscal side, rates of inflation are nothing to complain about. The Dominican Republic and Guyana got into trouble in the late eighties, but have brought inflation down in the past few years. Exchange rate problems have occurred at different periods, but recent efforts to bring about real depreciation of the exchange rate have been successful, for example in Trinidad and Tobago. Barbados and the Bahamas are keeping their exchange rates reasonably competitive, though at high cost.[1]

Thus the ingredients for export growth are there. The difference between East Asia two decades ago and Caribbean economies today is the Caribbean's much greater reliance on traditional, primary commodity exports. Relying on these exports makes the Caribbean countries more vulnerable to terms of trade decline, to Dutch disease in the case of Trinidad and Tobago, and, of course, to the vagaries of protection by the consuming countries. In the consuming countries, the market for these exports is unlikely to improve and may even worsen. (Moreover, were Cuba to re-enter the international community, it would have a tremendous comparative advantage in agriculture, with very extensive human

---

[1] The CFA countries of West Africa also paid a high price for pushing austerity to keep their exchange rates sufficiently depreciated, but eventually took a nominal devaluation.

Figure 2.3 Guyana: Recurrent Public Expenditures in the Social Sectors, 1986-92
(Percent of GDP)

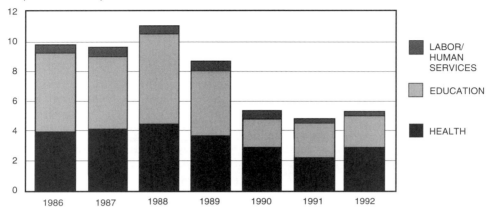

Source: Ministry of Finance.

resources, a solid scientific base, and favorable physical circumstances.)

It is therefore absolutely critical for the Caribbean countries to diversify their exports, using comparative advantage that ensures a degree of labor intensity. They must also concentrate more on services, on tourism, and on value-added, natural resource-based exports, thereby taking advantage of their relatively well-educated labor force.

Chile, for example, now produces 50 percent of its exports in nontraditional sectors, including fruits and vegetables, pulp and paper. While these are natural resource-based exports, tremendous value is added by means of marketing, packaging, refrigeration, and containers. Caribbean economies can also learn from the success of places like Indonesia, which overcame the beginnings of Dutch disease—a model perhaps for Trinidad and Tobago—and Hong Kong, which succeeded in services by having a very open approach to foreign investment. Export diversification, however, relies heavily on ensuring that private investors are comfortable—a point I will return to shortly.

What about the second E, education? In a snapshot view, Caribbean education looks quite successful. Most Caribbean countries have a distinguished record of attention to the social sectors, including education. Barbados and Trinidad and Tobago had secondary enrollment rates above 85 percent in the late 1980s, compared to 50 percent on average in Latin America. Jamaica's secondary school enrollment rate is more than 25 percent higher than would be predicted, based on its per capita income. In fact, Jamaica is the largest outlier in Latin America and the Caribbean in terms of its achievements in secondary education and health, another form of human capital investment. Jamaica and Trinidad and Tobago have the lowest under-five mortality in the entire Latin America and Caribbean region. So, education in a static sense, and human capital in general look fairly good.

On the other hand, this success in education is at risk. Figure 2.3 shows the decline in public expenditures in the social sectors in Guyana during its successful adjustment period.

Guyana is not the only case. In many other Caribbean countries, public expenditures have decreased, and the quality of education has declined. An increasing proportion of public expenditures is going to salaries and less is being spent on nonsalary inputs like in-service teacher training, books and other materials, and maintenance of infrastructure. In addition, the school directors and teachers receiving these higher salaries have neither power nor incentives to make their schools more effective. Therefore, although Caribbean education looks good compared to the rest of the developing world, it is at risk.

The Next Challenge for Caribbean Development

The third E, enabling government, is the missing ingredient and the next challenge for Caribbean development. As a development economist, I view that challenge as the need to build a new consensus around the idea of government—not as the engine of growth, or as the caretaker of the population—but as the enabler or catalyst for the private sector to operate effectively in every respect. We may call this the deepening of the reform of the state.

Initial stabilization reforms, though politically difficult, are technically straightforward. A dedicated and competent cadre of technocrats with political support from the top can manage the exchange rate more effectively, or address the first round of cuts in fiscal expenditures. But the second round of deeper reforms is more complex and more demanding institutionally, and involves a two-part agenda.

The first part of the agenda is reducing government's role—eliminating government interventions and government-owned monopolies that inhibit private investors. The second part is to strengthen government's role: its regulatory capacity, its judicial institutions, and in general, its ability to establish and enforce the rules that are essential to a sound, stable climate in which investors are willing to risk their resources.

The first part of the agenda begins with privatization. The Caribbean's limited progress in privatization is surprising when compared to its more southern neighbors. Some Caribbean countries still carry an enormous fiscal burden due to state-owned enterprises. For example, the Dominican Republic, though a star adjuster in the last few years, still has some twenty-five state-owned enterprises, ranging from airlines to blue jeans fabric factories. These state-owned enterprises lose the equivalent of roughly 3 percent of GDP per year, which equals public sector expenditures on education and health combined. In Guyana, another recent star in the first stage of adjustment, about twenty state-owned enterprises had similar overall losses in GDP terms in 1993.

Even in Trinidad and Tobago, where divestitures have yielded millions of dollars in the last few years, current public enterprises are projected to lose more than 3 percent of GDP again in 1994. Furthermore, the state still holds a large proportion of the land in Trinidad and Tobago, inhibiting private investment in agriculture. Such losses and restrictions are a long-term burden on the entire society. Fortunately, however, Barbados, Guyana and Jamaica have shown renewed interest in completing privatization programs.

The problem is that privatization requires a strong government in order to ensure that private monopolies do not simply replace public monopolies, with all the costs that this entails. Privatization is more than a technical procedure: It requires building a political and social consensus around removing the state from certain activities, as well as defusing concerns about who will gain and who will lose from privatization. In Africa, this political barrier is now the biggest single problem with privatization. It can only be addressed by building a national consensus, which in turn requires building a strong government.

The first part of the agenda also requires deregulation. In the Caribbean, deregulation is likely to be disruptive for the labor market. Many Caribbean countries have very rigid and inefficient entitlements for workers: these entitlements inhibit private investment, reduce efficiency, and exacerbate problems of inequity by reducing employment possibilities. And of course, who suffers when employment possibilities are reduced? Those who are driven to the informal sector—women and sometimes children, but certainly not the privileged.

However, governments cannot eliminate labor market inflexibility without constructing a new, market-enhancing, progressive labor policy. Such a policy should establish labor standards and, while recognizing collective bargaining rights, leave government out of bilateral negotiations between management and labor. Active policies to enhance labor mobility are critical, such as replacing severance pay obligations of employers with some form of unemployment insurance. The role of government in enhancing a free, fair and competitive labor market will become increasingly important in the Caribbean countries, given their interest in new free trade arrangements with the United States.

Another area of deregulation, restrictions on foreign investment, seems particularly perverse. Given that on the trade side Caribbean countries are very open economies, it makes sense to become more open to foreign investment. While on paper Caribbean countries appear open to foreign investment, in fact, most are not. In Trinidad and Tobago, foreign investors are restricted from more than twenty-five sectors, including land development, management services (which, given the high level of education, could emerge as a major area of comparative advantage), tire retreading, and the manufacture of cement blocks. By way of contrast, Chile has only two sectors where private investors cannot enter (defense and television), and in Bolivia there are no sectors that foreign investors cannot enter.

Finally, the civil service in many Caribbean countries is burdened with too many employees and with wages too low to attract the necessary experience and skills to the public sector. For example, about 30 percent of the work force in Trinidad and Tobago is employed by government. This means that, with close to 20 percent unemployed, the private sector employs only half the labor force.

Government cannot privatize industries and services without a regulatory framework. Similarly, it cannot withdraw from the financial sector without first ensuring adequate government supervision and prudent regulation. Social programs, environmental programs, and public expenditure reforms, all require a state that is an enabler of the private sector—not a big government, but a lean and strong one.

In short, the missing ingredient in structural reform in the Caribbean, and thus the region's next challenge, is to deepen reform of the state—to reduce further the government's involvement in productive sectors where private initiative can be more efficient, and to enhance government's role as an effective manager of the enabling environment. This is the key to higher private rates of investment, and thus higher employment and growth.

The role of the Inter-American Development Bank and other international institutions is to work with officials and others in those countries, taking into account their political and social constraints, and to support them in overcoming these constraints. However, what the IDB and the other multilaterals do matters much less than what happens in the countries themselves, as they address the fundamental institutional challenges of deepening reform of the state.

Bibliography

Pfeffermann, Guy, and Andrea Madarassy. 1992. Trends in Private Investment in Developing Countries. Discussion Paper #14. Washington, D.C.: International Finance Corporation.

World Bank. 1993. *The East Asian Miracle: Economic Growth and Public Policy*. New York: Oxford Univ. Press.

Chapter 3

Caribbean Identity and Survival in a Global Economy

Charles A. T. Skeete

We start not as foreigners but with identity.
Sir Shridath Ramphal

The best, unique, most lasting rationale for Caribbean
Community is cultural identity and kinship.
Havelock Ross-Brewster

Unless otherwise indicated, the term "Caribbean" is used in this paper to refer to the thirteen member countries of the Caribbean Community (CARICOM), all of whom, with the exception of Belize and Guyana, are island countries that form part of the archipelago of the Caribbean Sea. This admittedly restricted definition is chosen because of the diversity in historical experiences, legal systems, and linguistic traditions, in the region normally defined as the Caribbean.[1] The broad range of cultural values and approaches to self-determination in that region permits a definition of Caribbean identity only at the highest level of abstraction. This more restricted definition does not, however, imply any judgment about the value of wider Caribbean cooperation.

Advocates of Caribbean "unity" frequently promote it as a useful tool for the achievement of a variety of goals, including economic viability, the promotion and preservation of democracy, and the enhancement of negotiating and diplomatic leverage. On the other hand, the day-to-day conduct of Caribbean foreign economic policy increasingly suggests a preoccupation with economic survival, even at the expense of unity. This reality has led to recurring calls for

---

[1] CARICOM's member countries in 1993 were Antigua and Barbuda, the Bahamas, Barbados, Belize, Dominica, Grenada, Guyana, Jamaica, Montserrat, St. Kitts and Nevis, St. Lucia, St. Vincent and the Grenadines, and Trinidad and Tobago. When the definition of the Caribbean is relaxed to include the non-English-speaking Caribbean, common identity would appear to be confined to a history of European and/or U.S. domination and similarity in patterns of social organization. See Mintz (1966).

commitment to the goal of unity as an indispensable precondition for Caribbean economic viability and survival.

Nevertheless, political separateness and democratic forms of government have made the pursuit of improvements in material well-being the overriding and inescapable goal of the governments of Caribbean countries. We would therefore argue that the potential contribution of political union and economic integration to Caribbean survival and economic well-being is at best marginal. Caribbean unity ought to be pursued as an end in itself.

Survival and Unity: Complementary or Conflicting Goals?

Caribbean unity and economic viability are recurring themes in post-colonial reflections on the survival and future prospects of Caribbean societies. The case for unity, in whatever form, is usually presented in terms of a strategy for economic progress and collective self-reliance. According to this argument, unity appears to be a necessary condition for survival and economic viability in a world that confers disproportionate advantages on countries or conglomerations of relatively large size.[2] Yet a more persuasive and defensible case, in my opinion, can be made for approaching Caribbean unity as an understandable response to a deep-seated, if not always well-defined, sense of Caribbean identity.

Caribbean experience suggests that of the three main forms of unity—functional cooperation, political union, and economic integration—the latter two have little potential contribution to make to Caribbean survival. The frequently lamented failure of governments to implement commitments for unity is evidence of a perceived conflict between such commitments and the imperatives of economic viability at the national level. (The terms survival and economic viability, used synonymously here, refer to fiscal viability, balance of payments viability, or both.)

The first in a series of experiments with political union was the ill-fated West Indies Federation (1958–1962). During this period, the actual conduct of the affairs of the federal government was concerned mainly with constitutional and fiscal issues, rather than with a medium- or long-term strategy for economic survival.[3] The general perception, from ordinary people to government

---

[2] A notable exception to this more frequently encountered approach can be found in Brewster (1992). Brewster's paper deals with the content or the *how* of a form of Caribbean unity based on kinship and shared identity. This paper is more concerned with the justification for such an approach.

[3] A customs union was drawn up, but never implemented.

ministers, was that the smaller territories could not bear the fiscal burden of the institutions and trappings of independence without the participation of the larger territories. Not surprisingly, the notion that tax revenues from the larger territories would subsidize services in the smaller territories was unpopular with both politicians and taxpayers in the larger countries. Indeed, Jamaica withdrew from the Federation when the question of participation was put to its electorate.

Proposals for some form of political union without Jamaica were pursued but never realized in the years immediately following the collapse of the West Indies Federation (1962–1967). First, Trinidad and Tobago offered unitary statehood to the other eight islands that had been Federation members, but only Grenada showed any interest in setting up a single state with Trinidad and Tobago. After the U.K. government declined to provide financial assistance to the proposed state, the proposal foundered.

Next, a new federation of the "Little Eight" was proposed, between Barbados and the seven Windward/Leeward Islands. Barbados withdrew from these discussions, however, in disagreement over whether the services provided to the seven other territories would be similar to those already enjoyed by Barbados. Subsequent discussions among the Little Seven about some form of political union were also inconclusive.

These efforts to achieve political union in the 1960s raise two questions: Why did Caribbean governments try to achieve some form of political union before proceeding to independence on their own, and why did these attempts at political union prove abortive?

It appears that those Caribbean governments and electorates that would form the nucleus of a political union (namely Jamaica, Trinidad and Tobago, and Barbados) were not persuaded that such a union would confer fiscal benefits on their countries commensurate with their share of the costs. In Jamaica, the only country that placed the matter before its electorate for decision by popular vote, the proposition was roundly defeated. While consultation with the electorate prior to proceeding to independence was not undertaken in either Trinidad and Tobago or in Barbados, there was no popular outcry in either country against the decision of their respective governments to do so. Indeed, those political figures in Barbados who opposed independence were consigned to prolonged political oblivion.

The attempts at political union cited above do not exhaust the actual list.[4] For example, in 1991 St. Vincent proposed a political union between the Leeward and Windward Islands, or Organization of Eastern Caribbean States

---

[4] For a chronology of attempts at political union in the 1960s and early 1970s, see CARICOM (1973).

(OECS); and Trinidad and Tobago proposed a political union with Barbados and Guyana in 1992. These, too, were abortive. Nevertheless, the search for some form of Caribbean unity is likely to be an enduring feature of the Caribbean scene.

The Caribbean experiment with economic integration has, in a formal sense, been a more viable form of unity. Its tangible benefits are difficult both to identify and to measure. On the asset side of the balance sheet are the cost savings realized from various forms of functional cooperation, such as the University of the West Indies and the Caribbean Meteorology Institute. On the debit side are recurring concerns of some countries that burden-sharing formulas could impose a disproportionate share of the costs on their national treasuries. In spite of these complaints and of some notable failures (for example, in air and sea services), Caribbean functional cooperation may be said to represent the more positive side of their shared economic arrangements. Indeed, this aspect of the Caribbean Community may well account for the perception that, as developing country economic integration arrangements go, CARICOM is a success. The common market area of the Community's activities, by contrast, has yielded far less positive results.

Caribbean goals for economic progress are explicitly stated in both the Caribbean Free Trade Association (CARIFTA), which came into effect in May 1968, and the Caribbean Community (CARICOM) treaty, signed in April 1973. Prominent goals include expansion and diversification of intraregional trade, employment generation, and improved living standards. Importance was also attached to the goals of balanced growth and economic independence. The interrelationship between these diverse goals has posed interesting dilemmas for the integration movement. For example, these countries achieved growth in employment generation and intraregional trade by reliance on import substitution activities carried out behind high protective trade barriers. But these protective arrangements have not reduced CARICOM dependence on external markets for imports or exports. On the other hand, they have reduced and inhibited Caribbean export competitiveness, with concomitant costs in economic welfare.[5]

Although there is agreement on the failure of CARICOM to achieve its economic goals, there is less agreement on the reasons for this failure. The most frequently advanced explanations are as follows:

- The extremely small size of the individual Caribbean economies leaves them with little alternative but to achieve economic viability by means of various forms of economic cooperation, including economic integration.

---

[5] See for example, Group of Caribbean Experts (1981); World Bank (1990); and West Indian Commission (1992), ch. 2.

- In spite of the above, the provisions of the CARICOM treaty have never been fully embraced or implemented.
- The model of integration represented by the CARICOM treaty makes it unlikely that CARICOM would make a positive contribution to the material well-being of the people of the Caribbean Community.

The CARICOM approach to integration and economic prosperity is defended by respected thinkers and writers on the problems of Caribbean development. On these grounds alone, it ought not to be lightly dismissed. As I understand it, the substance of the case is that CARICOM is not a "classical common market with a fully integrated market for goods, totally free movement of capital and labor, and the unqualified right to establish and to provide services" (Group of Experts 1981, 20). Instead, the CARICOM treaty places as much stress on coordination, cooperation and joint effort in production and development as on a common external tariff.

In short, CARICOM is a package tailored to the needs of a specific region. Neither the failure of its members to embrace the package as a whole (economic integration, functional cooperation, and coordination of foreign policy), nor evaluations of its constituent parts separately, do justice to the CARICOM treaty.

In defending CARICOM, the West Indian Commission (1992) pointed to the absence of an effective mechanism for implementing its decisions and provisions as "the Achilles Heel" of CARICOM. Conceding that the treaty was perhaps outdated, they recommended implementing the declarations of two previous heads of governments : (1) to create a single market and economy, and (2) to work towards the establishment of a monetary union. They pointed out that a single market and economy implied, inter alia: the free movement of goods and services; a common external tariff (CET), "structured so as to reflect the trade and production situation in the Region" (ibid.); and the free movement of capital and labor.

According to the Commission, "a common currency would serve to eliminate transaction costs of national currencies, as well as exchange rate uncertainties in trade and investment decisions. This in turn would serve to facilitate expansion of regional trade and investment and deepen Caribbean integration." The Commission also suggested that a single currency could make an "important... symbolic and political" contribution to Caribbean unity (ibid., 110).

It may be fairly stated that the Commission's recommendations looked forward as well as backward. Forward, because they acknowledged that trends in the international economy made the original treaty, as they put it, "a child of its time." Backward, because they stated the view that foremost among "the benefits to production and development... of a genuine Single Market ... is *the increase in the size of the home market* which will allow for significant cooperation in production, transport and marketing" (ibid., emphasis added).

Contrary to the Commission's optimism about the benefits of a more closely integrated CARICOM market, I believe that key features of the Caribbean economy pose daunting obstacles to a Caribbean common market and drastically reduce the likelihood that an integrated market could contribute directly to Caribbean material well-being in any significant way. Caribbean markets are small and highly fragmented; their import capacity, either from regional or extraregional sources, is dependent on Caribbean exports to extraregional markets; and Caribbean economies are similar in structure and by international standards are high-cost producers. These features of the CARICOM economy suggest that any growth in intraregional trade is likely to come from trade diversion, rather than trade creation. The employment creation benefits of intraregional trade, in these circumstances, would be obtained at the expense of a loss in total economic welfare.[6] Moreover, the Commission's proposals for overcoming the admitted shortcomings of its original scheme are no less likely than the unamended CARICOM to be casualties of a globalized international economy, as Brewster (1992) has pointed out.[7] These realities of the Caribbean economy call into question the notion that economic integration can or will—however strengthened and deepened—bring about sustained development for Caribbean economies, collectively or separately.

Skepticism about the relevance of the existing economic integration arrangements to Caribbean economic progress may be summarized as follows. Unless CARICOM is geographically expanded to embrace a wider Caribbean, it is unlikely to become a critical mass for the realization of production economies of scale. In any case, such critical mass would be irrelevant in a globalized economy, in which Caribbean comparative advantage is more likely to be determined by services and knowledge-intensive activities.

The Case for Caribbean Unity

In the current debate about the relevance of economic integration arrangements to Caribbean survival, many of CARICOM's critics agree that Caribbean economic viability is dependent on success in exporting traditional and non-

---

[6] For a fuller treatment of the potential of Caribbean integration arrangements to contribute to the welfare of Caribbean peoples, see World Bank (1990), ch. 3.

[7] For an evaluation of the likely failure of the proposed single market and common currency to contribute to the goal of increased intraregional trade and investment, see Brewster (1992).

traditional products to extraregional markets.[8] Economic integration has not contributed in any significant way to this goal, however, except in terms of enhanced negotiating leverage with the European Community, Canada, and the United States. Why then do Caribbean governments repeatedly declare their commitment to economic integration?

These recurrent, even predictable, calls for unity in general, and economic integration in particular, seem to be evidence of a deeply felt need for unity for its own sake. I believe that the so-called implementation failures by the governments of the member countries of CARICOM, and reluctance to correct them, are evidence of a conflict between the integration approach and the economic welfare of the people of the individual member countries. Consider, for example, the potential cost-of-living increases and economic welfare costs of the new CET to the OECS countries.

In my view, the case for Caribbean unity rests on nothing more or less than an enduring need for a sense of identity and community. I believe too that this need is based on shared values, commonality in historical experiences and forms of cultural expression, and similarities in social and economic organization. These common features are reinforced by geography and exposure to common external influences. From a development perspective, Caribbean identity might define the area to some degree. Nevertheless, Caribbean development is constrained by high rates of unemployment, acute vulnerability to external shocks, and the lack of diversified economic structures.

This approach immediately raises the question: is the feeling of kinship and the need for a sense of identity that transcends national boundaries an adequate basis for a meaningful and enduring form of unity? In answering this question, I believe it is as important to confront the things that divide the people and countries of the Caribbean as it is to identify the features that unite its people. Caribbean countries have been traditionally divided by island uniqueness and insularity; class, racial, and ethnic distinctions; jealousy; and, because they are competing rather than complementary economies, the fear that unity might impose on them, individually, unacceptable economic costs. Because of these divisive factors, the association must be one that does not require democratically elected governments to sacrifice themselves on the altar of unity.

Brewster (1992, 11-13) suggests certain practical arrangements and criteria by which functional, cooperative activities could complement these

---

[8] Both the Group of Experts (1981) and the West Indian Commission (1992) stressed the importance of exports to extraregional markets to Caribbean growth and balance of payments performance. They also recognized that as the prospects for Caribbean traditional exports declined (bananas, sugar, bauxite, and petroleum), export growth increasingly implies growth in nontraditional exports.

constitutional arrangements.[9] For my part, candidates for functional cooperation would include higher education, cultural expression, and the appeal levels of the judiciary. The West Indian Commission report has also outlined possible plans for cooperation in the field of culture and sport.[10]

The third dimension to this approach of unity for its own sake could be diplomatic and negotiating leverage. However, individual countries should not be required to make heroic sacrifices in national welfare that cannot be compensated by gains from a unified approach. In the first place, there would no longer be the pretense of negotiating on the basis of a single, integrated, regional economy. This might at first appear a daunting task; however, in the vital area of trade negotiations, and in the absence of a pretense at a single market, what would be the leverage for negotiations?

The Jamaican journalist Frank Hill has explained how Jamaica once entered a federation, but later withdrew: "Our minds dragged our hearts into it." We should not repeat that mistake. In the first place, Caribbean successes in Lomé and the Caribbean Basin Initiative were not based on the market aspect of Caribbean unity; rather, they were based on the leverage of pooled talents, a united front, and a careful choice of tactics and allies. In the second place, the Caribbean strategy of negotiating preferential access to selected OECD markets has been undermined by the OECD embrace, under the Uruguay Round, of lowering tariff barriers on a most-favored-nation basis.[11] These developments suggest the need for a reevaluation—and separation—of the bases of Caribbean unity and Caribbean diplomatic leverage. Unlike Caribbean unity, diplomatic leverage must be a product of the head, rather than the heart.

---

[9] Not surprisingly, I regard Brewster's actual choice of functions of a West Indian Union as perhaps overly ambitious. For example, I am not as sanguine as he would appear to be about the prospects for, or benefits of, economic policy coordination.

[10] See West Indian Commission (1992), ch. 7.

[11] The implications of the Uruguay Round for Caribbean trade prospects are analyzed by the World Bank (1994).

Bibliography

Brewster, H. R. 1992. *The Caribbean Community in a Changing International Environment: Towards the Next Century.* Mona, Jamaica: Institute of Social and Economic Research, University of the West Indies.

CARICOM. 1973. *The Caribbean Community: A Guide.* Georgetown, Guyana: Caribbean Community Secretariat.

Group of Caribbean Experts. 1981. *The Caribbean Community in the 1980s.* Georgetown, Guyana: Caribbean Community Secretariat.

Lowenthal, David. 1961. "The Social Background of Federation," in *The West Indies Federation: Perspectives on a New Nation*, ed. David Lowenthal. New York: Columbia Univ. Press.

Mintz, Sidney W. 1966. "The Caribbean as a Sociological Area," in *The Peoples and Cultures of the Caribbean*, ed. Michael M. Horowitz. Garden City, NY: American Museum of Natural History.

West Indian Commission. 1992. *Report of the West Indian Commission: Time for Action.* Black Rock, Barbados: The West Indian Commission.

World Bank. 1990. The Caribbean Common Market: Trade Policies and Regional Integration in the 1990s. Report No. 8381, CRG, Washington, D.C.

———. 1994. Coping with Changes in the International Environment. Report No. 12821, March. Latin American and the Caribbean Regional Office, Washington, D.C.

Chapter 4

The Future of the Caribbean Community

Havelock R. H. Ross-Brewster

This paper argues that neither the traditional conceptions of political unification, nor the present and proposed approaches to economic integration in the Caribbean, are likely to succeed. Instead, we propose a form of political unity that draws its strength and institutional expression from the sociocultural affinities of the West Indian people. Such an alliance could be combined with the best options for regional integration, wherever they may be present. This approach leaves much of the field of production and trade open to integration on a global scale.

Federation and CARICOM

As in other developing regions, the course of events in the Caribbean has often been determined by outmoded concepts imposed or borrowed from outside. The British pushed federation for the West Indies, as well as for Malaysia, Singapore, Rhodesia and Nyasaland, thinking it a good solution for the small, nonviable colonies they had created, in particular for their diseconomies of scale in government and administration. But by the time the West Indies had formed a federation, it was already a bankrupt idea.

So the West Indian Federation fell apart, as was inevitable under the strains of the politics of sovereignty in newly independent countries. Thereafter the region's intellectual elite supported a functionalist approach to integration, eschewing the federalist notion of political unification, and emphasizing economic integration in its place. The conventional wisdom of the time was taken from the European Common Market. Underpinning that model, the effort at economic integration in the Caribbean, as in every other regional grouping in the developing world, began with a mandatory reassertion of certain dogma derived from Viner, and later Balassa. This model, which progresses from a free trade area through a customs union and common market, has of course been a failure in all developing regions, as it has been in CARICOM. The more mature stages of that Community experimented with neofunctionalism, including foreign policy coordination. The spillover of limited, discrete acts of cooperation in selected functional areas has not induced a progression to higher levels of collective decisionmaking. Instead, such cooperative events have grown rather promiscuously, without deepening the level of Community decisionmaking.

The economic integration strategy has failed, basically because it was always a second-best solution, predicated on the acceptance, out of necessity, of substantial protectionist costs and the implementation of effective compensatory mechanisms for maldistributed costs and benefits. Perhaps this was not altogether unreasonable at the time, when protectionism in the industrial world seemed insurmountably high and enduring. In the event, individual states have always been prepared to defect, in deed if not in word, from second-best arrangements, while the reality of uneven costs and benefits has served to curtail the deepening of integrationist ventures. Neofunctionalism has failed not only because the strategy lacked coherence and premeditated design on the part of the Community bureaucracy, but because it was always seen as ceding some of the fruits of state sovereignty for negligible gains.

The West Indian Commission's Missed Opportunity

The West Indian Commission, under the chair of Sir Shridath Ramphal, published their massive report in 1992, offering directions for the Caribbean Community into the next century (West Indian Commission 1992). So far as our present interests are concerned, the basic shortcoming of this substantial effort is that the Commission, in attempting to straddle three stools at the same time—West Indian integration, Caribbean regional-wide integration, and global integration—fell between them. No cogent new directions are therefore discernible in the heavily compromised schema it offers. It avoids commitment in the foreseeable future to political integration, and instead seeks to perfect the economic integration instruments of CARICOM. This, in my view, is regrettable, because in confining its sights to conventional notions of political integration (parliamentary union) and economic integration (single market), it has not only preserved a false dichotomy between them, and needlessly sparked off an unproductive debate among political leaders, the media and the public, but precluded consideration of more creative and fruitful options.

The Commission's approach has inevitably given rise to serious contradictions, as well. In seeking to perfect the instruments of CARICOM, such as those constituting the single market, it fails to address the more important question as to whether those instruments in the first place, and under contemporary conditions, can truly be efficacious in promoting regional development.

Similarly, the support given to monetary union is directly contradictory to the expressed intention of the Commission not to politicize, and thereby stymie, the integration process at this stage. Viewing monetary union as a more or less exclusively economic process is, of course, a result of the artificial separation of the economic from the political.

It is also difficult to see the consistency of the logic in insisting on the formalized widening of CARICOM into an Association of Caribbean States as the first phase of a strategy of widening concentric circles of integration. For one thing, the history of Central American and Latin American integration hardly suggests either a seriousness of purpose, or that there are any significant economic gains to be made or learning to be derived that would be useful for the further stage of North American and global integration. For another, the political and economic complications that would arise in this much more heterogeneous environment would surely be at the expense of the Commission's aim of advancing CARICOM, and would be a financially costly diversion, to boot. However, the worldwide process of trade liberalization is, in any case, making as much progress in this direction as seems to be practicable at this stage.

Lastly, the emphasis on export-led development, and its corollary of global integration, does not sit comfortably with the Commission's inward-looking CARICOM development strategy, for the question naturally arises as to whether it is realistic to assume that CARICOM integration can lead the drive into global integration. Would not the reverse be nearer the mark, that it will isolate the region? If so, the whole question of deliberately creating a single market with all the difficult technical and political issues it generates could be left aside, to take its natural course.

Towards a Future Without a Past

My vision of the future unfolds in three dimensions. The centerpiece of this vision is a Union of West Indian States, including West Indian citizenship, carrying with it generally agreed rights and duties, and coexisting with citizenship of the individual member states. In much the same way, the European Union (EU) and European citizenship were selectively defined to suit the peculiar needs and limits of the European states concerned. The EU coexists with the statehood and sovereignty of the individual states. It neither establishes a European parliament with legislative powers nor eliminates its member states' diplomatic representation and UN membership. Nor does it allow immediate and complete freedom of movement to resident aliens. Likewise, the Union of West Indian States could be defined to suit our evolving requirements and possibilities. Thus, West Indian union can be an indigenous and dynamic concept, rather than a fixed legal framework.

Cultural identity and kinship are already to a good extent part of West Indian reality and are thus the core of any institutional expression of political unity. Indeed, these essential ingredients are far more developed in West Indian society than in its political institutions: political expression needs to catch up with social reality. West Indian society is more united in many ways than the present European Union. A more formal expression of West Indian states as a distinctive society would not only correspond better to reality, but would enhance our people's pride, self-esteem, and confidence. A West Indian union could also have practical benefits, such as improved governance and civil society, administrative economies of scale, enhanced negotiating status, more effective self-protection, and stronger international diplomatic and cultural influence.

In my view, such a political union is now necessary, because the CARICOM states have become increasingly peripheral and isolated, with tenuous, virtually nonexistent links to Africa, Asia, Europe, Latin America and North America. The Caribbean may well be the most isolated community of people in the world: even the strategic, colonial and migrant ties of the recent past have disappeared, while its diaspora has become more remote with the passing years. At the same time that the nations of the world become more economically open, they are becoming more culturally and racially self-conscious and closed.

Political leaders of the region are aware of the need to move in these directions. The OECS member states have already committed themselves to work towards a unitary state. At the CARICOM summit meeting in June 1992, Prime Minister Manning of Trinidad and Tobago called for "those actions which will not only build on our common heritage and aspirations but strengthen the common identity of our peoples...." He proposed that the time has come for CARICOM members "to take the incremental approach to political union." President Jagan of Guyana also called for the establishment of a Union of West Indian States. He stated that the "lessons we should draw from the experiences of the Federation is not that political unity is a lost cause, but that we should be sensitive with respect to the nature and character of that concept.... Parliamentary and constitutional union is not the unique conception of or approach to a Union of States" (Jagan 1994). Together with Prime Minister Manning and President Jagan, Prime Minister Sandiford of Barbados was assigned the task of putting forward proposals to take these ideas further.

Developments along these lines will ultimately strengthen CARICOM's relations with the non-Anglophone Caribbean, Central America, and the rest of Latin America. Enhancement of the CARICOM peoples' own cultural identification, self-knowledge and self-confidence will enable them to reach out to their neighbors, who are so culturally and geographically cohesive. Where mutually advantageous opportunities for trade and other forms of economic cooperation exist, full advantage should be taken of them. But this does not require the paraphernalia of international treaties and costly intergovernmental institutions.

Second, I see the economic and functional dimensions of the Union revolving around activities of the first priority that cannot be pursued nationally or regionally. This means activities that are unique, or least-cost, or for which there are no alternative options. The latter, for example, concern regional commons, public goods, and complementary resources. Regional commons are commonly shared benevolent or malevolent resources, such as the sea, airspace, the weather, disease, and pest infestation. Regional public goods are goods and services that would otherwise not be provided at all, such as regional security, social infrastructure like high technology and advanced scientific training and medical facilities, physical infrastructure like sea and air transportation, and telecommunications. Regional resource complementarity refers to combinations of resources that are usually exploited through regional arrangements, such as food demand/arable land, mineral smelting/hydroelectricity, and diversified financial services.

The Community's future economic and functional institutions would no longer, for example, manage the various instruments that constitute and support the common market. Instead they would be devoted to such issues as energizing the private sector for its role in region-wide enterprise development; identifying and promoting the development of those truly first-best regional activities, including regional infrastructure and regional services. They would further support and guide the regional governments in undertaking regular, research-based consultations on macroeconomic and exchange rate policy, and national and regional policy assessment and outlook analysis.

Third, production and trade activities that cannot meet the first-best test on a regional scale would be left to the dictates of comparative advantage in the global market. This policy should allow reasonable adjustment periods for critical industries, especially agriculture, that cannot immediately compete internationally. Moreover, it must be determined that international trading partners are not themselves using protectionist subsidies and other unfair trading practices.

This proposition is not as remote as it appears, particularly since the individual CARICOM states are progressively moving in this direction under the stimulus of structural adjustment programs. They are moving towards this goal at different rates, some more quickly and comprehensively than others. It serves no good purpose to pretend that intra-CARICOM production and trade are being developed under the impetus of Community regimes. Regimes like the Common External Tariff (among others) have neither conferred common protection, nor have they been effective in promoting resource-based industries and trade within the region. Accession to NAFTA under mutually agreeable terms would be consistent with, indeed would enhance, this third dimension of CARICOM's future. Participation in NAFTA could be an important component in shaping a strategy for the future of CARICOM, particularly on the economic side. However, it cannot be a substitute for fostering our identity as a distinctive people and a nation-of-states, and for organizing the region's public goods and services and exploiting its commons.

Bibliography

Jagan, C. B. 1994. *The Caribbean Community: Cross Roads to the Future.* St. Augustine, Trinidad and Tobago: Institute of International Relations, University of the West Indies.

Ross-Brewster, H. R. 1992. *The Caribbean Community in a Changing International Environment: Towards the Next Century.* Mona, Jamaica: Institute of Social and Economic Research, University of the West Indies (ISER-UWI).

West Indian Commission. 1992. *The Report of the West Indian Commission: Time for Action.* Black Rock, Barbados: The West Indian Commission.

Chapter 5

Caribbean Regional Cooperation and Strategic Alliances

David E. Lewis

The central thesis of this paper is that the external and regional resources and conditions no longer exist for the continuation of traditional Caribbean subregionalized cooperation and integration processes. Whereas in the past there existed both regional and external rationalizations and justifications for restricting and limiting the scope of regional initiatives, the regional, hemispheric and global scenario of the 1990s requires both the Caribbean states and the external powers to cooperate beyond the subregional initiatives of the past.

The impetus for this change of direction, scope and strategy is not only regional but sectoral, including business, labor, and non-governmental organizations in a way never seen before. Hemispheric and global factors are also involved. External alliances such as the proposed single European market, NAFTA, and Western Hemisphere Free Trade Area (WHFTA), signal the obsolescence of regional, exclusive schemes for cooperation and integration.

Regional cooperation and economic integration in the Caribbean have been the subject of many diverse studies. Those that mostly concentrate on the CARICOM experience include Bourne (1988), Brewster and Thomas (1967), CARICOM Secretariat (1984), Chernick (1978), Derné et al. (1990, 1992), Group of Caribbean Experts (1981), Harker (1989), Manigat (1991), Samuel (1989a-b, 1990), Vega (1987), and Will (1991), among others. Of this sampling, only Samuel and Harker have analyzed the subject from a truly regional perspective, going beyond the central CARICOM experience. The Samuel studies emerge out of research initiatives developed by the regional Association of Caribbean Economists (ACE), integrating researchers from territories throughout the region. However, most of these studies are evaluative, do not incorporate prospective analyses, and are already quite dated.

Some recent studies have identified and developed the initial format of what I have called a "beyond CARICOM" agenda for the region, incorporating cooperation and integration with the non-CARICOM Caribbean, Central

America, Latin America, and even the state of Florida.[1] These studies cover matters ranging from joint trade and investment policies to common negotiating positions vis-a-vis NAFTA and hemispheric trade liberalization. Here, I believe, the future strategies and policies of a competitive Caribbean will originate and develop.

Within the Caribbean, especially at the national level, there are major trends and initiatives toward cooperation and integration. From the impact of economic liberalization in Cuba, to collaboration with Central America and the special role that the Dominican Republic can play as a subregional "bridge," a wide realm of action and commitment exists for supporting various proposals discussed herein. Private sector groupings, regional governmental organizations, and the nongovernmental sectors have also played important roles and merit a separate analysis. By understanding the intertwining of these initiatives, we can gauge the strategic planning that is taking place and define specific policy actions and initiatives that will best serve the needs and interests of the region.

Cuba: Economic Liberalization and Political Democratization

A market-oriented Cuba reintegrated into the Caribbean economy will have substantial impact on the Dominican Republic, Jamaica, and the smaller CARICOM states, in areas such as tourism, nontraditional agriculture, and some assembly industries. Some trade will be created and some diverted, as Cuban growth in trade and investment either adds to or displaces levels elsewhere in the region. Trade-creating effects are more likely for tourism, and trade-diverting effects for assembly industry, with nontraditional agricultural exports somewhere in between. Puerto Rico, for example, could service the new Cuban market economy in areas such as investment, financial services, construction, and technical assistance. Likewise, such opportunities would face stiff competition from U.S.-based businesses, especially in Florida.

Economic and political reforms leading to an open Cuban economy, with normalized relations with the United States, would bring immediate Cuban accession to CBI and NAFTA benefits, as well as direct economic assistance. Cuba would thereby gain access to the U.S. market for such sectors as textiles, agricultural products, and some manufactures, while its investment climate

---

[1] See for example, Bernal (1993), Bryan (1989, 1991), Bryan and Serbin (1990), CAIC (1993), CBTAG (1992), C/LAA (1993), FEDEPRICAP (1992), Gill, (1992), Lewis (1992a-c, 1993c), Rosenberg and Hiskey (1993), Segal (1992), Serbin (1993), the West India Committee (1991) and West Indian Commission (1992).

would improve. Cuba's participation as an open market economy in the Caribbean would not only transform trade and investment patterns, but would result in greater Cuban and regional interdependence with the U.S. economy.

Lastly, the human and financial resources of Cuban expatriates and the growing interests of U.S. multinational corporations are critical factors that would well serve Cuba's economic restructuring and positively assist in developing its new regional and hemispheric competitiveness. No Caribbean country, not even Puerto Rico, has the resources to counter or balance such support. In sum, the region should look to Cuba as an economic complement, and not as a zero-sum competitor.

The potential implications of such changes in Cuba should be fully assessed. While CARICOM has established a CARICOM–Cuba Joint Council (c. July 1993, with an official signing in December 1993), most consideration of the impact of change is taking place at the level of the private sector. In March 1993, however, Prime Minister Charles of Dominica called for an end to the U.S. embargo on Cuba and stressed the need for CARICOM states to actively engage in business in Cuba.

Still, for CARICOM, the interests of political democratization and economic liberalization in Cuba are contradictory. If and when the United States ends its embargo on the island, U.S. multinational corporations could challenge and displace current CARICOM business in Cuba. In the present situation, while major U.S. business interests are excluded from the Cuban market, Caribbean entrepreneurs can take full advantage of the opportunities offered in Cuba by economic liberalization. The Joint CARICOM–Cuba Technical Cooperation Agreement of July 1993 should further strengthen these processes and help guarantee and safeguard the interests of both sides during this uncertain period.

The Dominican Republic as a Bridge Between the Caribbean and Central America

In a sense, the main issues presented in the 1974 study of the implications of the Dominican Republic's entry into CARICOM (Vega 1978) are at the center of Dominican–CARICOM relations today. There is still debate concerning the cost-benefit ratio of complete Dominican participation in CARICOM.

Throughout 1992 and 1993, the Dominican Republic embarked on an unprecedented initiative to establish trade linkages with both the CARICOM grouping and the Central American Common Market countries. At the CARICOM level, the Dominican Republic has emphasized political, cultural and geographic reasons for cementing a relationship that has often fluctuated.

Since its 1991 request for full membership, presented at the CARICOM summit in St. Kitts, the Dominican Republic's interest in CARICOM is best described as haphazard. However, since the first CARICOM–Central America ministerial summit in Honduras in 1991, the Dominican Republic has embarked on an aggressive strategy towards the two subregions, since it is capable of participating in both groupings.

Toward Central America, the Dominican initiative has been impressive and aggressive. At the December 1992 Central American presidential summit in Panama, Vice President Carlos Morales Troncoso laid political foundations for a Dominican entry into the Central American integration process. Emphasizing the shared cultural-linguistic heritage and similar reforms in trade and economic liberalization, the country is able to fully exploit trade opportunities with Central America.[2]

Among Caribbean countries, the Dominican Republic has the most dynamic posture regarding the Association of Caribbean States (ACS), suggesting itself as the ideal central location for a future ACS secretariat. The second ACS technical meeting was hosted in Santo Domingo on 9–10 May 1993, a week before national elections, a clear sign the country is committed to maximizing its regional linkages.

Two major points, one negative and one positive, must form part of this strategic summary. On the one hand, the Dominican Republic's commitment to a bona fide relationship within CARICOM is still questioned by many in the Community. It is no secret that CARICOM's failure to respond to the Dominican request for full membership presented in 1991 was due to lack of confidence in the Dominican Republic's commitment to abiding to a "CARICOM position" on regional and international matters.

The positive point is that for the first time there is a public–private sector consensus within the Dominican Republic on the strategic importance of establishing these linkages with its CARICOM and Central American neighbors. This two-track approach to regional integration should continue as a coherent, well-directed effort. As these initiatives progress within the Dominican Republic, they should also receive political reinforcement from CARICOM and the rest of the region.[3]

---

[2] Both groups have lowered their external tariffs to less than 20 percent and have argued vehemently for immediate inclusion into the NAFTA and a complete willingness to abide by the NAFTA eligibility criteria established by the USTR in 1991.

[3] The *Consejo Nacional de Hombres de Empresa* (CNHE) commissioned a study of the integration options available to the Dominican Republic both within CARICOM and Central America. The study was conducted by Bernardo Vega and Carlos Despradel, two former Central Bank governors, under the title *Estudio de las alternativas de integración económica de la República Dominicana* (mimeo, August 1993). Results were expected for early 1994.

Most of the obstacles in CARICOM–Dominican Republic collaboration are due to a long controversy over the preferential trade regime for Caribbean bananas in Europe. The Dominican Republic has used its new Lomé status to compete in this market, in direct contradiction of the agreement with CARICOM prior to the December 1989 accession.[4] The institutionalization of the Lomé Regional Indicative Program under the CARIFORUM, and the Dominican Republic's special role in the European Community's drive to utilize Lomé programs to strengthen the Caribbean integration process, should form the basis for a qualitative improvement in CARICOM–Dominican relations.[5] If cooperation at the technical level is strengthened and complemented by similar processes in Dominican foreign policy towards the region, the Dominican Republic can become the bridge for bona fide regional cooperation.

Strengthening this public policy initiative would complement recent initiatives by the Dominican private sector (traditionally focused on ties to the U.S. and not known for its integrationist commitment) to mobilize resources for trade, investment, and capital market ventures with CARICOM and Central American neighbors.[6] In the final analysis, the bridging role can succeed only with support and participation from the Dominican private sector.

As long as the Dominican Republic is viewed by CARICOM and CARIFORUM as seeking to take advantage of potential business, financial and commercial schemes, the relationship is bound to remain in crisis and in flux. Unless recent private sector initiatives are complemented by an *institutionalization of a Caribbean policy within the government* (especially in the Ministry of Foreign Affairs and the National Palace), there will be no true Dominican commitment to Caribbean cooperation. While the Dominican linkage towards CARICOM has been characterized by uncertainties and doubts on their

---

[4] As early as January 1990, the Dominican Republic was in violation of this agreement, as bananas were being shipped and marketed from Manzanillo to England by the British conglomerate Fyffes. Moreover, despite the three-year banana conflict with CARICOM, the Dominican Republic's Lomé Minister Roberto Martínez Villanueva announced that by the end of 1993 the country would have shipped two million tons of bananas to the European market, paying the 20 percent tariff which applies to exports beyond its 175,000-ton quota.

[5] Curiously, the director and deputy director of the CARIFORUM Programming Unit in Guyana, Percival Marie and Renso Herrara-Franco respectively, are from Dominica and the Dominican Republic. The rapid success of their collaboration in the first year of CARIFORUM should be seen as an indicator of future relations.

[6] See, for example, the seminar on The Dominican Republic and the Challenge of Regional Integration, organized by the Santo Domingo Chamber of Commerce and Industry and the government's Commission on Integration Schemes, headed by Vice President Morales Troncoso (*Listín Diario* and *Hoy*, Santo Domingo, 29 July 1993). Also note the convening in Santo Domingo of the VIth Europe\Caribbean Conference of the Caribbean Council for Europe, on 10–12 November 1993, with full support of the Dominican government and private sector.

part, CARICOM's performance towards the Dominicans has been one of nonchalance, if not outright neglect and disinterest.

If the Caribbean region as a whole is to face the new global trading environment, the potential for collaboration must materialize in an effective and productive manner. The Dominican Republic's contribution to the regional integration and cooperation process could indeed be great, given its size, production structures, and unique participation in both the CBI and Lomé. The opportunity and the responsibility now rest in both camps.

Puerto Rico: Beyond 936 and the Future of the Caribbeanization Process

The central issue for the next few years will be Puerto Rico's overall commitment to collaboration with the rest of the Caribbean beyond the financial and technical specifics of the 936 Caribbean Development Program.[7] As Edwin Carrington said in 1992 before becoming CARICOM secretary general: "The Caribbean expects much more than 936 from Puerto Rico." In some forty years of Puerto Rico–Caribbean relations, this has been the crux of the matter (Lewis 1992c; Rivera Ortiz 1992). To what degree is Puerto Rico committed to the institutionalization of relations with the rest of the Caribbean?

These collaborative initiatives have served both the United States and Puerto Rico well; moreover, they have served the region as a whole. They were developed on the basis of collaboration between the private and public sectors in Puerto Rico, recognizing that political, economic, and cultural involvement in the Caribbean Basin is positive. This process of economic collaboration has placed Puerto Rico at the center stage of regional economic development and the transfer of technology and resources to the Caribbean Basin. Transportation, tourism and manufacturing have all benefitted from this involvement. Investment promotion efforts have also strengthened regional trade, as Puerto Rico's exports to the Caribbean Basin increased by 63 percent between 1985 and 1992 (from $518 million to $812 million), and Caribbean exports to Puerto Rico increased by 64 percent over the same period (from $616 million to $960 million).[8]

Another important initiative in this direction began in 1991–92, under the loose coordination of the government of Puerto Rico's Department of State. The Caribbean Basin Technical Advisory Group (CBTAG) was an informal attempt by Puerto Rico to establish a technical-level forum for private sector,

---

[7] For an in-depth analysis of this issue and its linkage to the Puerto Rican identity and status problems, see García-Passalacqua (1993).

[8] All dollar amounts are in U.S. dollars unless stated otherwise.

government, academia, NGOs, and civil society from the Caribbean and Central America, including non-independent territories. CBTAG was an effort to develop technical analyses and policy recommendations regarding the economic impact of the proposed NAFTA and SEM on the economies of the Caribbean and Central America.[9]

Moreover, CBTAG saw its role as providing the technical foundation necessary for justifying Caribbean–Central American strategic collaboration. This "critical economic mass" of 50 million people represented a GNP of $50 billion, which could become a negotiating bloc vis-a-vis the NAFTA–EAI process and other hemispheric trade and economic liberalization processes, and could operate efficiently in the regional, hemispheric and international markets. During its existence,[10] CBTAG sought to coordinate efforts and prepare regional briefings concerning economic policy related to NAFTA, SEM, and specific public policy initiatives.

CARICOM governments have always viewed Puerto Rico with varying degrees of trust over the Caribbean linkage issue, and historically they have been correct. Unless Puerto Rico can prove that its self-interest in developing Caribbean ties to save 936 is matched by a bona fide regional commitment, then under the pro-statehood New Progressive Party (NPP) administration (in power until 1997), Puerto Rico's role in regional cooperation initiatives will be very limited.

That the CBTAG initiative was dormant under this administration is definitely not a positive sign in regard to Puerto Rico's involvement in regional and hemispheric trade, cooperation and integration schemes. Similarly, reports that the government plans to end its membership in some international and regional organizations do not bode well for its commitment to regional and hemispheric cooperation initiatives. As a matter of fact, Secretary of State Corrada del Río has stated that Puerto Rico will participate in international forums as part of the U.S. delegations.[11]

---

[9] *Proposal to Establish the Caribbean Basin Technical Advisory Group–CBTAG* (San Juan, Puerto Rico: IVth Point Four Conference, 29 April–1 May 1991). Technical briefings on these matters were prepared and circulated regionally on 29 August 1991, 24 September 1991, January 1992, and September 1992.

[10] Since January 1993, the Puerto Rico government has suspended all CBTAG activities and its mandate, much to the chagrin of regional government and business leaders who valued and supported the CBTAG's work and saw it as a potential bridge in U.S.–Caribbean relations, as well as in Caribbean–Central American relations. Moreover, Puerto Rico opted not to participate in the ACS convening meetings of 18–20 March (Jamaica), 9–10 May (Dominican Republic), and 3–5 June (Mexico), and curiously offered to host the June meeting of the Southern Governors Association with the countries of Central America and the Caribbean.

[11] *El Nuevo Día* (San Juan), 23 August 1993, p. 4. The government has sought to end its membership in the World Tourism Organization, the U.N. Food and Agriculture Organization (FAO), and the

It is curious that within the framework of union with the United States, Puerto Rican statehooders have never looked to the examples of Florida and the southwestern states of Texas, Arizona, New Mexico and California in their respective linkages with the countries of the Caribbean and Central America, as well as Mexico. Florida actually has a Caribbean policy linking private and public sectors, a policy that seeks to safeguard the relationship with the Caribbean Basin.

The current Florida legislative proposals for CBI NAFTA parity (H.R. 1403 and S.R. 1155) began in August 1992 under the government of then-Resident Commissioner Antonio J. Colorado, a clear indication of how deeply Puerto Rico has become involved and committed to regional economic development matters. Already, for example, there are two associations, a very active Gulf States Association and a Southern Governors Association, which serve as vehicles for linkage and collaboration with U.S. states and Mexico on matters such as NAFTA, immigration, environmental management, and regional economic development.

Puerto Rico's use of 936 is but another instance of a continuing problem, however. The San Juan administration has effectively avoided the larger question: What kind of linkage should Puerto Rico have with the rest of the Caribbean? With or without 936, Puerto Rico should actively participate in matters relating to economic development initiatives and regional collaboration, and the region should strongly communicate to Puerto Rico that this will serve their interests as well. Even if Puerto Rico were to achieve statehood, both sides can benefit if current linkages are maintained and strengthened.

Both CARICOM and Puerto Rico need to look at this issue from a perspective of enlightened self-interest and avoid being ensnared in the perennial ups and downs of Puerto Rican status politics. Regional collaboration is not incompatible with closer ties to the U.S., or even with statehood. Similarly, a strategy of external economic linkages is the prerequisite for Puerto Rico's future economic development under any status, whether it be statehood, commonwealth, or independence.

Every economy in the region—whether a sovereign state, a dependent colonial state, or any other constitutional format— should consider economic and strategic participation in NAFTA and in the impending WHFTA. If one thing is clear from the nonmajority results of the 1993 status consultation in Puerto

---

U.N. Economic Commission on Latin American and the Caribbean (ECLAC), of which the U.S. Virgin Islands has been a member since 1976. Membership will apparently be maintained in the World Health Organization (WHO) and the Pan American Health Organization (PAHO). Observer status in CARICOM will be maintained, possibly an indication of the Roselló administration's short-term 936 commitment vis-a-vis CARICOM.

Rico,[12] it is that Puerto Rico's regional agenda cannot wait for the status issue to be resolved.

To date, Puerto Rico has participated in regional initiatives not by promoting its own model of economic development, but by understanding the needs and interests of other countries in the region and identifying ways that its human, financial, and political resources can complement regional resources to mutual advantage. The countries of the Caribbean Basin—CARICOM especially—have learned that Puerto Rico's potential commitment in 1985 is now a solid commitment to economic collaboration. But Puerto Rico must confirm to the rest of the Caribbean that regionalism can be politically and economically profitable. In a world of global trading blocs and regional groupings, assisting Caribbean Basin economic cooperation and integration is a viable public policy that can have positive results for Puerto Rico, the Caribbean, and the United States as well.[13]

Central America: Between Bananas and Cooperation

The preferential market for Caribbean bananas in Europe, and challenges posed by the so-called dollar-banana producers of Central and South America, have been a stumbling block in subregional relations. Nevertheless, advances in the past few years have established a foundation for future efforts at cooperation. The institutionalization of the CARICOM–Central America ministerial forum via the CARICOM and SIECA secretariats will allow technical-level collaborative efforts to develop and will complement ministerial-level policy initiatives, strengthening the linkages between the two subregions from below and above.

Specific attention must be given to the CARICOM–Central America ministerial forum, established in January 1992 in San Pedro Sula, Honduras, which has become a permanent forum for CARICOM–Central America collaboration. The second meeting took place in Kingston in May 1993, and a proposed third

---

[12] The final tally of votes on 14 November 1993 gave no real majority to either status option, resulting in various anti-colonial, anti-commonwealth, anti-statehood interpretations: Commonwealth–48.4 percent, Statehood–46.2 percent, Independence–4.4 percent. Adding Independence support to either of the remaining major status options results in an anti-statehood vote of 52.4 percent or an anti-commonwealth/colony vote of 50.2 percent. While no commanding majority, most regional observers see the vote as a short-term victory against statehood, with the caveat that the Puerto Rican electorate is clearly split 50–50 on this issue. Since the vote, neither the U.S. Congress nor President Clinton have indicated any willingness to tackle the Puerto Rico status question.

[13] The State of Florida and its Caribbean Basin and Latin American initiatives should be an important point of reference for the current administration in Puerto Rico, given its obvious zero-sum vision of statehood and regionalism.

meeting was scheduled for mid-1994 in Costa Rica (CARICOM 1992 and 1993).[14] So far the ministerial forum has served as a regional convener for the discussion of a common interest agenda, and also has become a critical institutional arena for the development of collaborative proposals in a variety of areas, such as trade and investment, tourism, transportation, agriculture, drug trafficking, environmental management, education, and technology, among others.

Moreover, through the forum, various sensitive subjects of Caribbean–Central American relations, such as the trade preference regime for bananas in Europe, have been addressed, thus strengthening the arguments for a true regional collaboration agenda. The ministerial forum is also expected to review the matter of a common stance towards NAFTA. Of particular importance in this venture has been the commitment and support of CARICOM member states and the secretariat. However, commitment and support on the one hand must be balanced by functional collaboration on the other. Here the role of non-CARICOM member states, such as the Dominican Republic, Puerto Rico, the French and Dutch Antilles, and even Cuba in some instances, will be critically important, as their involvement will advance the integrationist agenda on behalf of these initiatives.

The May 1993 signing of a cooperation agreement between SIECA and CARICOM allowed for developing a common policy agenda in light of the trade liberalization processes of NAFTA–EAI and the GATT, and for developing joint strategies in trade and investment promotion and functional cooperation (health, education, culture and language, sports, environmental management, disaster preparedness, and drug trafficking). This includes establishing institutional mechanisms within each subregion that will help to strengthen cooperative ventures.[15]

All these initiatives have served to complement the ACS effort, whose success hinges on the effective participation and commitment of three major regional groupings: CARICOM, Central America, and the Group of Three (G-3: Colombia, Mexico, and Venezuela). Whatever the form of the ACS or the policy decision by CARICOM on this matter, CARICOM will eventually have to face the need to establish formal external linkages as part of a regionwide effort to

---

[14] A five-point basic cooperation agreement was signed between the CARICOM secretary general, Edwin Carrington, and the secretary general of the General Treaty of Central American Economic Integration (SIECA), Rafael Rodríguez Loucel, on 28 May 1993 in Kingston, Jamaica, the final day of the IInd CARICOM–Central America Ministerial Conference. The agreement established an inter-institutional cooperation program aimed at furthering greater interregional linkages.

[15] Unfortunately, during the ministerial forum meeting, the Central American representatives sought to remove the issue of bananas from the agenda, while CARICOM wanted the matter discussed. The result was a one-day standoff and its noninclusion in the final communiqué, and the release of a separate CARICOM statement on bananas. Clearly the banana issue can become the political obstacle to any future collaboration initiatives.

avoid marginalization and to develop regional and hemispheric-wide strategic alliances in support of economic and political viability.

Moreover, given the advent of recent private sector initiatives to develop closer linkages between both subregions and the commitment to establishing a common regional agenda vis-a-vis the NAFTA and regional economic competitiveness, CARICOM governments should not only respond positively to the Central American initiatives, but begin to formulate and present their own vision of collaboration to the Central Americans (FEDEPRICAP 1992; CAIC 1993; C/LAA 1993).[16] These gains may have been dealt a mortal blow by the CARICOM states' failure to fully support the Central American candidate for OAS secretary general, Foreign Minister Bernd Niehaus, during the March 1993 elections. Whether this "voting strategy fiasco" will impair the institutional cooperation envisioned by the ACS, or bilateral cooperation between Central America and CARICOM, remains to be seen.

Finally, the linkage taking place between Central America and the Dominican Republic is a sign of potential strategic alliances at the public policy level. More importantly, this linkage is the basis for export production complementarity, market penetration initiatives, CBI and GSP trade benefits, free trade zone strategy, and trade and production coordination with mainland U.S. industries, as well as the lobbying efforts mentioned earlier with regard to specific industries.

With the exception of Jamaica, the countries of Central America, together with the Dominican Republic, have the most at stake concerning NAFTA and WHFTA, and can participate more effectively in these new hemispheric schemes. The potential value of such alliances as part of an ACS or CARICOM regional and hemispheric strategy must be carefully evaluated within the CARICOM-ACS realm.

Playing the Latin American Card: the Rise of Economic Interests

For most of the 1970s and 1980s, Latin American interests in the Caribbean region—mostly expressed by policy initiatives from the Group of Three—focused on the strategic and security aspects of political instability in the region. Whether it meant bringing the Caribbean states into the forefront of the external debt movement, or playing the "strategic buffer" vis-a-vis the Cold War

---

[16] For example, the June 1993 decision by the Caribbean and Central American Textile and Apparel Council to retain the lobbying services of the Miami-based law firm of Greenberg, Traurig indicates that the regional textile industry has realized the need to develop firm and institutional joint positions on matters pertaining to trade, investment, and production. Likewise, FEDEPRICAP and CAIC met in December 1993 in Miami under the auspices of the OAS, resulting in a new collaboration strategy, Prospects for Cross-Caribbean Business Relationships and Trade.

hegemonic policies of the United States in the region, the dominant trend in relations with the Caribbean was based on security concerns.

Moreover, given increased Caribbean participation in international forums and organizations, Mexico and Venezuela in particular aimed to strengthen ties with the Caribbean as a means to ensuring greater Latin American (and Caribbean) voting power in these groupings. However, despite such proactive policy initiatives, most countries in the Caribbean—the CARICOM member states especially—saw ulterior "subimperialist" motivations at hand, and shied away from developing closer political and economic ties with Latin American countries.

Due to major changes in the regional and international political economy (trade liberalization, integration initiatives, global trading blocs, et cetera), efforts at closer Caribbean–Latin American collaboration have intensified, and both subregions have prioritized the strengthening of relations. Curiously, though, even with Venezuela's active "shared responsibility" Caribbean policy in the late eighties (Serbin 1991–1992), or Mexico's new regional commitments to CARICOM and the CDB, the Latin American countries have always viewed the region as a rather unimportant, though necessary player in the hemispheric configuration of politics and economics.

In the 1990s, both the Caribbean and Latin America are accelerating the processes of subregional integration, revitalizing some previous schemes such as the Andean Pact and the Central American Common Market, and creating new schemes such as the G-3 and MERCOSUR, together with bilateral initiatives for trade liberalization and commercial expansion. The January 1993 trade and investment agreement between CARICOM and Venezuela (with the potential development of a similar scheme with Colombia) signalled a major watershed, in which the previous economic-interest justification for Caribbean–Latin American relations was nonexistent.

The West Indian Commission's emphasis on CARICOM linkages with the wider Caribbean and Latin America, coupled with the G-3 initiative to become observer members in CARICOM and to advance nonreciprocal trade agreements, have now opened a new door in this relationship. The concern for regional stability is now balanced by an interest in economic gains and opportunities. The proposed 1994 free trade agreement between the G-3 and Central America, as well as confirmation of a political and economic cooperation agenda for the October 1993 CARICOM–G-3 summit in Trinidad and Tobago, signal the new strategic importance of economic opportunities in this relationship.[17]

Likewise, recent Mexican overtures at promoting manufacturing investments in Central American and Caribbean countries must be seen in light of

---

[17] These initiatives formed the foundation of the G-3's early commitment to the ACS proposal, spelled out in the October 1993 Port of Spain declaration.

Mexico's need to expand its area of economic activity, in order to maintain manufacturing competitiveness within NAFTA. As production costs in Mexico rise with NAFTA, sourcing production in more labor-competitive countries like El Salvador, Guatemala and the Dominican Republic will be increasingly attractive to Mexican firms being displaced by free trade.

These initiatives may not necessarily signal the end of the strategic interests era, especially since G-3 and Latin American collective subregional interests are focusing on the Cuban political transition, Haitian democratization, the stabilization of Suriname, and curtailment of drug trafficking. Still, economic concerns are becoming part of the formula for defining Caribbean policy. As countries in Latin America and the Caribbean begin to advocate a stronger role for OAS and UN bodies in safeguarding collective security, the emphasis on Caribbean regional economic initiatives will become stronger.

Latin American participation in an ACS proposal led by CARICOM will be a critical determinant of the degree of future political and economic attention given to the Caribbean. As Caribbean trade liberalization and regionalization processes result in greater economic growth and competitiveness, countries like Mexico, Venezuela and Colombia will seek to draw the region into complementary economic agreements.

Florida: Making Geography Destiny?

Florida's call for the development of a strategic consensus with the Caribbean Basin, exemplified in the legislative proposals in Congress (H.R. 1403 and S.R. 1155, The Caribbean Basin Free Trade Agreements Act) to provide NAFTA parity benefits to the region, is the most advanced initiative for the securing of trade and investment stability in the region. Florida's state government and private sector have begun to take on the role of the benign hegemon, whose participation is necessary for effective cooperation.[18] Moreover, Florida's notion of the need for a strategic alliance is paralleled by similar initiatives in Central America and, to a lesser extent, in the Caribbean.

As Florida continues to lead in terms of regional and hemispheric strategic planning and proactive initiatives (mostly via this government–private sector collaboration),[19] its Caribbean Basin partners will need to determine how to respond to and complement the Florida effort. While Florida is clearly safe-

---

[18] The Florida International Affairs Commission (FIAC, c. 1992) agenda is by far the most advanced and progressive initiative on the Caribbean by any government. The Florida–Caribbean Institute is only one of a dozen international programs coordinated by FIAC.

[19] See Florida's recent success in having Miami selected by President Clinton as the site for the December 1994 hemispheric summit.

guarding its own self-interests—a $4 billion export trade to the Basin in 1992, representing 30 percent of its total exports and creating 80,000 jobs in the state (Rosenberg and Hiskey 1993, 2–4)—it is virtually impossible to separate where its own interests end and Caribbean Basin interests begin. The region should address this issue, not as a point of contention, but rather to establish the institutional linkages (in government and the private sector) to strengthen this very important partnership. As stated by Rosenberg and Hiskey:

> Florida is as much a part of the Caribbean as it is of the Southeastern United States. As the social bonds between Florida and the Caribbean proliferate and deepen, the economies of the two areas are showing greater complementarity. Any complete economic development strategy crafted by either misses a critical component if the geographic and commercial contiguity of the other is ignored. *However, given the rapid emergence of trade blocs and the historic trade and integration-oriented efforts of Mexico, Canada, and the United States, the development of greater pan-Caribbean cooperation is not just far-sighted, but a strategic necessity as a means to maintain and expand the Caribbean Basin standard of living* (ibid., 1, emphasis added).

Curiously, neither the West Indian Commission Report, nor any other region-based studies, reports or CARICOM meetings have even raised the issue of the role of Florida in regional integration and cooperation schemes. CARICOM has not responded to Florida's initiative regarding the so-called CBI NAFTA Parity bill or to Florida's interest in safeguarding Caribbean Basin economic interests. Although Florida and Miami serve as trade, transportation, finance and human resource hubs for the region, no Caribbean plan has sought to incorporate these initiatives into a strategy for regional cooperation and integration.

In the hemispheric political economy of the 1990s, the route to integration and cooperation will have to pass through Florida and Miami. If CARICOM or any other grouping within the Caribbean Basin cannot yet understand this, we must question how seriously the concept of a wider Caribbean is being used. Just as various Caribbean-based initiatives involve cooperation and integration, so too must we undertake a detailed analysis of how Florida is linked to the rest of the Caribbean, and how that linkage can help the region strengthen its hemispheric competitive position.

Moreover, in the eventual case of economic and political liberalization in Cuba, the linkages with Florida and Miami (geographic, financial, commercial, human and demographic) will ensure that Caribbean islands are not economically marginalized due to the attraction of the larger, unpenetrated Cuban market. Because of these factors, as mentioned earlier, the strategic alliance between the region and Florida must be developed now and not later.

Beyond CARICOM: The Cost of Not Cooperating

As the Caribbean Basin prepares to enter the twenty-first century, the prevailing winds of economic change are related to economic liberalization and competitiveness. Yet most of the small economies of the region lack the necessary resources to meet the challenge of economic liberalization and hemispheric free trade. Small size may be a disadvantage, but it is not the major obstacle preventing the countries of the Caribbean Basin from competing effectively in a free trade area. Rather, the rapid development of global trading blocs and the decline of protectionist tenets in the international trading system have transformed the region, so that 'survival of the fittest' prevails.

The region needs to focus less on threats and challenges posed by free trade and NAFTA and more on opportunities for economic reform and restructuring to become more competitive internationally. Such an endeavor should not only focus on the traditional trade preferential markets of the United States (CBI), Canada (CARIBCAN), and Europe (Lomé), but should prioritize the Latin American trade and investment markets. Mexico, Venezuela and Colombia are most important initially, and the region should seek to develop and exploit a comparative advantage vis-a-vis these economies. Central American and CARICOM countries have already established nonreciprocal free trade agreements with Mexico and Venezuela, respectively, but have not significantly advanced their own strategic alliance in trade and investment matters.

Efforts are being intensified to remove remaining obstacles to integration, while at the same time engaging the process of truly regional and hemispheric-wide cooperation. The CARICOM countries fully realize that they must work together to consolidate past gains in integration and to resolve internal differences while also reaching out to other countries, lest they be overtaken by the tide of global economic change. In addition to the actual physical difficulties to integration posed by an island region, regional efforts must now address coordination in fiscal, trade and monetary policies, as well as specific measures to achieve a more outward, extraregional orientation.

The common arrangements being proposed by CARICOM will continue to experience difficulties, unless greater progress is made on reconciling diverse systems and economic policies and on trade policy reform. Acceleration of tariff reductions; the harmonization of investment incentives; and trade, financial and monetary policy coordination are vital for the grouping, if it is to take full advantage of benefits which may eventually become available under other trading arrangements, and for collaborating with other regional and hemispheric ventures.

Moreover, there exists great concern within CARICOM countries, especially the smaller ones, over how larger countries like Mexico, Venezuela and even the Dominican Republic can be integrated into a community like CARICOM or ACS without overwhelming the developing economies and small populations of the present member states. This kind of political dilemma could be the Achilles heel of these initiatives. As long as efforts towards widening are relegated to the ACS—whose mandate, functions and resources are completely undetermined and undefined—there is no clear indication that such proposals will advance.

The degree of action, or inaction, on the many national, sectoral and regional initiatives discussed here will necessarily influence the prospects for both positive and negative regional economic development and the competitiveness that could strengthen cooperation and integration efforts. A synthesis of these various proposals and initiatives is needed in order to develop effective and practical options.

Given the public-private sector mandate currently enjoyed by CARICOM's ACS proposal, coupled with various sectoral and national initiatives, the region should consider establishing a joint ACS secretariat, to be staffed by public and private sector representatives from the various subregional groupings. As a pan-regional initiative, the secretariat would need to incorporate a highly developed communications capacity,[20] blending public policy needs with entrepreneurial criteria and speed, while serving to implement the various mandates that already exist.

With the proper regional and international support, such an infrastructure could not only complement current regional needs and interests, but also tackle some pending issues and initiatives that are unattended by existing institutional mechanisms. The advisory and executive capabilities of such a structure should be defined a priori by the proper national and regional bodies. As a bridge institution, its physical location and administrative mandate would have to serve the strategic and tactical political needs of both subregions' interests.

In much the way that NAFTA negotiations have established the need for a North American development bank, so too these diverse cooperative experiences will have to consider establishing an institutional mechanism for channeling interregional and intraregional policy initiatives and negotiations. Only

---

[20] For example, the regional communications gap is getting worse, yet the timely collection and dissemination of information, both internal and external to the region, must be a top priority for any cooperation and integration agenda.

if these initiatives are institutionalized so as to complement, support and strengthen existing forms of regional cooperation and integration, will there be the capacity and commitment to advance these ideas into policy actions.

Bibliography

Bernal, Richard L. 1992. Impact of NAFTA on the Economic Development of the Caribbean and U.S./Caribbean Trade. Statement at the Hearing of the House Committee on Small Business, U.S. Congress, 16 December.

———. 1993. CARICOM: Externally Vulnerable Regional Economic Integration. Paper presented at workshop, Economic Integration in the Western Hemisphere: Prospects for Latin America, at the Kellogg Institute for International Studies, University of Notre Dame, 17-18 April.

Bourne, Compton. 1988. *Caribbean Development to the Year 2000: Prospects and Policies.* London: Commonwealth Secretariat.

Brewster, Havelock, and Clive Y. Thomas. 1967. *The Dynamics of West Indian Economic Integration.* Jamaica: ISER-UWI.

———. 1993. "The Report of the West Indian Commission, *Time for Action:* Critique and Agenda for Further Work." *Caribbean Affairs* 6(1): 56-72.

Bryan, Anthony. 1989. "The New International Relations Agenda." *Caribbean Affairs* 2(4): 49-63.

———. 1991. "El Caribe y el Nuevo Marco Internacional." In *El Caribe hacia el año 2000: desafíos y opciones*, ed. Anthony Bryan and Andrés Serbin, 35-57. Caracas: Editorial Nueva Sociedad.

———. 1993. A Wider Caribbean. Paper presented to the OAS Seminar, Trade Liberalization in the Western Hemisphere. Washington, D.C., 19-20 April.

Bryan, Anthony and Andrés Serbin, eds. 1990. *¿Vecinos indiferentes? El Caribe de habla inglesa y América Latina.* Caracas: Editorial Nueva Sociedad.

CAIC (Caribbean Association of Industry and Commerce). 1993. Strategies for Strengthening the Regional Private Sector to Help CARICOM Governments Meet the Challenges and Opportunities of the 1990s and Beyond. Presentation to the XIVth Meeting of the Conference of Heads of Government of the Caribbean Community. Nassau, The Bahamas, 6 July.

C/LAA (Caribbean/Latin America Action). 1993. Confronting the Future in the Caribbean Basin—Challenges for 1993. Washington, D.C., June.

CARICOM Secretariat. 1992. Final Communique of the First Ministerial Summit of the Countries of the Caribbean Community and the Central American Isthmus. San Pedro Sula, Honduras, 29-31 January.

———. 1993. Final Communique of the Second Ministerial Forum of CARICOM and Central American Foreign Ministers. Kingston, Jamaica, 27-28 May.

Castañer, Juan A. 1993. El Tratado de Libre Comercio México–Estados Unidos–Canadá: los casos de las industrias de ropa y farmacéuticos en Puerto Rico. Paper presented at the Fourth Conference of the Association of Caribbean Economists (ACE). Willemstad, Curacao, 22-25 June.

CBTAG (Caribbean Basin Technical Advisory Group). Proposal and Briefings 1 May 1991; 30 August 1991; 24 September 1991; January 1992; September 1992. San Juan: Department of State.

Ceara Hatton, Miguel. 1994. La República Dominicana y la región del Caribe: su potencial geopolítico y comercial ante el nuevo orden mundial. Presentation to the British–Dominican Chamber of Commerce. Santo Domingo, 14 January.

CNIRD (Caribbean Network for Integrated Rural Development). 1990. "The CNIRD Initiative: Mobilising the NGO Sector for Rural Transformation." *Caribbean Affairs* 3(2): 120-134.

Consejo para el Desarrollo Estratégico de Puerto Rico. 1992. Normalización de relaciones entre Cuba y los Estados Unidos: retos y oportunidades para Puerto Rico. San Juan, Puerto Rico: Oficina del Gobernador, 31 December.

Chernick, S. 1978. *The Commonwealth Caribbean: The Integration Experience.* Baltimore: Johns Hopkins Univ. Press.

Deere, Carment Diana, et al. 1990. *In the Shadows of the Sun: Caribbean Development and U.S. Policy.* Policy Alternatives for Central America and the Caribbean (PACCA). Boulder, CO: Westview.

Derné, Marie-Claude, Enid Osbourne and Wendell Samuel. 1992. "Business Opportunities in Caribbean Cooperation." *Social and Economic Studies* 41 (3): 65-100.

Fajardo Maldonado, Arturo. 1993. Las relaciones entre los paises del istmo centroamericano y la Comunidad del Caribe (CARICOM): propuesta para un Programa de asistencia técnica. Consultant's report prepared for SIECA, Guatemala (Secretaría de Integración Económica de Centroamérica).

FEDEPRICAP. 1992. "A New Partnership for Development and Competitiveness: A Caribbean Basin Proposal." Costa Rica: Federación de Empresas Privadas de Centroamérica y Panamá (FEDEPRICAP). December.

García-Passalacqua, Juan M. 1993. "Towards a History of Their Own Making: The Role of the Puerto Rican People in the Caribbean of the 21st Century." In *Democracy in the Caribbean: Political, Economic, and Social Perspectives*, ed. Jorge I. Domínguez, Robert A. Pastor, and R. DeLisle Worrell. Baltimore: Johns Hopkins Univ. Press.

Gill, Henry. 1992. "The Caribbean in a World of Economic Blocs." *Social and Economic Studies* 4(3): 25-36.

———. 1993. Defining a Caribbean Position on NAFTA. Paper presented at the Fourth Conference of the Association of Caribbean Economists (ACE), Willemstad, Curacao, 22-25 June.

Gonzales, Anthony P. 1989. "Recent Trends in International Economic Relations of the CARICOM States." *Journal of InterAmerican Studies and World Affairs* 31(3): 63-95.

González, Gerardo. 1992. *El Caribe en la política exterior de Cuba: balance de 30 años, 1959-1989*. Santo Domingo: Ediciones CIPROS.

———. 1993. Las relaciones Cuba-Caribe: cambios y continuidad en los 90. Paper presented at seminar, The Caribbean and Cuba in a Post–Cold War World. INVESP–Wilson Center, Caracas, 20-22 May.

Griffith, Ivelaw L. 1993. Caribbean Security: An Agenda for the 21st Century. Paper presented at Caribbean Studies Association Conference held in Jamaica, 24-28 May.

Group of Caribbean Experts. 1981. *The Caribbean Community in the 1980s. Report to the Caribbean Common Market Council of Ministers*. Georgetown, Guyana: CARICOM Secretariat.

Harker, Trevor. 1989. Cooperation between CARICOM and Non-CARICOM Countries. ECLAC LC/CAR/G.269, 5 April.

Hernández, Rafael. 1993. Cuba y la seguridad del Caribe. Paper presented at seminar, The Caribbean and Cuba in a Post–Cold War World. INVESP–Wilson Center, Caracas, 20-22 May.

Landau, Georges D. 1990. "La cooperación internacional para el desarrollo de América Latina y el Caribe." *Comercio Exterior* (Mexico) 40 (1): 34-40.

Lewis, David E. 1992a. Cooperación intra-regional e integración económica en el Caribe. Prepared for project, Percepciones etno-históricas en las relaciones entre América Latina y el Caribe non-hispánico. INVESP/OAS, Caracas, February.

———. 1992b. Maximizing Regional Collaboration: Puerto Rico's Changing Caribbean Role. Paper presented at Seventeenth Congress of the Latin American Studies Association (LASA), Los Angeles, 24-27 September.

———. 1993a. Las posibilidades de cooperación entre Centroamérica y el Caribe. Paper presented at the Fourth ACE Conference, Willemstad, Curacao, 22-25 June.

Maingot, Anthony P. 1989. "Caribbean International Relations." In *The Modern Caribbean*, ed. Franklin Knight and Colin Palmer. Chapel Hill: Univ. of North Carolina Press.

Manigat, Mirlande. 1991. Regional Cooperation between the OECS and the DOMs. Paper presented at the SICAD 91 Third International Exhibition for Cooperation and North-South Exchanges, Marseilles, 14-17 October.

McAfee, Kathy. 1991. *Storm Signals: Structural Adjustment and Development Alternatives in the Caribbean*. London: Zed Books.

Pastor, Robert, and Richard Fletcher. 1992. "The Caribbean in the 21st Century." *Foreign Affairs* 70(1): 98-114.

Payne, Anthony and Paul Sutton. 1992. "Commonwealth Caribbean Diplomacy: A New Strategy for the New World Order." *Caribbean Affairs* 5(2): 47-63.

———. 1993. "The Commonwealth Caribbean in the New World Order: Between Europe and North America." *Journal of InterAmerican Studies and World Affairs* 34(4): 39-75.

Preeg, Ernest and Jonathan Levine. 1993. *Cuba and the New Caribbean Economic Order*. Washington, D.C.: Center for Strategic and International Studies.

Rivera Ortiz, Angel Israel. 1992. ¿Un lugar para Puerto Rico en el mundo de la integración regional? Paper presented at IVth Meeting of the CLACSO (Consejo Latinoamericano de Ciencias Sociales) Working Group in Caribbean/Central American International Relations. St. Thomas, U.S. Virgin Islands, 9-13 June.

Rodríquez, Ennio. 1993. Central America: Common Market, Trade Liberalization and Trade Agreements. Paper presented at academic workshop, Economic Integration in the Western Hemisphere: Prospects for Latin America, at the Kellogg Institute for International Studies, University of Notre Dame. 17-18 April.

Rosenberg, Mark B., ed. 1991. *The Changing Hemispheric Trade Environment: Opportunities and Obstacles*. Miami: FIU-LACC/White & Case.

Rosenberg, Mark B. and J.T. Hiskey. 1993. "Florida and the Caribbean Basin Countries in the 21st Century: Is Geography Destiny?" *Caribbean Affairs* 6(1): 13-30.

Saborío, Sylvia, ed. 1992a. *The Premise and the Promise: Free Trade in the Americas*. New Brunswick: Transaction Publishers.

Saborío, Sylvia and Constantine Michalopoulos. 1992b. Central America at a Crossroads. Policy Research Working Paper WPS 922, International Economics Department. Washington, D.C.: World Bank.

Samuel, Wendell. 1989a. "An Assessment of the CARICOM Integration Experience." In *Development in Suspense: Proceedings from the First Conference of the Association of Caribbean Economists*, ed. George Beckford and Norman Girvan, 223-236. Kingston: Friedrich Ebert Stiftung (FES).

———. 1990. "Regional Cooperation as an Element of Caribbean Development Strategy." In *Integration and Participatory Development*, ed. Judith Wedderburn, 7-79. Kingston: FES.

Segal, Aaron. 1992. Caribbean Trade Options: Playing the North American, European and Latin American Cards. Paper presented at Conference of the Association of Caribbean Universities and Research Institutes (UNICA). Santo Domingo, November.

SELA (Sistema Económico Latinoamericano). 1992. *La nueva etapa de la integración regional*. México: Fondo de Cultura Económica.

Serbin, Andrés. 1991. "The CARICOM States and the Group of Three: A New Partnership between Latin America and the Non-Hispanic Caribbean?" *Journal of Interamerican Studies and World Affairs* 33(2): 53-80.

———. 1992. "Ménage à Trois ou Partouze? The Caribbean, the United States, and Latin America in the 1990s." *Caribbean Affairs* 5(2): 70-80.

———. 1993. El contexto geopolítico de la Cuenca del Caribe en la decada del noventa: reconfiguraciones geoeconómicas y transiciones políticas. Paper presented at seminar, The Caribbean and Cuba in a Post–Cold War World. INVESP–Wilson Center. Caracas, 20-22 May.

Tirado de Alonso, Irma, ed. 1992. *Trade Issues in the Caribbean*. Philadelphia: Gordon and Breach.

Vega, Bernardo. 1978. *Estudio de las implicaciones de la incorporación de la República Dominicana a la Comunidad del Caribe*. Santo Domingo: Fondo para el Avance de las Ciencias Sociales, Editora Taller.

Watson, Hilbourne. 1993. Global Restructuring for the Establishment of a Caribbean Council for Europe (CCE). Kingston: Caribbean Association of Industry and Commerce (CAIC) and the Private Sector Organisation of Jamaica (PSOJ).

West India Committee. 1991. Proposal for the Establishment of a Caribbean Council for Europe (CCE). Kingston: CAIC and PSOJ.

West Indian Commission. 1992. *Report of the West Indian Commission: Time for Action*. Black Rock, Barbados: West Indian Commission.

Will, Marvin W. 1991. "A Nation Divided: The Quest for Caribbean Integration." *Latin American Research Review* 26 (1): 3-37.

Chapter 6

Adjustment, Reform, and Growth in Caribbean Economies

Bertus J. Meins[1]

The Caribbean region is one of the most diverse in the world, with populations varying from 260,000 in Barbados, to 6.7 million in Haiti, and 7.5 million in the Dominican Republic. The region's total population (excluding the 10.5 million people in Cuba) was estimated in 1993 at 20 million. Per capita GDP ranged in 1993 from less than $300 in Haiti, to more than $11,400 in the Bahamas, the third richest country in the Western Hemisphere.[2] Whereas the Dominican Republic and Haiti gained their independence in the first half of the nineteenth century, the others became independent only in the 1960s (Barbados, Guyana, Jamaica, Trinidad and Tobago) or even the 1970s (the Bahamas and Suriname). As a result of this colonial past, the region has four different languages, numerous dialects, and a rich ethnic and cultural diversity.

Also, its economic mainstays differ greatly. The Bahamas and Barbados have become dependent mainly on tourism and services; the Dominican Republic and Jamaica, on tourism, mining, and light export manufacturing. Suriname and Guyana rely heavily on mining combined with agriculture; Haiti, on agriculture and light manufacturing; while Trinidad and Tobago's mainstay remains the export of oil, oil derivatives, and natural gas-based petrochemicals such as ammonia, urea, and methanol. Because of this diversity, it is difficult to arrive at meaningful consolidated figures for the region. Therefore, while describing some broad trends, this paper also highlights examples and exceptions on a country basis.

Buoyed by strong private and public investment, low global interest rates, favorable terms of trade for regional commodities, and an agile, adaptive labor force, the Caribbean economies achieved substantial real GDP growth rates on average during both the 1960s (4.3 percent) and the 1970s (3.8 percent). Thus, per capita real growth was above 2 percent per annum for the region as a whole, and continued progress was expected toward political stability, so-

---

[1] The author is indebted to IDB economist Dougal Martin for his assistance.

[2] All dollar amounts herein refer to U.S. dollars.

Table 6.1 Caribbean Real GDP Growth, 1970-93
(Percentages)

	1970-79	1980-89	1984	1985	1986	1987	1988	1989	1990	1991	1992	1993
Bahamas	2.7	3.0	2.5	4.2	2.3	3.8	2.3	2.0	1.0	-4.0	-2.0	0.8
Barbados	2.1	2.1	3.3	0.6	9.5	3.8	3.1	5.0	-4.8	-3.0	-5.0	1.5
Dominican Republic	7.0	-2.7	0.3	-2.6	3.2	9.1	0.5	4.1	-5.1	-0.9	7.8	3.0
Guyana	1.7	-3.2	-0.8	0.3	1.0	-3.9	-7.9	-5.9	-3.3	8.3	8.0	7.2
Haiti	4.5	-0.8	0.3	0.3	0.6	0.6	-1.5	-1.5	-3.0	-4.0	-10.0	-4.0
Jamaica	-0.2	2.1	-0.9	-4.7	1.7	7.7	2.9	6.8	5.5	0.5	1.4	1.0
Suriname	5.6	-0.6	-2.9	0.6	-2.6	7.2	9.5	4.7	0.3	2.8	-5.0	-5.0
Trinidad and Tobago	5.3	-3.1	-5.8	-4.1	-3.3	-4.6	-3.9	-0.8	1.5	2.5	-1.6	-1.3
Caribbean Region	3.8	0.1		-2.3	-0.6	2.2	0.1	2.7	-0.6	-0.2	0.2	0.6

Source: IDB, ESDB.

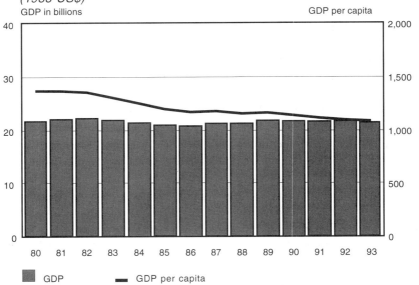

Figure 6.1 Caribbean Regional GDP and GDP per capita, 1980-93
(1988 US$)

Source: IDB, Statistics Unit.

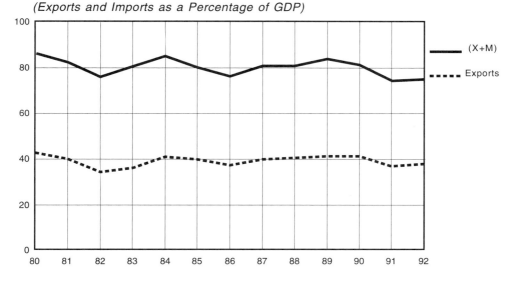

Figure 6.2 Caribbean Openness, 1980-92
(Exports and Imports as a Percentage of GDP)

Source: IDB, Statistics Unit.

cioeconomic prosperity, creation of ample and meaningful employment, and the eradication of poverty.

Unfortunately, the 1980s and early 1990s have turned out less favorably: the consolidated real growth was marginal during the 1980s, and the sum total for the period 1990–93 has been zero growth, albeit with an improving trend (see Table 6.1 and Figure 6.1). This implies that in the early 1990s regional per capita GDP on average fell between 1 and 2 percent per annum, thus reversing part of the earlier gains. Leaving out Haiti because of its very dire current situation improves this picture, but not substantially. The Caribbean is clearly lagging in growth behind many other regions in the world.

Of the eight regional countries that are IDB members,[3] only Haiti experienced negative per capita GDP growth during the 1960s, whereas in the 1970s both Guyana and Jamaica lagged behind. However, during the 1980s, the per capita GDP of the Dominican Republic, Guyana, Haiti, Suriname, and Trinidad

---

[3] The Bahamas, Barbados, Dominican Republic, Guyana, Haiti, Jamaica, Suriname, and Trinidad and Tobago; the IDB contributes to the smaller island states through financial contributions to the Caribbean Development Bank (CDB). For the sake of this paper, Belize is considered to be part of Central America.

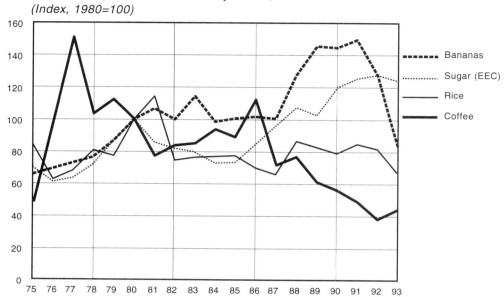

Figure 6.3 Agricultural Commodity Prices, 1975-93
(Index, 1980=100)

Source: IMF, International Financial Statistics.

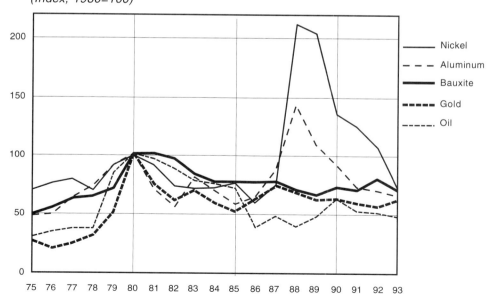

Figure 6.4 Mineral Commodity Prices, 1975-93
(Index, 1980=100)

Source: IMF, International Financial Statistics.

and Tobago contracted, whereas that of Jamaica grew only marginally. So far, in the decade of the 1990s, the economies of mature tourist destinations Barbados and the Bahamas have been struggling, along with those of nonadjusting Suriname, Haiti, and hydrocarbon exporter Trinidad and Tobago, which remains vulnerable to slides in global oil prices.

Common Characteristics of Caribbean Economies

Salient features of most Caribbean countries (with the partial exception of Haiti and the Dominican Republic) are a relatively high degree of formal education of the population; a limited size of the domestic market and thus of the local private sector; a strong regulatory and locomotive role for the state in the economy, partly due to insufficient popular confidence in the capacity of global market forces to bring order and proper priorities in the economy or prosperity to the people; a track record of risk aversion and rent-seeking by the local private sector; limited and arguably declining bargaining power in daily dealings with major trading partners; a relatively good, but progressively outmoded physical infrastructure (particularly critical in Guyana and Suriname, due to years of inadequate maintenance). Last but not least, their economies are extremely open and highly vulnerable to external shocks, such as fluctuations in growth in the industrialized countries, terms of trade, and global interest rates (Figure 6.2).

The regional economies are so open that the weighted average of the sum of exports and imports oscillated around 80 percent of GDP throughout the 1980s, before sliding to 75 percent in the early 1990s. Thus the oil price shocks of 1973 and 1979 took their toll on the region's external accounts. An exception was Trinidad and Tobago, where an oil boom resulted; the subsequent investment spike eventually introduced "Dutch disease" into the country, from which it has yet to recover.

During the last decade the region's economies underwent a formidable transition. As the trend towards urbanization continued, employment moved away from agriculture and fisheries towards manufacturing, tourism, and other services. Notable exceptions were Guyana, Haiti and Suriname, which lacked the basic prerequisites for rapid development of these sectors. Another exception was Trinidad and Tobago, where the oil boom and an ill-designed and implemented public works program led to an exodus from the primary sector in the early 1980s. It also led the authorities to ignore the potential for tapping into the rapidly expanding Caribbean tourism market. Therefore, the recent increase in Trinidad's agricultural GDP contribution must be viewed as a natural recovery, a welcome diversification of employment opportunities in a country unduly dominated by the hydrocarbon sector.

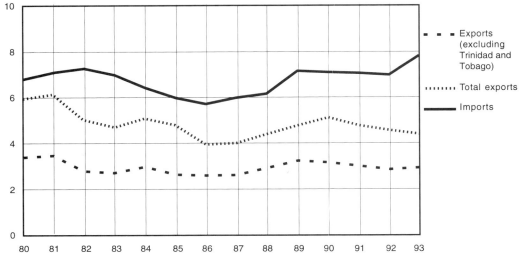

Figure 6.5 Exports and Imports of Goods, 1980-93
(Billions of US dollars)

Source: IDB, Statistics Unit.

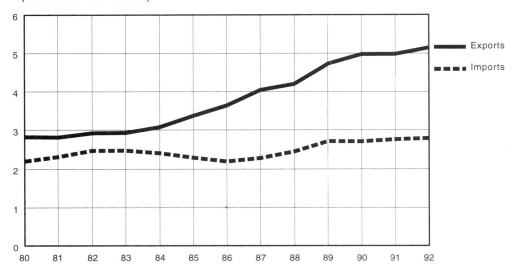

Figure 6.6 Exports and Imports of Non-Factor Services, 1980-92
(Billions of US dollars)

Source: IDB, Statistics Unit.

External Shocks and Policy Response

The impact of the second oil price shock was initially mitigated by a commodity price boom that inflated export revenues from the region's most important export products: tropical agricultural produce and minerals, notably bauxite and alumina (Guyana, Jamaica, and Suriname); gold (Dominican Republic, Guyana, and Suriname); and ferronickel in the Dominican Republic (Figures 6.3 and 6.4). The real hit to the region's prosperity came when monetary policies tightened in the industrialized world in the early 1980s. That induced a spike in global interest rates, putting a high price tag on the servicing cost of external indebtedness. Foreign debt had rapidly expanded during the 1970s, an era of strong growth of global trade and promising investment opportunities, and electoral demand for public services and a proactive productive sector role for the public sector.[4]

Very stringent monetary policies were employed in the industrialized world to mitigate the inflationary impact of the second oil price hike and subsequent commodity boom, and these policies had a severe impact on the region. Apart from inflating the burden of external debt servicing (which, by 1982, had led to the Latin American and Caribbean debt crisis), they substantially slowed down international growth rates and investment propensities (and thus demand for Caribbean goods and services) and diverted capital flows. Not only was direct foreign investment reduced, but the prevailing high interest rates in the industrialized world attracted private capital away from the region, especially after exchange rate stability was broken. Even worse, labor market conditions in the industrialized world induced popular support for measures to restrict immigration from the region, which worsened regional unemployment.

The initial policy response to these external shocks was ambivalent. Perhaps unduly reassured by the commodity boom, and subsequent relatively solid reserve positions, most of the region's governments expected the global recession would be short lived. Trinidad and Tobago even adopted an outright countercyclical policy stance, by almost doubling public sector wages on top of an ongoing investment boom in the hydrocarbon sector. In retrospect, it is evident that the region's economies stayed too long in an expansionary mode, despite growing evidence that the major trading partners (United States, European Union, and Canada) were slipping into a rather prolonged recession.

These circumstances led to external current-account fluctuations and fiscal disequilibria. Exports and imports of goods, which grew in step during the 1970s, have widely diverged since 1982, resulting in a regional trade gap that averaged almost $1 billion per annum between 1983 and 1993 (Figure 6.5).

---

[4] Many regional countries adhered to the so-called "control the commanding heights of the economy" doctrine.

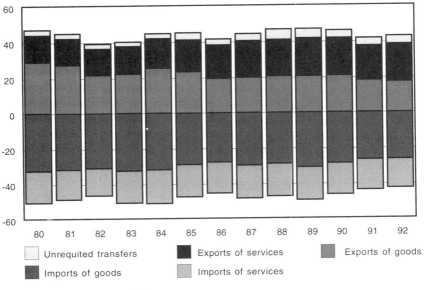

Figure 6.7 Components of the Current Account, 1980-92
(Percentage of GDP)

Source: IDB, Statistics Unit.

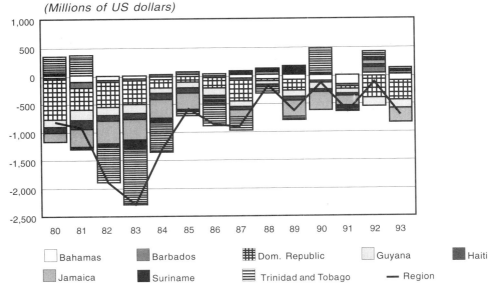

Figure 6.8 Current Account Balances by Country, 1980-93
(Millions of US dollars)

Source: IDB, Statistics Unit.

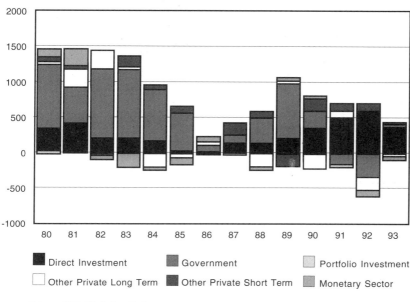

Figure 6.9 Capital Flows to the Caribbean, 1980-93
(Millions of US dollars)

Source: IDB, Statistics Unit.

Fortunately, with the onset of major tourist resort developments and export processing zones (EPZs), notably in Jamaica and the Dominican Republic, the region's balance of services became progressively positive (Figure 6.6). Combined with increasing family remittance transfers (Jamaica, the Dominican Republic, Guyana, Haiti, and Suriname are estimated to have received some $800 million in 1993), this mitigated the consolidated external current-account deficit. The latter, which spiked in 1982 and 1983 to around $2 billion for the region as a whole, has returned to more manageable levels since the late 1980s (Figures 6.7 and 6.8). Nevertheless, at no point in the last decade has there been a regional current surplus.

These deficits on the current account were initially financed in the early 1980s by large inflows of external savings, averaging some $1.4 billion between 1980 and 1983 (Figure 6.9). While governments were delaying structural adjustment measures, private long-term capital inflows into the region peaked between 1981 and 1982. Government borrowing abroad, in part from the IMF, accelerated between 1982 and 1985. In the wake of increased international investor uncertainty and attractive real interest rates in the United States, in 1986 the sum of private and official capital inflows fell to only $200 million. Direct investment was even virtually nil in 1985–86. Subsequently, the total inflow averaged some $550 million per annum between 1987 and 1993. In 1992,

Figure 6.10 External Debt Stock by Country, 1980-93
(Billions of US dollars)

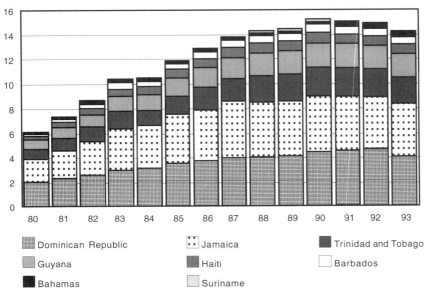

Source: IDB, Statistics Unit.

Figure 6.11 External Debt Indicators, 1980-93
(Percentages)

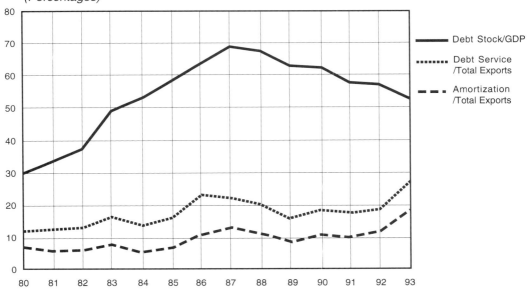

Source: IDB, Statistics Unit.

Figure 6.12 Structure of External Debt

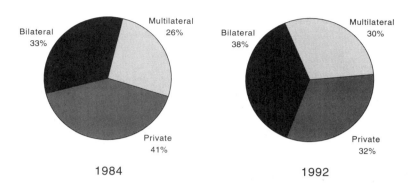

exceptionally large debt amortizations were compensated by sharply increased direct foreign investment.

Between 1988 and 1990, the bulk constituted official borrowing, in part related to implementation of IMF- and IBRD-supported structural adjustment programs (and, since the early 1990s, IDB sector adjustment loans) and to restore adequate reserve buffers. Since 1990, private capital inflows recovered to $440 per annum, as stabilization and liberalization efforts began to bear fruit and structural reform measures shifted the role of engine of growth and innovation from the public enterprise to the private sector. As a result, direct foreign investment averaged 2 percent of regional GDP (or $700 million per annum) in the early 1990s, in response to the privatization policies.

Dimensions of the External Debt Crisis

During the 1970s, the region's consolidated external debt averaged between 35 percent and 40 percent of GDP. However, as of the onset of the 1980s, a rapid increase took place, climbing to around 70 percent of GDP by 1987–88. Subsequently, a steady reduction is observable, to roughly 55 percent of GDP in 1993. More importantly, the debt service ratio, and especially its interest component, has improved considerably since its peak in 1986 (Figures 6.10 and 6.11). However, in 1993, a reversal due to a bunching of amortizations was observable, despite low international interest rates.

The structure of the region's external debt has substantially improved since the mid-1980s, to the extent that high, mostly variable, interest lending from private banks was progressively replaced by a mix of multilateral and bilateral loans (Figure 6.12) that carry more favorable interest rates in exchange for more stringent conditions on the use of the funds. Nevertheless, a number

Figure 6.13 Guyana: Developments in the Official and Parallel Exchange Rates, 1980-92
(Guyana dollars per US dollar)

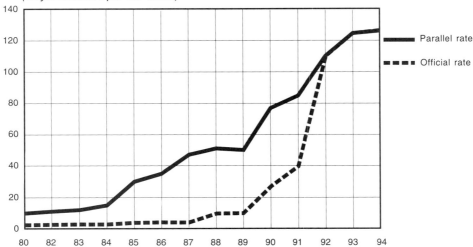

Source: IMF IFS, and IDB estimates.
N.B. The parallel rate shown is an unofficial estimate.

Figure 6.14 Guyana: Gross Official International Reserves, 1980-93

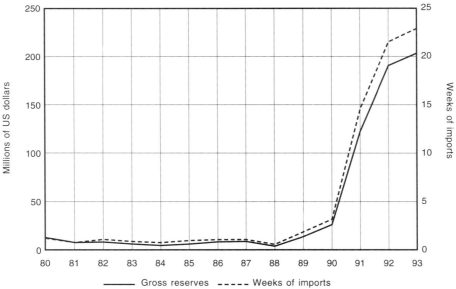

Source: Bank of Guyana, IMF.

of Caribbean countries, most notably Jamaica, the Dominican Republic, Guyana, Haiti, and even Trinidad and Tobago, experienced difficulties in meeting their external debt servicing obligations. After occasionally falling into arrears, they had to rely on special arrangements with the Paris Club (for bilateral and officially guaranteed loans) and the London Club (for private bank loans) to reschedule their obligations to longer maturities and sometimes more favorable terms. The Dominican Republic and Guyana were also enabled to use soft-term bilateral and multilateral funds to buy back a substantial part of their outstanding borrowing from private banks.

International Reserves and Exchange Rate Policies

International reserves are more than a nation's stock of wealth: they also mirror the relationship between its public and private sectors, its consumption and savings behavior, and its foreign exchange earning and retention capacity. Reserve levels are also considered a prime indicator of the adequacy of exchange rate policies. To track a country's creditworthiness, the international financial community closely follows reserve trends: if reserves start falling below prudent levels, international bank loans and export credits rapidly dry up. Once this happens, the domestic banking and business communities are likely to fall in step with hoarding of foreign exchange and, if conditions worsen, with capital flight (for the reverse, see the case of Guyana, Figures 6.13 and 6.14). Maintaining adequate reserve levels is a necessity for small and open economies. (Depending on a country's vulnerability to external shocks, these levels may vary from the equivalent of between three and six months of imports for gross reserves.)

Adequate reserve levels greatly facilitate the private sector's chances of obtaining international financing for imports of intermediate and capital goods. They are a necessary, if insufficient, precondition for sustained economic growth. From Table 6.2 and Figure 6.15 it is obvious that, with the notable exceptions of the Dominican Republic and recently Guyana, the region could not fulfill these conditions during the last decade, and thus may have substantially damaged its growth potential.[5]

A similar reasoning applies to exchange rate policies. This crucial instrument (especially for small and extremely open economies, such as those in the Caribbean region) can be seen as both a reflection of the adequacy of the domestic policy stance (the political argument); as simply the equation price for supply and demand of foreign exchange (the rational argument); or as a powerful instrument to promote a country's foreign exchange earning capacity in

---

[5] Table 6.2 shows the Net Reserve position divided by imports and converted on a week-basis.

Table 6.2 Net Reserves: Import Coverage in Weeks, 1984–92

	1984	1985	1986	1987	1988	1989	1990	1991	1992
Bahamas	7	7	7	4	4	3	3	0	0
Barbados	9	9	9	8	7	5	5	4	8
Dominican Republic	9	10	10	3	5	3	1	7	7
Guyana	1	1	1	1	1	2	3	14	14
Haiti	1	1	1	1	1	1	0	1	0
Jamaica	4	6	3	4	3	2	3	2	0
Suriname	3	3	2	2	1	1	2	0	0
Trinidad and Tobago	28	26	11	4	3	7	13	7	4
Region	12	11	7	4	4	3	4	4	4
Region minus Trinidad and Tobago	6	7	6	4	4	3	2	3	4

Source: IDB, ESDB.

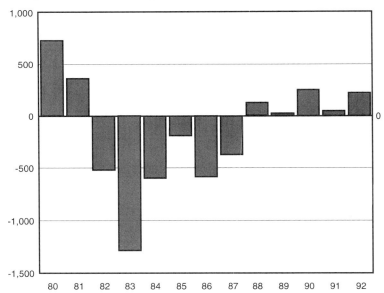

Figure 6.15 Change in International Reserves, 1980-92
(Millions of US dollars)

Note: Positive indicates increase.

Source: IDB, Statistics Unit.

agriculture, manufacturing, and services such as tourism, by reducing otherwise "sticky" labor costs (the strategic development argument).

History has shown that the vast majority of governments, not only those in the Caribbean, intuitively adhere to the first approach, quite often under pressure from an urban class interested in keeping the price of imported consumer goods and foreign travel low. Also, in the heyday of the import substitution model, domestic manufacturing industries with high import components (CKD car assembly industries in Trinidad and Tobago, for instance) represented a formidable pressure group to keep exchange rates overvalued. Eventually, this became self-defeating, however: in the long run, fiscal necessity and/or international competition will phase out highly protected industries, and persistent reserve losses will eventually necessitate exchange rate corrections. The Dominican Republic, Guyana (see Figures 6.16 and 6.17), Jamaica, Trinidad and Tobago and, since recently, Suriname, all went through the traumatic experience of unduly delayed, and thus substantial, devaluations in the second half of the 1980s and the early 1990s. In most cases this induced substantial short-term inflationary consequences, as domestic price levels had often been artificially repressed (see Table 6.3).

As experience in other parts of the world has shown, there is a considerable potential for the exchange rate instrument to help a country build up a foothold in certain sectors where it has potential comparative advantages. This assumes that the vicious-circle effects of subsequent inflation and wage claims can to a large extent be avoided, which is more likely when a slack capacity prevails in the economy.

From the regional experience so far, one can tentatively conclude that, because of the extreme openness of the regional economies with regard to trade and private capital flows, there is a considerable long-term cost associated with maintaining overvalued exchange rates in terms of missed export and job-creation opportunities, as well as missed opportunities to diversify the exports and job base. Corrections towards realistic exchange rates do have a substantial impact, as illustrated by the remarkable expansion of the tourism and EPZ sectors in the Dominican Republic and Jamaica, and the ongoing economic recovery in Guyana.

The Dominican Republic and Jamaica have greatly increased their share in Caribbean tourism, both in terms of foreign exchange revenues and market share. In the case of the Dominican Republic, in addition to highly competitive exchange rates, another factor contributing to the massive investment in tourism accommodations was strong government support: one of the branches of the central bank, for instance, extended substantial amounts of credit to the sector at preferential rates. In addition, tourism revenues and 50 percent of revenues from reinvested profits were exempted from income taxes for a ten-year period (see Table 6.4).

Figure 6.16 Guyana: Annual Change in the Consumer Price Index
(Percentages)

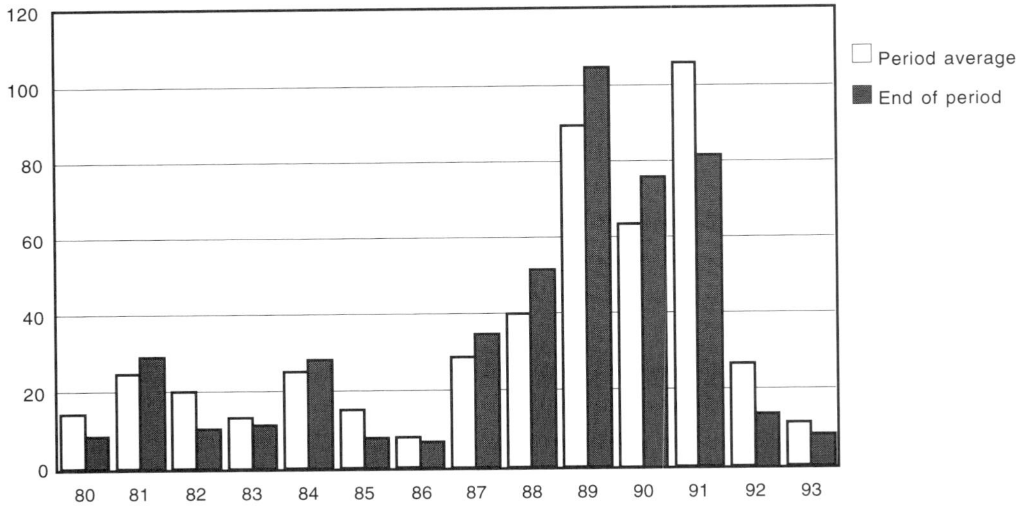

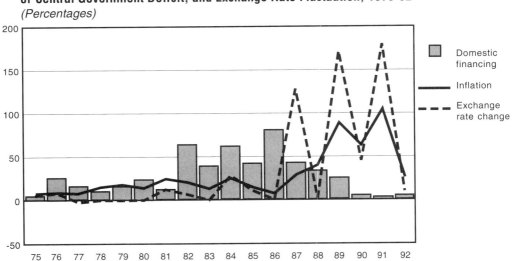

Source: Statistical Bureau, IMF, and IDB estimates.

Figure 6.17 Guyana: Inflation, Domestic Financing of Central Government Deficit, and Exchange Rate Fluctuation, 1975-92
(Percentages)

Source: Ministry of Finance, Bank of Guyana.

Table 6.3 Average Inflation Rates and Causes, 1984-93

		1984	1985	1986	1987	1988	1989	1990	1991	1992	1993
Bahamas	Inflation	4.0	4.6	5.4	5.8	4.4	5.4	4.6	7.1	5.7	2.8
	Pch XR	0.0	0.0	0.0	0.0	0.0	0.0	0.0	0.0	0.0	0.0
	M1/GDP	10.6	9.7	9.8	10.4	9.4	9.8	10.1	11.0	11.2	12.3
	FisD/GDP	-0.9	-1.4	-0.5	-0.6	-3.0	-4.1	-2.4	-4.3	-2.3	-0.7
Barbados	Inflation	4.7	4.0	1.3	3.4	4.9	6.2	3.1	6.2	6.0	1.2
	Pch XR	0.0	0.0	0.0	0.0	0.0	0.0	0.0	0.0	0.0	0.0
	M1/GDP	13.1	12.9	15.2	14.0	15.3	14.8	13.9	15.0	13.6	14.7
	FisD/GDP	-4.2	-4.2	-5.3	-5.3	-2.3	-0.8	-6.7	-2.1	-1.1	-3.2
Dominican Rep.	Inflation	27.1	37.6	9.7	16.0	44.4	45.4	59.5	53.9	4.6	4.7
	Pch XR	0.0	210.0	-6.5	31.0	60.5	31.0	34.9	49.4	0.1	-0.1
	M1/GDP	8.6	0.7	9.6	11.8	11.9	10.4	9.4	7.2	8.7	9.3
	FisD/GDP	-0.3	-2.8	-0.4	-1.5	-0.1	0.7	0.6	3.5	3.9	1.2
Guyana	Inflation	25.2	15.0	7.9	28.7	39.9	90.0	65.0	80.0	26.3	10.0
	Pch XR	26.7	13.2	0.0	127.9	2.0	172.0	45.2	183.0	11.8	1.4
	M1/GDP	28.1	30.0	35.2	31.0	33.2	22.5	14.8	10.8	13.1	14.0
	FisD/GDP	-43.1	-54.2	-54.0	-49.0	-35.8	-14.1	-31.0	-25.2	-17.1	-7.2
Haiti	Inflation	6.5	10.6	3.3	-11.4	4.0	6.9	21.5	20.4	25.3	46.2
	Pch XR	0.0	0.0	0.0	12.0	7.1	10.0	13.6	2.7	18.2	36.3
	M1/GDP	14.2	14.4	12.3	11.2	19.9	25.0	14.1	13.6	15.7	14.9
	FisD/GDP	-7.3	-3.7	-1.5	-2.7	-2.3	-3.1	-3.4	-2.6	-2.0	-2.4
Jamaica	Inflation	27.8	25.7	15.1	6.6	8.3	14.3	22.0	51.1	77.3	22.0
	Pch XR	105.3	35.9	-1.8	0.0	0.0	3.6	26.3	68.1	90.0	8.3
	M1/GDP	10.2	11.1	11.9	13.7	13.6	11.2	11.0	11.4	13.2	16.3
	FisD/GDP	-5.4	-3.8	0.7	1.5	-1.5	1.2	3.0	4.4	4.2	3.2
Suriname	Inflation	3.7	11.3	18.7	53.4	7.3	0.8	21.7	25.9	43.7	148.1
	Pch XR	0.0	0.0	0.0	0.0	0.0	0.0	0.0	0.0	0.0	0.0
	M1/GDP	29.2	39.5	59.6	67.5	74.2	75.5	69.9	75.5	67.8	52.9
	FisD/GDP	-16.9	-21.4	-24.8	-24.4	-21.1	-13.6	-5.7	-18.5	-12.1	-5.6
Trinidad and Tobago	Inflation	13.3	7.6	7.7	10.8	7.7	11.4	11.0	3.8	6.5	10.8
	Pch XR	0.0	4.2	44.0	0.0	5.6	13.2	0.0	0.0	0.0	25.6
	M1/GDP	12.1	11.6	12.4	12.1	11.0	11.0	10.4	11.3	11.8	12.3
	FisD/GDP	-8.9	-5.1	-5.9	-5.9	-5.7	-4.2	-1.2	-0.2	-2.9	0.2

Note: Pch XR = percentage change in OFFICIAL exchange rate.
M1 = Narrow money supply ratio to Gross Domestic Product.
FisD/GDP = Fiscal deficit ratio to GDP.
Source: IDB, ESDB, IMF, IFS.

Figure 6.18 Barbados: Real Effective Exchange Rates, 1980-92
(Index 1980=100)

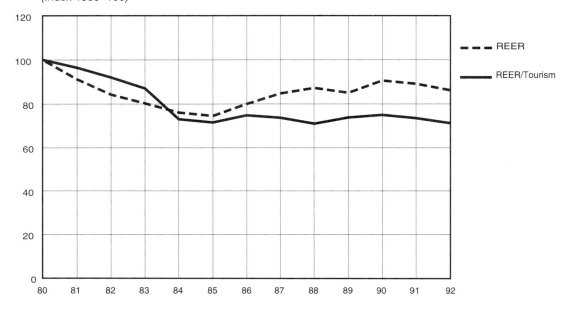

Note: Decrease = Appreciation
Increase = Depreciation
Source: IDB, IMF

Figure 6.19 Comparison of Barbados' Real Effective Exchange Rates with Competitors, 1980-92
(In percentages)

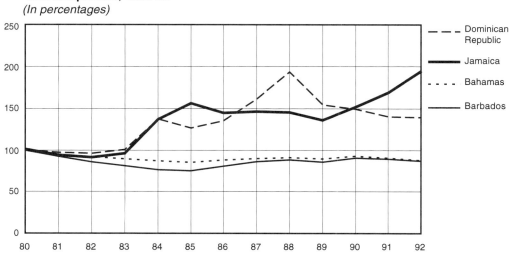

Source: IDB, IMF.

Furthermore, both the Dominican Republic and Jamaica made remarkable headway between the early 1980s and 1993 in the development of their EPZs, which boosted their service balance and strongly contributed to alleviating their pressing unemployment problems. In the case of the former, foreign exchange revenues from EPZ activities increased from $45 million in 1980 to $1.25 billion in 1993 ($300 million in net value added), while total employment in export processing increased from 19,000 to more than 150,000 in the same period, or from less than 1 percent to around 5 percent of the labor force.

The Bahamas and Barbados, on the other hand, have continued their commitment to staving off the need for depreciating exchange rates by adopting instead austere fiscal and monetary policies, as well as income policies. While these policies are achieving their stabilization goal quite satisfactorily, the long-term cost in terms of foregone employment possibilities still needs to be assessed. Figures 6.18 and 6.19 illustrate how these two countries experienced a gradual appreciation of the real effective exchange rate, while their strong competitors, the Dominican Republic and Jamaica, allowed for a sizeable depreciation. Aside from the question of whether the latter was the result of good (strategic use of the exchange rate to penetrate the international tourism market) or failing economic policies (the exchange rate depreciated because of failure to contain fiscal deficits and monetary expansion, resulting in destabilizing reserve losses), there is a strong prima facie coincidence between exchange rate appreciation and loss of tourism market share in the Bahamas and Barbados.

Guiding the Reform Process: The "Washington Consensus"

With the hindsight of the failures of the so-called heterodox adjustment efforts in Latin America, and the relative successes of more orthodox adjustment processes in Bolivia, Chile and Mexico, in the latter part of the 1980s a consensus gradually emerged among macroeconomic and development scholars, policy research institutes and multilateral institutions, as to which combination of policies might be most effective in restoring the internal and external equilibria most conducive to sustainable economic growth. This came to be referred to as the "Washington Consensus." It entailed a number of policy recommendations that together form an integral system for stimulation of economic recovery by reinvigorating dormant or suppressed market forces. While the depth of the proposed reforms is crucial, their sequencing and timing have turned out to be of equal importance.

The following body of recommendations constitute the backbone of the consensus:

Table 6.4 Evolution of Caribbean Tourism Revenues, 1984–92
(In US$ millions and percent of Caribbean total tourism revenue)

	1984		1985		1986		1987		1988		1989		1990		1991		1992	
	$	%	$	%	$	%	$	%	$	%	$	%	$	%	$	%	$	%
Bahamas	797	19.1	990	21.0	1,100	20.6	1,170	18.6	1,144	16.3	1,272	16.9	1,272	16.9	1,264	15.3	1,244	13.4
Barbados	286	6.9	311	6.6	326	6.1	381	6.1	460	6.6	529	7.0	500	6.0	461	5.4	464	5.0
Dominican Rep.	371	8.9	451	9.6	506	9.5	571	9.1	768	10.9	818	10.8	899	10.9	877	10.3	1,096	11.8
Guyana	11	0.3	18	0.4	19	0.4	24	0.4	30	0.4	28	0.4	27	0.3	30	0.4	31	0.3
Haiti	85	2.0	93	2.0	82	1.5	90	1.4	74	1.1	70	0.9	66	0.8	66	0.8	46	0.5
Jamaica	408	9.7	407	8.6	516	9.7	595	9.5	527	7.5	593	7.8	740	8.9	764	9.0	882	9.5
Suriname	4	0.1	5	0.1	6	0.1	4	0.1	6	0.1	4	0.1	1	0.0	1	0.0	2	0.0
Trinidad and Tobago	99	2.4	97	2.1	83	1.6	94	1.5	92	1.3	85	1.1	95	1.1	103	1.2	111	1.2
Total for above eight countries	2,061	49.4	2,372	50.2	2,638	49.5	2,929	46.7	3,101	44.2	3,399	41.1	3,592	43.4	3,524	41.4	3,876	41.7
Total Caribbean (US$ million)	4,174		4,722		5,333		6,277		7,018		7,583		8,273		8,511		9,302	
Note:																		
Cuba (percent of total Caribbean)		2.3		2.5		2.8		2.9		2.7		2.7		3.0		3.5		4.1

Source: IDB, CTO, WTO.

- Fiscal Discipline: Fiscal deficits should be small enough to be financed without recourse to inflation tax; a primary surplus is needed, as is an operational deficit not larger than 2 percent of GDP.
- Public Expenditure Priorities: Fiscal expenditures should be redirected away from low-efficiency areas to those with high economic returns and the potential to improve future income distribution, such as health, education and infrastructure.
- Tax Reform: The tax base should be broadened and marginal tax rates lowered to reduce fraud and evasion, to improve the economy's incentive structure, and to improve tax administration.
- Financial Liberalization: The ultimate objective is market-determined interest rates; in the interim, the abolition of preferential interest rates for privileged borrowers, and moderately positive real interest rates.
- Exchange Rates: The goal is a unified (at least for trade) exchange rate at a sufficiently competitive level to induce a rapid growth of nontraditional exports.
- Trade Liberalization: Quantitative restrictions to be replaced by tariffs progressively reduced, as macroeconomic conditions permit.
- Direct Foreign Investment: Legal and procedural barriers to foreign investment should be abolished; domestic and foreign investors should essentially be treated equally.
- Privatization: The state should focus its scarce fiscal and human resources and management skills on its core functions; in most cases it is more efficient to have enterprises and utilities run privately.
- Deregulation: Regulations that impede the entry of new firms, or otherwise restrict efficient competition, should be abolished; regulations should concentrate on aspects of environmental protection, labor safety, and prudential supervision of the financial sector.
- Property Rights: To stimulate productive investment, the legal system should provide secure property rights to the private sector, including the informal sector and microbusinesses.

In the context of various adjustment and sector adjustment loans (SAL) extended by the multilateral institutions to the Caribbean region during the last decade, several of these reforms have been introduced, in many instances with positive results. The most outstanding example has been Guyana, which teetered on the brink of disaster in the mid-1980s, but has made a remarkable turnaround since the introduction of its economic recovery program in 1988.

However, in a number of cases, the results so far have lagged behind expectations, basically because the prescribed reforms were not completed fully or in a timely manner, not implemented in the proper sequence, or were

Figure 6.20 Fiscal Operations, 1980-92
(Percentage of GDP)

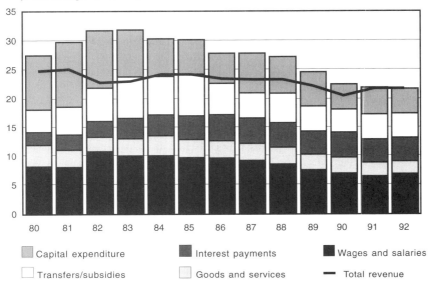

Note: Excluding Suriname.
Source: IDB, Statistics Unit.

Figure 6.21 Savings and Investment, 1980-92
(Percentage of GDP)

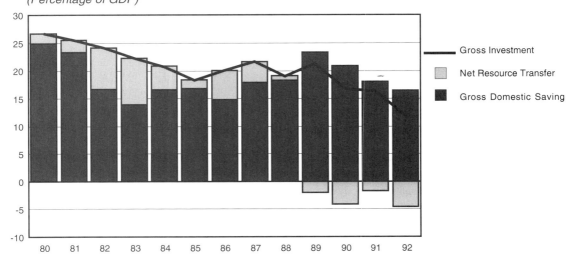

Note: Excludes Jamaica and the Bahamas because of lack of data.
Source: IDB, Statistics Unit.

simply overtaken by unforeseen external shocks. A striking example in this respect is Trinidad and Tobago, which started a trade reform process in the framework of an IBRD-SAL loan in 1990. Initially it benefitted strongly from the oil price spike of 1990, causing its terms of trade to improve by more than 20 percent. However, the subsequent relaxation of fiscal policies in the face of elections in late 1991, probably instigated by an increase in fiscal revenue of 4.5 percent of GDP partly due to the oil-price spike, induced a strong increase in aggregate demand that led to a more than 25 percent increase in imports, which was in turn greatly facilitated by the ongoing trade reforms. The resulting reserve loss turned out to be too much for the country to bear, and it was forced to float its currency in March 1993, resulting in a nominal depreciation by one-third.

Evidence of Recovery

Fiscal Reforms

Substantial fiscal deficits have more often than not been the norm in the Caribbean region. Arguably as a long-range result of the colonial era, the peoples of the Caribbean have come to appreciate a broadly defined role for the public sector: not only were governments expected to provide external and internal security, health care and education for vast strata of the population, and basic infrastructure, they were also expected to regulate many aspects of economic life, as well as provide a myriad of goods and services. They were also pressed to provide a wide array of employment opportunities, either in the administration or in the parastatals, and act as employment-provider of last resort in adverse economic situations.

As the Caribbean economies were running out of steam in the 1980s, the region's public sectors generally could not adjust expenditures downward fast enough to keep pace with the drop in revenues, or were even inclined to follow countercyclical policies, as was the case in Trinidad and Tobago in 1982. As a result, the regional public sectors incurred huge deficits (see Figure 6.20). Extreme cases in this respect were Guyana and Suriname, where fiscal deficits, often widely surpassing 20 percent of GDP, occurred between the early 1980s and 1993. Consequently, interest and amortization obligations absorb an ever increasing share of the budget, so that both countries have only been able to keep essential public services going with substantial external assistance. The Dominican Republic, on the other hand, incurred destabilizing fiscal deficits in the second half of the 1980s, but these were basically the result of a sharp acceleration of public investment (especially in construction activities) insufficiently paired with financial improvement in state-owned enterprises and utilities. Nevertheless, its final effect was also a crowding out of social expenditures and public-sector salaries.

The useful lesson to be derived from the era of excessive fiscal deficits in the Caribbean context is that they are highly inflationary and self-defeating in the end, because of limited long-term external financing possibilities. They often induce excess domestic demand, which translates into additional imports. When added to government's usual hesitancy to correct exchange rates despite falling reserves, exports (especially nontraditional exports, which generally tend to have a higher labor content) are discouraged, which places the economy at risk of sliding into recession. Similarly, experience with high, direct government financial involvement in the tourism sector (Jamaica, Barbados, Trinidad and Tobago, and lately the Bahamas) has unveiled the budgetary as well as the moral hazards (Why sell during a boom period?) involved.

Savings and Investment

Figure 6.9 shows that the region has made headway in attracting direct foreign investment in recent years. This can mainly be attributed to improved fiscal policies and incentive structures, a reduction of unnecessary government interference in the economy, more outward-oriented trade policies, and the removal of red tape for investors. Notable exceptions to this were Barbados, Haiti, and Suriname, where investment has dropped sharply. The falling investment trend in Figure 6.21 indicates that additional measures need to be taken to bring investment back to at least 20 percent of GDP in these countries.

The Role of the Private Sector: Supply-Side Measures

Mostly in the context of multilateral lending designed to stimulate reforms in the agricultural, financial and investment sectors, regional countries so far have made substantial headway in removing obstacles to private investment, both local and foreign. While such obstacles may have been necessary or desirable in earlier decades, they have outlived their usefulness in the current competitive world. The most striking examples of these are export taxes levied on exports of agricultural produce and minerals, import prohibitions and quantitative restrictions, investment prohibitions and/or restrictions in certain sectors, high government involvement in productive enterprises and utilities, and discriminatory practices in the financial sectors. The latter often entailed preferential rates for certain activities or enterprises at the cost of the local taxpayer. Over the years, many of these practices had evolved into inefficient state or private monopolies.

Although reforms to reinvigorate the private sector by removing such obstacles are far from complete, positive private sector response to improved incentives for export-oriented activities is noticeable. However, one sticky point remains virtually untouched—the labor market. As other areas in the world move rapidly toward greater efficiency and flexibility, the Caribbean region is slow to adopt structural changes in its labor markets. Due to the traditionally strong links between the political body and labor unions, this is understandable. Moreover, in ethnically diverse countries like Trinidad and Tobago, Guyana and Suriname, where professions *grosso modo* run along ethnic lines, the political platform for privatizing state enterprises in the agricultural and mineral sectors is often not available. As long as such standoffs last, these sectors cannot reach the high efficiency standards required for successful international competition, and they risk becoming extinct in the longer term.

The Medium-Term Outlook

The international environment in which the region's productive activities will have to operate in the medium and long term is characterized by progressively stronger global competition; a process of rapidly increasing technological innovation spurred by hardly imaginable advancements in telecommunications; the creation of strong—and possible increasingly exclusive—trade blocs; the globalization of international enterprises that, by far, transcends that of national authorities; and donor fatigue, especially if the region is not capable of rapidly implementing the reforms deemed necessary for advancement.

The chances are that the region will increasingly be confronted with demands for bilateral concessions (in the case of replacement of unilateral Caribbean Basin Initiative preferences by NAFTA conditions), which will harden the terms of external assistance. Similarly, new GATT-WTO conditions will stress trade over aid. In the same vein, as electorates become more informed about the fiscal consequences of current agricultural policies in the United States and the European Union, agricultural price supports are likely to be reduced. This will have a substantial impact on sugar exports, as virtually all the Caribbean countries can only remain operating in this sector at the preferential prices offered in the U.S. and Europe. Once Cuba re-enters the hemispheric trade world, regional competition is likely to further increase, not only in sugar, but also in rice, vegetables and citrus, tourism, services, and manufacturing.

In this environment, Barbados and the Bahamas may consider giving their highest priority to achieving higher cost efficiencies in their respective tourism and service sectors and to better defining the niches where they have the most comparative advantages. They may have to determine whether stayover tourism and cruise-ship tourism are mutually reinforcing, or just the opposite, and act accordingly.

Jamaica could improve its potential by concentrating on improving the consistency of its macroeconomic policies, so that the investment climate is no longer periodically disturbed by emergency measures. Haiti, for the time being, cannot be expected to advance unless its constitutional problems are solved, so that aid flows can be resumed in anticipation of more structural measures.

The Dominican Republic and Guyana need to devote a substantially larger share of their budgets to investment in human resources, including health and education, and allow the private sector to play a much larger role in housing.

Trinidad and Tobago needs to concentrate on overcoming its Dutch disease symptoms, basically by no longer allowing the revenues from the dominant hydrocarbon sector to set the parameters for the country's consumption. For the sake of the employability of its future generations, it will have to take a hard look at supply side measures and institutional necessities not yet in place, and adopt a policy framework conducive to the rapid growth of nontraditional exports.

Both Guyana and Suriname will have to solve the structural problems confronting their bauxite industries. In addition, Suriname will finally have to make the long postponed structural adjustment measures that can make it a viable economic entity, once external aid flows are phased out.

The Social Dimensions of Adjustment

Not merely as an afterthought, but as an integral component of the recuperation process, the social dimensions of the adjustment process deserve adequate attention, lest medium-term gains become lost in social polarization and strife. In this respect, the recent erosion of social expenditures in most regional budgets raises concern. The same goes for the fall in real purchasing power of public sector wages and salaries, particularly in the Dominican Republic, Jamaica, Guyana, and Suriname. In these countries it is hard to imagine how the public sector can attract and retain sufficiently qualified professionals at current remuneration levels, and keep them honest and motivated.

Impact on Social Indicators

The dissemination of improved medical prevention and intervention skills has to a large extent offset the negative distributive impact of adjustment. Considering the Caribbean's crude death rates, infant mortality, and life expectancy (see Table 6.5), it can be concluded that, between 1980 and 1992, health indicators improved throughout the region, with the exception of the crude death rates in Guyana. In addition, crude birth rates fell in all countries except Suriname.

Table 6.5 Health Indicators in the Caribbean Region, 1980 and 1992

	Crude Birth Rate per 1000		Crude Death Rate per 1000		Infant Mortality Rate per 1000 Live Births		Life Expectancy Years at Birth	
	1980	1992	1980	1992	1980	1992	1980	1992
Bahamas	24.2	20.0	6.6	5.7	30.0	25.0	66.6	69.6
Barbados	16.6	15.7	8.0	8.8	21.0	9.7	72.3	75.1
Dominican Republic	34.1	26.8	7.9	6.1	70.8	59.0	63.3	67.2
Guyana	30.3	24.8	7.3	7.7	64.6	49.6	61.0	64.7
Haiti	36.7	34.7	15.1	13.0	113.2	94.0	51.9	54.5
Jamaica	27.6	23.9	6.7	6.4	21.2	15.0	70.9	73.6
Suriname	27.6	30.5	7.8	6.3	46.6	37.0	64.8	68.6
Trinidad and Tobago	28.6	23.4	7.1	6.3	35.0	18.0	68.0	71.3

Source: IDB Pocket Profiles and National Data.

Unfortunately, a similarly positive conclusion does not extend to the education sector, as fiscal austerity forced governments to rationalize education expenditures, both current and (especially) capital. This happened most notably in Guyana, where recurrent education expenditures were slashed from 5.6 percent of GDP in 1986 to a mere 2.2 percent in 1992, basically to make room for interest expenditures related to servicing external and internal debt. This resulted in a sharp deterioration in the country's average educational achievements, as reflected in regional examination scores.

While the region as a whole had earlier established impressive educational standards substantially above Latin American averages, reduced fiscal allocations to the sector during the past decade have eroded the predominantly public education systems. In the interest of social cohesion and future competitiveness, education expenditures, with their high economic rate of return in the long term, warrant high public and private priority in the future.

Employment and Real Wages

The economic transformation process required to reduce the fiscal deficits and to attain the shift of the manufacturing sector away from import substitution and towards export orientation has taken its toll on the region, especially in the high real-wage countries/late adjusters; namely, Barbados, which saw a major part of its high tech assembly industry depart by the mid-1980s, and Trinidad and Tobago, which has not been able to kickstart its ailing EPZ, basically for lack of wage competitiveness. Late reformer Guyana saw its real wages plummet, especially in the nonskilled bracket, where they now range between two and three U.S. dollars per day. This is substantially below the average remuneration in the EPZs of the Dominican Republic and Jamaica, which have thrived on low real wages in an era of very high labor force expansion. Nevertheless, even these low real wages cannot attract foreign export processing firms, unless major improvements are realized in physical infrastructure (airport, port accommodations and storage facilities, roads, and electricity supply).

Suriname has had difficulty starting a comprehensive adjustment program, although it could secure very substantial bilateral grant assistance by accepting IMF monitoring of its program. Here the long-suppressed depreciation of the exchange rate has resulted in teacher salaries of between $12.50 and $19.00 per month, a fraction of their value just two years ago. While these salaries are likely to be reviewed in the near future, they are nevertheless a cause of great concern for the longer-term quality of the education system, as well as the public sector at large.

The Final Tally: Successful and Incomplete Adjustment Efforts

The jury is still out with regard to the real degree of success of recent adjustment and reform measures in the Caribbean region. One measure, namely the degree of economic recovery, employment generation, and reserve accumulation, would place the efforts of the Dominican Republic, Guyana, and partly Jamaica in the category of successes.

In addition, it can be concluded that both the Bahamas and Barbados successfully achieved their more modest adjustment goals by conscientiously implementing fiscal austerity and monetary prudence. In the case of Barbados, the income policy designed in 1993 also seems to have been reasonably successful. However, in both countries this policy stance had substantial negative employment effects.

The Dominican Republic has implemented a consistent set of policies with the assistance of the IMF since mid-1990. This eventually resulted in restoration of adequate reserve levels, fiscal surpluses, sizable external capital inflows, and a gradual improvement of the unemployment situation. Unsolved so far remain excessive trade deficits, highly skewed income distribution, and social deficits in the areas of health, education, and housing. Moreover, state ownership of some twenty-five enterprises (CORDE, inherited from the Trujillo era) perpetuates the unchallenged existence of monopolies and certainly crowds out private-sector investment propensities.

The structural adjustment efforts of Jamaica, which originated in the early 1980s, and the recent efforts in Trinidad and Tobago have a more mixed record. Major improvements were made in terms of fiscal balances, but part of this was achieved by postponing public investment. Because of the interrelationship between public and private investment in these economies, the investment propensities of the private sector have been eroded, resulting in reduced growth prospects. In some cases attractive fiscal terms were needed to persuade investors to make substantial investments in certain sectors. In the future, attention must shift towards policy-based rather than deal-based investment.

Suriname is the classic example of an economy gone bust because of inadequate policy adjustment, as well as the second variant of the Dutch disease; namely, excessive dependence on external assistance, both official and private. As a result, it is at risk of losing its economic mainstay, the bauxite and alumina industry, which would have far-reaching income and employment effects. The exchange rate depreciated from 1.8 per U.S. dollar in the early 1980s to around 160 in the parallel market in 1994 (not by design, but by default!), improving the chance of popular acceptance of a consistent adjustment program.

Guyana is a shining example of a country on its way back from a deep abyss. After draconian adjustment measures taken since the introduction of the ERP in 1988, it has reduced its external and fiscal deficit by roughly one-half; reigned in monetary expansion so that inflation fell to just 10 percent in 1993 (down from 105 percent in 1991); and restored international reserves from the equivalent of one week of imports in 1988, to some eight months in early 1994. All of this took place while the country produced an average real growth rate of 7 percent in the last three years. This track record enabled the multilateral institutions and the Paris Club to give maximum assistance and debt relief.

To sustain its current recuperation pace, Guyana will have to continue implementing reform measures so as to support private sector expansion. So far, it has received extensive interest and investment from foreign investors, especially in the agricultural, forestry, and mining sectors. The financial sector also seems set for a drastic improvement in efficiency, assuming that privatization plans are implemented. Still unresolved are Guyana's excessive external debt servicing obligations; fiscal deficits still out of line with prudent financing possibilities; a very weakly staffed public sector involved in many productive activities, but not investing adequately in improving the human resource base; and the need for maintenance and upgrading of physical infrastructure, a condition *sine qua non* for attracting foreign investment in manufacturing.

Fortunately, the region has not been subjected to the destabilizing forces of hyperinflation, except for the spikes in the Dominican Republic in 1990 and Guyana in 1989–91, and in Suriname, as repressed inflationary forces are released after major exchange rate corrections. There is no need, therefore, for heterodox adjustment policies. What is needed, however, is public awareness that the region is increasingly lagging behind others in its growth achievements and employment prospects. While its situation is not directly comparable, nevertheless, some lessons from the East Asian miracle might be taken to heart.[6]

An Emerging Regional Policy Consensus for the Nineties

Despite occasional evidence of adjustment fatigue among the region's electorate (which has in some cases led to a political changing of the guard), it is increasingly clear that adjustment is both a global and continuous phenomena. Under the influence of scientific, managerial, and technological innovations, spearheaded by computerization and telecommunications advances, and with dramatic changes occurring in the political arena (as in Eastern Europe and China), global competition has widened and accelerated. The traditional distinction between high-wage and low-wage countries is rapidly fading: technology now takes only a few years to disseminate, resulting in a technology trickle-down that, in the foreseeable future, will weigh heavily against low-skilled and/or low-productive labor. Indeed, some Eastern European nations with highly trained labor forces have real wage levels below those in relatively high-wage Caribbean countries (the Bahamas, Barbados, and Trinidad and Tobago).

Against this background, the multilateral development institutions stand ready to assist the region in structural reforms, which must transcend mere considerations of economic efficiency. Future competition will be based not only on price, but especially on non-price considerations, as well as social equity and environmental concerns. In this respect, the region should be able to tap multilateral and bilateral support capacity to the fullest extent, for tackling the following medium-term challenges that are critical to its long-term prosperity:

- Ensure that the modernization and reform processes are economically viable.
- Promote social and distributive equity, including that between generations.
- Establish an optimal size and role for the state, by moving it away from productive activities and reassigning the managerial and implementation

---

[6] Miracle is actually a misnomer in this case. All the achievements were hard-won by well-coordinated, prudent macroeconomic policies: deliberate undervaluation of the exchange rate, import restrictions, substantial financial and logistic government support for export-oriented sectors, and exceptionally high investment in human resources.

capacity to areas where intervention by the state is indispensable, such as education, health, social safety, and environmental protection.
- Assist the private sector in increasing its price and non-price competitiveness. This should include institutional reforms in trade and investment promotion; establishing and/or upgrading bureaus of standards; export quality control measures (especially in agriculture); and measures to establish, register, and protect intellectual property rights.
- Improve the investment climate for the private sector by removing unnecessary controls and institutional obstacles.
- Assist the regional private sector in reaching a state of up-to-date preparation to meet global competitive forces.
- Attract the most appropriate technologies to bolster the region's competitiveness and adequately protect the environment.
- Support a comprehensive investment effort to bring the region's human resource base up to par with the emerging competitive challenges.
- Define the most appropriate future regional and supraregional trade linkages, given the rapid emergence of global trade blocs.
- Consolidate democratic structures through political consensus building and the promotion of good governance. The latter must be interpreted broadly, to include legislative and judicial efficiency, equity and accountability, and efficient and equitable taxation, social expenditures, income distribution, and incentive structures.

Conclusion

While the future holds formidable challenges for the Caribbean, the region's remarkable resilience in the adverse international climate of the 1980s, and its ongoing recovery, suggest its potential to overcome future adversity as well. Governments, unions, and the private sector show greater understanding for the need to improve the region's competitive position. Moreover, there are signs that the initially defensive reaction is yielding to a more forward- and outward-looking strategic orientation on the region's natural comparative advantages, aimed at defining niches in the international market of goods and services where the region can successfully compete.

The Caribbean region as a whole is not yet doing as well as it could and should. Too much tension still prevails between public and private sectors, between employees and employers, between export orientation and import substitution, and, last but not least, between the desire to preserve current standards of living and the economic imperative to devote resources to generating productive employment for future generations. Scarce public sector management skills are overly committed to stabilization, instead of being used to solidify the preconditions for sustained economic growth.

As the world economy makes a quantum leap towards integration, the region must take a final, hard look at the conditions, policies, regulations, and institutional arrangements that could inhibit future growth. With the combined forces of the national governments and private sectors, and efficient use of available external assistance, especially to invest in its human resources, the Caribbean region can be trusted to make the mental transition from the aid to the trade mode, which is the precondition for the advancement and prosperity of its future generations.

Bibliography

Bernal, R.L. 1992. *Recent Developments in the Western Hemisphere and their Implications for Jamaica.* Kingston, Jamaica.

———. 1993. The Caribbean Basin Free Trade Agreements Act. Statement before the U.S. House Ways and Means Committee, Subcommittee on Trade.

Birdsall, N. 1993. *Social Development is Economic Development.* Washington D.C.: World Bank Human Resources Development and Operations Policy Research Paper.

CARICOM. 1991. *Guidelines for Economic Development Strategy for CARICOM Countries into the Twenty-First Century.* Working Document Prepared by the Planning Committee for the Regional Economic Conference.

Corbo, V. 1991. "Estrategias y políticas de desarrollo en América Latina: Una perspectiva histórica." Economía 14 (27).

Edwards, S. 1988. *Exchange Rate Misalignment in Developing Countries.* Baltimore and London: The Johns Hopkins Univ. Press.

———. 1993. *Latin America and the Caribbean.* Washington D.C: The World Bank.

Esquel Group Foundation. 1993. Civil Society, State and Market: An Emerging Partnership for Equitable Development. Paper presented to the Social Forum convened by the IDB and UNDP, Washington D.C., February.

Harris, D.J. 1994. *Comparative Analysis of Export Performance in Five Caribbean-Basin Countries.* Washington D.C.: IDB Visiting Scholar Paper.

IDB (Inter-American Development Bank). *Economic and Social Progress Report, 1984–1993.* Washington D.C.: IDB.

IBRD (International Bank for Reconstruction and Development). 1993. *The East Asian Miracle: Economic Growth and Public Policy.* Washington D.C.: The World Bank.

———. 1993. *Caribbean Region: Current Economic Situation, Regional Issues, and Capital Flows, 1992.* Washington D.C.: The World Bank.

Iglesias, E.V. 1992. *Reflections on Economic Development: Towards a New Latin American Consensus.* Washington D.C.: IDB/Johns Hopkins Univ. Press.

IMF (International Monetary Fund). 1993. *International Financial Statistics: Yearbook 1993.* Washington D.C.: IMF.

Jaspersen, F.Z., and C.G. Ginarte. 1993. *Capital Flows to Latin America 1982–92: Trends and Prospects.* Washington D.C.: IDB Research Paper.

Loser, C.M. 1983. *La función de los precios-clave en el proceso de ajuste.* Washington D.C.: IMF Institute.

McIntyre, Sir A. 1993. *Building National Consensus on Social Policy: Trinidad and Tobago.* Report of the Pilot Mission on Socio-Economic Reform of the Inter-American Development Bank. Washington D.C: IDB.

Smith, S.C. 1991. *Industrial Policy in Developing Countries: Reconsidering the Real Sources of Export-Led Growth.* Washington D.C.: Economic Policy Institute.

Teitel, S. 1993. *Industrial and Technological Development.* Washington D.C.: IDB/Johns Hopkins Univ. Press.

West Indian Commission. 1992. *Time for Action: The Report of the West Indian Commission.* St. Michael, Barbados: West Indian Commission Secretariat.

Williamson, J. 1993. In Search of a Manual for Technopols. Washington D.C.: Institute for International Economics.

Worrell, D. 1987. *Small Island Economies: Structure and Performance in the English-Speaking Caribbean since 1970.* New York: Praeger Publishers.

———. 1993. Economic Integration with Unequal Partners: The Caribbean and North America. Address to the Woodrow Wilson International Center for Scholars. Washington, D.C.

Chapter 7

The East Asian Experience and Its Relevance to the Caribbean

Sarath Rajapatirana

Economic development during the last thirty years provides a continuing experiment from which important lessons can be learned. These lessons are both positive and negative, from economies that have succeeded and others that have failed. Among the former, the East Asian countries provide valuable lessons that cannot be ignored by policymakers in other parts of the world. Of some twenty-three East Asian countries, eight stand out in terms of economic performance: Japan, the four original Tigers (Hong Kong, Singapore, South Korea, and Taiwan) and Indonesia, Malaysia, and Thailand.[1] Japan has sustained high growth over a fifty-year period, and is by no means a developing country. The success of the remaining seven countries poses two essential questions for Caribbean countries (as well as others). First, what policies led to the recorded and undisputed success of these seven developing countries in East Asia? Second, how relevant is that experience to Caribbean countries, not only in terms of their domestic policy environments, but also their external environment, such as the prospects posed by NAFTA?

In order to set the tone for the discussion, it is necessary to observe a few caveats. First, the East Asian experience has been widely interpreted by different protagonists as confirming their own special interpretations of the causes for success. But in order to examine the facts objectively, epithets such as neoclassical and revisionist must be discarded. Second, we can also learn from at least one hundred other developing countries that were not as successful as the East Asian countries.

Third, in speaking about East Asian countries, it is important to note the diversity among them. For example, Hong Kong and Singapore are small countries, wholly devoted to manufacturing, with small populations and high population densities. But South Korea, Malaysia, Indonesia, and Thailand are rela-

---

[1] A recent study by the World Bank considered these eight countries and part of China. See World Bank (1993a) and Leipziger and Thomas (1993).

tively large, not only in terms of population, but also in terms of their natural resource endowments. And even the two small countries (sometimes referred to as mere city-states) have different characteristics. Hong Kong's economy is much less interventionist than Singapore's; in fact, many consider Hong Kong a laissez-faire economy, despite the large public investment in housing to accommodate the ever increasing numbers of immigrants from mainland China. Singapore, on the other hand, intervenes more in the economy, but does so outside the production sector, in a manner based on both foreign and domestic competition.[2] Finally, the lessons from the experience of one group of countries can be transplanted to another group only after careful consideration of their initial conditions, institutions and political economy.[3]

The plan of the paper is as follows. The next section gives an account of the facts of the seven East Asian countries that are relevant for the Caribbean context. Then the factors commonly assumed to have led to their success are examined. Recently, the success of East Asian countries has been attributed to a combination of fundamentals, such as stable macroeconomic policies and sound incentive policies, as well as selective interventions. Mainstream economists would agree that their success was facilitated by the fundamentals.[4] This reinterpretation, which explicitly recognizes the institutional ethos of these countries, renders at least part of the East Asian experience irrelevant to many other developing countries, including those in the Caribbean, with different institutional structures.

The third section considers the Caribbean context, noting similarities and differences among East Asian and Caribbean countries. The group of Caribbean countries is defined to include the members of the Caribbean Group for Cooperation in Economic Development, except for Belize, the Dominican Republic, Guyana, Haiti, and Suriname. The ten countries considered, therefore, are Antigua and Barbuda, the Bahamas, Barbados, Dominica, Grenada, Jamaica, St. Kitts and Nevis, St. Lucia, St. Vincent and the Grenadines, and Trinidad and Tobago. These ten countries can be thought of as belonging to the same set, not only in terms of resource endowments, but also because they are neighbors and have similar institutions and economic policies. The Caribbean countries are compared with the East Asian countries in order to examine the relevance of the factors in their success for Caribbean development. The fourth

---

[2] The differences between these two economies have been well documented by Krause (1988). The differences among the whole group are emphasized by others. See Petri (1993).

[3] Thus, Robert Lucas has remarked that asking countries to follow what South Korea did with its economy is like asking any aspiring basketball player to follow the Michael Jordan model. See Lucas (1993).

[4] See World Bank (1993a).

section of the paper examines the external environment for the Caribbean group with special reference to NAFTA. The last section draws the possible lessons and the conclusions of the paper.

Facts about the East Asian Experience

The undisputed facts about the East Asian experience are the high per capita income growth, greater macroeconomic stability, and export success of these countries. These achievements were combined with a greater equity, which has been sustained. Moreover, while the world economy was subject to large external shocks during the 1970s and the 1980s, these economies recovered faster than those of other countries. The economic performance of these countries is all the more creditable, considering their poor initial conditions when reforms began in the mid-1960s. While reforms at times were slow due to external shocks, there were no policy reversals. This policy consistency is another important feature of the performance of the East Asian countries.

The four Tigers—Hong Kong, Singapore, South Korea, and Taiwan—had initial per capita incomes in the range of $650 to $2,300 in 1965,[5] while per capita incomes in Indonesia, Malaysia, and Thailand ranged from $190 to $850.[6] Their rapid and sustained GDP growth of nearly 8 percent per year from 1965 to 1992 have made them the fastest-growing developing countries (see Appendix, Table 7A.1). Many other countries had higher per capita income levels in the mid-1960s, but slower GDP growth during this period. In fact some consider the performance of the East Asian countries a unique phenomenon in world economic history.[7]

An important feature of the East Asian countries is that they achieved declining levels of inequality with high income growth. Social indicators show steadily increasing life expectancy; fewer people living in absolute poverty; improved access to basic necessities, clean water, and adequate shelter; and higher standards of nutrition, when compared to other developing countries. Of course there are differences within the group. Indonesia, with its huge population and relatively poor initial conditions, has more poverty than the others. Singapore has a very low proportion of its population below the poverty line

---

[5] In 1965, per capita incomes were as follows: Hong Kong $2284, Singapore $1678, Korea $652 and Taiwan $1157, in 1987 US dollars.

[6] Indonesia's per capita income was $193, Malaysia's $846, and Thailand's $354, in 1987 US dollars.

[7] A host of studies have examined the industrial, trade and development issues of these countries, including Little et al. (1970), Balassa (1971), Bhagwati (1978), Krueger (1978), and Michaely et al. (1991).

and high income all round. These poverty and equity outcomes are closely related to the other features of their economic success.

A second characteristic of the East Asian countries is their macroeconomic stability. During the 1965–1992 period, the seven countries had an average inflation rate of 9.9 percent (Table 7A.2). (That average would be much smaller if the two inflation episodes of Indonesia and South Korea were excluded. But even these two countries rapidly brought down their rates of inflation.) Changes in domestic prices in the region were increasingly linked to international prices, through trade liberalization and exchange rate adjustments. Thus they understood that continued inflation would destroy their export competitiveness. The real exchange rates remained relatively stable and competitive in these countries. Strong fiscal measures were used, particularly in Singapore, Malaysia and Thailand. In addition to controlling inflation, these countries sustained their balance-of-payments positions, met their payment obligations, and avoided central bank financing. These practices, along with fiscal discipline and rapid export growth, helped them avert the debt crises that beset other countries.[8] In addition, they adjusted rapidly to adverse external shocks, so the negative shocks did not result in crises and low growth.[9]

The third feature of the performance of the East Asian countries is the rapid growth of exports, particularly manufactures, starting from a low base (Tables 7A.3 and 7A.4). As a group, the Tigers increased their share of the world market for exports from 1.5 percent in 1965 to 6.7 percent in 1990. The other three countries (Indonesia, Malaysia, and Thailand), raised their share of world trade from 1.5 percent to 2.2 percent over the same period. Due to rapid growth of both exports and imports, the trade ratios of the East Asian countries rose significantly between 1970 and 1988. South Korea's trade ratio doubled to 66 percent, and Hong Kong's trade ratio increased by more than 70 percent.

The rapid growth of exports of the East Asian countries was an important ingredient of their success. The period from the mid-1960s to the mid-1970s is considered the golden age of exports, as the rate of world trade growth was double that of world income growth. But most important is that these countries were able to raise their share of world trade significantly and change the composition of trade from the developing countries.[10] As a group they received no special trading preferences, but they captured the largest share of

---

[8] Indonesia was the exception. It had a debt crisis in 1975, when the state-owned oil company got into difficulties in servicing its large short-term debt. This produced the Pertamina crisis. That crisis had a cathartic effect on Indonesia, which has maintained a close watch of its public enterprises to avoid the possibility of another debt problem. See Woo and Glassburner (1994).

[9] The cases of South Korea, Thailand, and Indonesia have shown the rapid policy responses to external shocks and the beneficial effects of a fast recovery. See Little et al. (1993).

[10] See Riedel (1987).

preferences granted to the developing countries under the General System of Preferences (GSP), and a lion's share of the textile and garment trade subject to the Multi Fibre Arrangement (MFA).

A fourth feature of the success of the East Asian countries was their high investment rates (Table 7A.5). This was possible due to high savings rates that averaged about 30 percent of GDP during the 1965–1990 period. Their investment rates were significantly higher than the average for some 118 developing countries; more important, the share of private investment in total investment has remained higher than 40 percent. Public investments were not severely cut, as happened in most developing countries during the turbulent 1980s, while the provision of public goods remained relatively stable.

Fifth, direct foreign investment (DFI) played a critical role in these economies, providing for technology transfer, employment creation, labor force training, and foreign exchange generation. East Asian economies acquired technology rapidly and sought foreign technology through a variety of mechanisms, such as licenses, capital goods imports (embodied technology), and foreign training. Openness to DFI accelerated technology transfer in Hong Kong, Malaysia, Singapore, Indonesia and Thailand. South Korea and Taiwan restricted DFI, but obtained foreign technology through licenses and other means.

A sixth feature was the high educational achievement reached in these countries. The four Tigers achieved universal primary education by 1965. Even the most populous country in the group, Indonesia, had primary education coverage of some 70 percent by then. Among the four Tigers, secondary school enrollment reached nearly 50 percent of the cohort group by the early 1980s. In South Korea, secondary school enrollment reached 80 percent by 1987. In addition to the widening coverage, the quality of education improved steadily. By one account, South Korean secondary school students performed better than their American and European counterparts.[11]

Seventh, high growth achieved in these countries was due not only to the accumulation of physical and human capital, but also to total factor productivity (TFP) growth. This refers to growth independent of increased inputs— growth associated with efficient allocation, technological catch-up, increasing returns, and organizational changes. While some two-thirds of the growth in East Asia arose from factor accumulation, a full third was due to total factor productivity increase, substantially more than in other developing countries.[12]

---

[11] See Birdsall and Sabot (1993).

[12] IN TFP growth estimates for the 1950–1987 period, the four Tigers are at the top of a large sample of countries, according to Elias (1990). Young (1993) disputes the claim of high total factor productivity growth among the Tigers and ascribes their high growth to factor accumulation and better allocation.

Eighth, the labor markets functioned well in East Asia, in matching the needs of industries with the preferences of the labor force. The pool of skilled labor facilitated easy allocation of labor from one activity to another, and wages were largely market determined. While real wages increased with increased productivity, labor markets were virtually unsegmented, so workers of similar skills earned similar wages in different parts of the economy. Rapid economic growth increased labor market flexibility, and labor was prepared to accept performance-related wages, such as bonuses and incentive payments, that varied with profit levels. To be sure, South Korea, Indonesia, and Taiwan placed restrictions on labor union activities, but these governments did not repress wages.

Interpretation of the East Asian Experience

Most mainstream economists would agree that the remarkable achievement of the East Asian countries is due to a combination of good policies and appropriate institutions. Stable macroeconomic policies were reflected in the avoidance of large fiscal deficits, inflation, and appreciation of the exchange rate. These produced the conditions for high savings opportunities and the proper evaluation of investments, which in turn led to increases in physical and human capital. Both these types of investments had high payoffs in the East Asian countries. The consistent pursuit of stable macroeconomic policies, and strong measures to counter negative external shocks and to manage positive shocks, protected these countries from "stop-and-go" policy routines. Given the credible macroeconomic policies, private sector investment in total investment was relatively high. In this environment, private entrepreneurs made sound investment decisions. In South Korea and Taiwan, public sector officials played a leading role, particularly in the early stages of industrialization, once the private sector had chosen the avenues of investment. Thus, public interventions were "market driven," in that the private sector selected an activity for promotion. Singapore had more state direction as to the choice of technology during the 1980s: while it failed to increase the skill content of production, the country adjusted to its normal high growth during a short period.

Another sound policy was the emphasis on incentive reforms, beginning with adoption of outward-oriented trade policies. These included reduction of bias against exports by compensating for import controls through duty-free status, wastage allowances, and automatic access to imports. Some analysts have noted that these trade regimes were neutral.[13] However, neutrality was achieved through intervention, rather than by leaving production decisions

---

[13] See survey by Lal and Rajapatirana (1987).

entirely to the private sector, as was the case in Hong Kong.[14] Outward orientation, open access to private foreign capital, and the use of international and domestic markets in competitive and contestable environments were important ingredients of openness. Thus, savings were better allocated in high-return investments and access to new technology was facilitated, resulting in higher productivity of both physical and human capital.

A somewhat controversial aspect of the interpretation of East Asian policy arises in the area of selective intervention. While the steady hand of government assured credibility of economic policy, some argue that a deliberate choice was made to distort incentives through intervention. In other words, the institutional dice were loaded, with public officials "governing the market," and public policy deliberately distorting prices to reduce the price of capital and "to get the prices wrong."[15] The theoretical and empirical basis for this view is based largely on anecdotal evidence. Mainstream economists contend that distortions detract from better allocation and lead to departures from neutrality, and that such departures cannot be justified from the standpoint of productivity.[16]

According to other views, industrial targeting, picking winners, credit subsidies, and other instruments have been used with success in at least three of the four Tigers. Yet the weight of the empirical evidence does not indicate that the East Asian countries's success was the result of interventions through credit subsidies, deliberate underpricing of capital, and the use of quotas for promoting import substitution. Whether South Korea, Singapore, and Taiwan would have done better without selective intervention is debatable. The results of industrial targeting as inferred by productivity are at variance with the claims of its success. For example, the industrial and export structures of the countries using industrial targeting turned out to be what was predicted by comparative advantage. And where selective interventions did take place, total factor productivity in those activities remained below that of the nonpromoted industries.[17]

---

[14] It does not seem to matter for success whether neutrality is achieved through domestic subsidies or trade measures. In fact, neoclassical literature supports the use of domestic subsidies to offset domestic distortions (see Bhagwati, Ramaswamy, and Srinivasan 1969).

[15] See Wade (1990) and Amsden (1989).

[16] In the case of Taiwan, the government's selective promotion has had no effect on investment and productivity (Yang 1993). This is also confirmed in a recent study where the authors attempted to relate output growth in certain sectors in Japan to instruments of selective promotion (Beason and Weinstein 1993). In Korea, activities that were not promoted had higher TFP growth than those that were promoted (World Bank 1993a).

[17] Singapore had no total productivity growth in the early 1980s when it tried to intervene in labor markets to bring about the use of more advanced technology (World Bank 1993a).

Finally, the institutional aspect of the East Asian countries' success is based on high-quality technocrats, who are said to be isolated from political influence. While managing the provision of public goods, including macroeconomic stability and credible incentive policies, and promoting competition, they also monitored economic activities closely and effectively, to ensure their success. The symbiotic relationship between government and business may have been an essential ingredient for the success of these countries. Here, too, Hong Kong is the exception, since its government intervened only in public housing. The three newly industrializing countries, Indonesia, Malaysia, and Thailand, reduced intervention and the public sector's role in tradable activities in the 1980s, and achieved considerable success in exports and output growth following these reforms.

The Caribbean Countries in the Context of the East Asian Success

The ten Caribbean countries (Antigua and Barbuda, the Bahamas, Barbados, Dominica, Grenada, Jamaica, St. Kitts and Nevis, St. Lucia, St. Vincent and the Grenadines, and Trinidad and Tobago) share certain characteristics that affect their overall economic performance. Analytically, all can be thought of as small economies, since no single country can influence the terms of trade, interest rates, or wage rates prevailing outside the country. In this respect, all are similar to the East Asian countries, particularly the four Tigers. A large part of their GDP is related to the external sector. This is a matter of smallness in the geographical sense, since their resource bases tend to be narrow. Their exports are concentrated in two agricultural commodities, bananas and sugar, with the exceptions of Trinidad and Tobago (petroleum) and Jamaica (bauxite). Tourism is also an important foreign exchange earner for nearly all the Caribbean countries.

Although these countries have high trade ratios to their national income, they did not have open trade regimes in the policy sense until the late 1980s and early 1990s, which is much later than the East Asian countries. They had many trade barriers until then, and some have them even now. Hong Kong and Singapore have had open economies since the 1950s, South Korea and Taiwan since the mid-1960s, and Indonesia, Malaysia, and Thailand since the early 1980s.

Like the East Asian countries, there are significant differences among the ten Caribbean countries. First, the members of the Organization of the Eastern Caribbean States (OECS)—comprised of Antigua and Barbuda, Dominica, Grenada, St. Kitts and Nevis, St. Lucia, and St. Vincent and the Grenadines—have a common currency with a fixed exchange rate linked to the U.S. dollar. Monetary policy is set by a single authority, the Eastern Caribbean Central Bank (ECCB), based on pre-set rules limiting the ability of the governments in the organization to monetize government debt and prescribing the relationship of foreign exchange reserves to the money stock in each country. This is very much like the cases of Hong Kong and Singapore.

Second, of the ten countries, Trinidad and Tobago is the sole oil exporter, as are Malaysia and Indonesia. While all the other Caribbean countries experienced negative oil shocks during the early 1980s, Trinidad and Tobago sustained a positive shock (like Malaysia and Indonesia) and had to contend with the problems of a resource surfeit at that time.

Third, nearly all the countries have large tourist sectors, and these countries were relatively more affected by the recessions in the United States and Europe. Finally, all except the Bahamas are members of CARICOM, while the East Asian countries are members of a rather loose union, ASEAN, that gives a greater leeway to change their tariff regimes.

GDP Growth

The Caribbean countries are relatively well off compared to the other developing countries, and are certainly well off compared to the East Asian countries at the beginning of their reforms. Per capita income for the majority of the Caribbean countries in 1992 is from $2,000 to $5,000, with the Bahamas as an outlier having an income level of over $12,000, and Jamaica with an income level less than $1,350 (Table 7A.6). During the 1980s, many of them experienced declining income levels, due to the vicissitudes they faced.

The ten countries as a group had better GDP growth compared to the majority of the countries in the rest of the world, but they pale in comparison to the East Asian countries. Their average GDP growth was 3.2 percent for the 1981–1992 period: this compares with a 7.9 percent GDP growth rate for the seven East Asian countries for the 1966–1992 period. GDP growth was dispersed among the Caribbean group of countries as shown in Table 7.1. The highest GDP growth rates for the group, exceeding 4 percent, were those of Antigua and Barbuda, Dominica, St. Kitts and Nevis, St. Lucia, and St. Vincent and the Grenadines.

Table 7.1 GDP Growth, 1981–92 *(Percent)*

Country	GDP Growth
Antigua and Barbuda[1]	5.8
Bahamas[1]	2.1
Barbados	0.5
Dominica	5.3
Grenada	3.8
Jamaica	1.9
St. Kitts and Nevis	4.3
St. Lucia	4.4
St. Vincent and the Grenadines	6.0
Trinidad and Tobago	-2.4
Group	3.2

[1] 1981–91.
Source: World Bank.

Investment and Savings

The gross domestic investment rate exceeded 30 percent for Antigua and Barbuda. Dominica, Grenada, St. Kitts and Nevis, and St. Lucia were in the same range as the East Asian countries, but the latter have had this rate for three decades. Grenada had a high investment rate, but a GDP growth of 3.8 percent (Table 7.1).

As expected, low growth was associated with low investment rates, below 20 percent for the Bahamas and Barbados. All the other countries in the group had investment rates above 20 percent, but had varied output growth given different productivity levels. As in East Asian countries, high GDP growth was more related to the share of private investment in total investment.

The time path of savings parallels that of investment (Table 7.2). Savings remained below investment for the group, given that almost all were receiving capital and experiencing current-account deficits. This has been the historical pattern, with increased current-account deficits arising from the terms of trade shocks and interest rate increases of the early 1980s. One exception to the typical relationship of domestic savings to investment was the Bahamas, which had an excess of savings over investment, due to its status as an international financial center.

Table 7.2 Investment and Savings, 1980–92
(Percent)

Country	Investment/GDP	Savings/GDP
Antigua and Barbuda	34.3[a]	11.2[a]
Bahamas	19.0	25.2[b]
Barbados	19.4[b]	15.3
Dominica	31.1	3.4[f]
Grenada	37.5	8.2
Jamaica	21.4	18.3[e]
St. Kitts and Nevis	40.8[c]	11.0 c
St. Lucia	35.8[d]	n.a
St. Vincent and the Grenadines	29.9[e]	8.2[g]
Trinidad and Tobago	21.4[c]	24.7[e]
Group	29.1	13.9

Note: Based on averages for the periods.
[a] 1987–91; [b] 1980–87; [c] 1982–92; [d] 1986–91; [e] 1980–91; [f] 1980–89; [g] 1980–88.
Source: World Bank, IMF.

Macroeconomic Stability

Fiscal outcomes played a central place in the economic performance of the Caribbean countries. First, the large size of the government in these economies meant that fiscal outcomes had a strong impact. Second, fiscal policies were used to maintain aggregate demand in the face of the negative shocks these countries experienced. Consequently, the recovery was more protracted than that of the East Asian countries. Third, fiscal revenues in the Caribbean countries were more susceptible to commodity price movements, since revenues were dependent on tourism and a narrow export base. Finally, the public sector had a prominent role in gross domestic investment and savings.

Fiscal deficits as a proportion of GDP ranged from 2 percent to 8 percent for most of the Caribbean countries. In contrast, St. Vincent and the Grenadines and St. Lucia had fiscal surpluses (Table 7.3). Many countries continued to have large fiscal deficits that prevented stability and better growth performance. Antigua and Barbuda, Barbados, Jamaica, and Trinidad and Tobago still experienced fiscal problems of a more endemic nature.[18] The growth in deficits for most countries was affected by their inability to contain expenditures in the face of negative external shocks, as well as by expenditure booms from rising public sector wages and from transfers to state-owned enterprises.

Large deficits in some countries were initially financed from external sources, so fiscal deficits were less associated with inflation. But when access to foreign capital was reduced during the debt crisis in the early 1980s, the countries with high deficits resorted to money creation as the mode of financing, and the money stock expanded. This was not the case with the OECS countries. First, their ability to raise fiscal deficits was limited by the rules of that monetary arrangement. Second, there was a fixed ratio of reserves prescribed for money stock that limited the extent of credit expansion. Consequently, the OECS countries had relatively low inflation rates for the whole period. The same was true for Hong Kong and Singapore, which also have currency board systems. For all East Asian countries, the average inflation was 6.2 percent for the 1980–1992 period (see Appendix Table 7A.2). The average inflation rate for the Caribbean countries was 7.8 percent for the 1981–1992 period, with Jamaica and Trinidad and Tobago having the highest inflation rates.

Table 7.3 Fiscal Deficit and Inflation, 1981–92
(Percent)

Country	Fiscal Deficit/GDP	Inflation
Antigua and Barbuda	8.1[a]	5.5[b]
Bahamas	2.1[b]	6.2
Barbados	7.5[b]	6.5
Dominica	2.7[c]	6.5
Grenada	5.4[d]	6.2
Jamaica	6.7[e]	20.7
St. Kitts and Nevis	2.0[f]	4.7[b]
St. Lucia	-0.2[b]	5.7
St. Vincent and the Grenadines	-0.1[g]	5.5
Trinidad and Tobago	4.1[a]	10.7
Group	3.8	7.8

Note: Based on averages for the periods.
[a] 1987–92; [b] 1980–91; [c] 1985–90; [d] 1984–91; [e] 1980–85, 1988–91; [f] 1982–90; [g] 1980–90
Source: World Bank, IMF.

---

[18] These figures may overstate the extent of fiscal deficit, since a continuous time-series for the 1980–1992 period was unavailable. However, there was sporadic fiscal instability in these countries in the late 1980s, especially in the case of non-OECS countries. For instance, Antigua and Barbuda maintained high fiscal deficits in the late 1980s and early 1990s and "financed" them through external debt arrears.

The Exchange Rate Regimes

The Caribbean countries have two types of exchange rate regimes. The OECS has a fixed exchange rate system linked to the U.S. dollar under a single central bank, the ECCB, a monetary arrangement that has the characteristics of a currency board for each country. The fixed rate can only be changed by unanimous agreement, and the money stock must be determined by the level of external reserves with full convertibility.

Certain other countries in the group have fixed exchange rates without the self-imposed monetary rules or fiscal discipline of a currency board system; thus, Barbados and the Bahamas have fixed exchange rate systems pegged to the U.S. dollar. Except for Barbados, the others in the group have changed their peg in recent years.

Jamaica and Trinidad and Tobago have freely floating exchange rate systems. The adoption of freely floating rates in these countries was a phenomenon linked to the reforms of the late 1980s. With freely floating exchange rates, these countries have been able to allow the exchange rate to play its role as an adjustment instrument. Earlier, policymakers had a limited number of instruments to adjust to macroeconomic shocks and to maintain external competitiveness.

Table 7.4 Real Exchange Rate Evolution, 1980–91

Depreciating	Stable	Appreciating
Antigua and Barbuda	Dominica	Bahamas
Jamaica	Grenada	Barbados
St. Kitts and Nevis	St. Lucia	Trinidad and Tobago
	St. Vincent and the Grenadines	

Note: Based on averages for the period.
Source: World Bank, IMF.

Real effective exchange rates have evolved in predictable patterns (Table 7.4). Currency appreciation was greatest in the economies with high inflation and fixed exchange rates, like the Bahamas and Barbados. Many countries that had experienced appreciations during the mid-1980s chose to devalue their currencies or to adopt flexible exchange rates. Jamaica offset the appreciation of its currency by adopting floating exchange rates. The East Asian countries, however, had adopted flexible exchange rates in the early 1970s, and their real exchange rates remained relatively stable.

In sum, the macroeconomic outcome of the Caribbean countries contrasts with that of the East Asian countries in several important respects. The Caribbean countries had high fiscal deficits, high inflation rates, more appreciated exchange rates, large balance of payments deficits, rapid external debt accumulation, and lower public savings rates. Moreover, policy responses to external shocks were slower, leading to protracted periods of adjustment.

Trade Performance

The Caribbean countries have high trade-to-output ratios, since they are small economies (Table 7.5). The high trade ratios imply that terms-of-trade shocks figure prominently in these countries and that those shocks were large during the 1980s, arising from the oil and other commodity price shocks.[19] The other important feature of the trade system is that many had trade regimes that discriminated against exports and favored production for the domestic market. This is in sharp contrast to East Asian economies that reduced their import protection early and did not allow a bias against exports to develop.

Trade performance for these countries is indicated more accurately with export performance. Three important features of export performance stand out. First, export performance was an important determinant of GDP growth in these countries. Dominica, St. Vincent, and St. Lucia had export growth rates exceeding 16 percent per annum for the whole period. Their GDP growth performance paralleled that of their export performance. Second, the commodity composition of export trade was an important factor in the growth of exports. Finally, for each country, export growth rates varied considerably over the period.

The trade performance of these countries was related to preferential access to the U.S. and European markets, which helped them to increase export receipts. This is in contrast to the East Asian countries, which had no special preferential access. Instead, they utilized preferences available under the GSP to all developing countries and used the MFA quotas of others.

Table 7.5 Openness and Exports, 1980–91
(Percent)

Country	Trade/Output[1]	Growth of Exports
Antigua and Barbuda	108.4	9.8
Bahamas	55.9	-6.8
Barbados	61.0	1.7
Dominica	90.0	22.8
Grenada	82.8	8.3
Jamaica	68.3	2.2
St. Kitts and Nevis	97.1	5.9
St. Lucia	100.0	16.1
St. Vincent and the Grenadines	111.9	n.a
Trinidad and Tobago	56.4	-2.0
Group	83.2	6.5

Note: Based on averages for the period.
[1] Ratio of merchandise exports plus merchandise imports to GDP.
Source: World Bank.

---

[19] The extent of a terms of trade shock depends on the price change and the trade ratio for each country. For example, the external shock for Jamaica during the 1980s amounted to 4.3 percent of GDP on average. Trinidad and Tobago experienced large positive shocks in the 1970s of 10 percent and a negative shock of 7.6 percent of GDP in the 1980s (McCarthy and Zanalda 1993).

Direct Foreign Investment

The DFI experience of the Caribbean countries is in sharp contrast to the East Asian experience and has been restrictive in relation to the foreign ownership of firms, the right to buy land, the right to borrow locally, and limits to the issue of work permits. Between 1984 and 1990, almost US $2 billion in new investments flowed to the Caribbean countries as a result of the Caribbean Basin Initiative (CBI). However, DFI provisions in the Caribbean had a number of shortcomings. They had a pro-assembly/manufacturing bias, with information service operations ineligible for benefits, and there was also a lack of distinction between firms serving the export and domestic markets. The tax holidays for DFI favored quick payoffs and encouraged footloose industries. There is an overall lack of transparency, due to multiplicity of criteria in awarding licenses; moreover, whatever DFI took place could not lead to high productivity growth, given the distorted incentives.

Educational Achievements

Most indicators of educational achievement place the Caribbean countries, where the adult literacy rate is above 90 percent on average, well above the average for countries at a similar level of income. The Caribbean countries attained universal primary education earlier, if not at the same time as the four Tigers, but certainly earlier than Indonesia, Malaysia and Thailand. Secondary school enrollment is above the average for middle-income countries, but tertiary and university education is not as high as in other middle-income countries and certainly below that in the East Asian countries.

For productivity growth, primary and secondary school enrollment are crucial. This has been the experience of the East Asian countries, but Caribbean educational achievements did not lead to significant productivity growth. Several factors may explain this. First, ability to produce comes from employment, and structural unemployment in the Caribbean has been around 10 percent to 13 percent of the labor force. During the 1980s, there was also high cyclical unemployment of about 20 percent of the labor force. Second, the earlier inward-oriented trade policies and restrictions on foreign investment may have prevented increased access to both technical and management knowhow. In such a situation, the potential for learning-by-doing may have remained limited. Third, the quality of education appears to have declined. Reduced expenditures per pupil, the inability to replace incompetent teachers, and school administration deficiencies could have lowered educational standards, and the probability of primary school entrants completing secondary school is low, around 30 percent.[20] Furthermore, human capital is lost via migration, even though returns to the countries could be higher when the probability of unemployment is high and the loss in income taxes from migration is captured by remittances to relatives.[21]

Labor Market

The labor market in the Caribbean countries shows many characteristics of limited flexibility and segmentation. Labor is highly unionized, and unions influence the level of wages, labor practices, and labor legislation. Labor has higher educational achievements than most countries at similar levels of income. For the most part, wage determination, labor allocation, and nonwage payments are not market determined in these countries as they are in the East Asian countries. Consequently there is labor market rigidity and limited adjustment to external shocks. Labor costs are also high in some sectors and adversely affect the competitiveness of these economies, particularly on account of the sticky exchange rates. Public sector labor practices have a strong impact on private sector labor contracts. Public sector wages are higher for relatively less skilled labor compared to the private sector; conversely, public sector wages are low for skilled workers.

Relatively high levels of unemployment coexist with near constant real wages, implying that adjustments in the labor market are related to quantity rather than the price of labor, which explains the high levels of unemployment. Moreover, the presence of significant nonwage fixed payments robs the economies of a market-based matching of productivity increases to the wage rate. Until recently, the existing levels of import protection helped to sustain uncompetitive real wages, while total income declined or stagnated in many of the countries during the 1980s.

Conclusions from the Comparison

The main conclusions that follow from the above review of the performance of Caribbean countries in comparison to the East Asian countries are the following. First, these countries had lower GDP growth compared to the East Asian countries, but higher growth than other developing countries. The Caribbean countries faced large external shocks in the 1980s, like the East Asian countries, but the effects of these shocks were magnified in the Caribbean, because their exports were not diversified. The two small East Asian economies, Hong

---

[20] See World Bank (1993b).

[21] The immigration rates were 14 per thousand for Antigua and Barbuda, 22 per thousand for St. Kitts and Nevis, and 10 per thousand for Barbados (World Bank 1993b).

Kong and Singapore, experienced large shocks that did not significantly change their performance. This was due to their greater export diversification, the flexibility of their factor markets, and their strong and rapid policy response to the shocks.

Second, the Caribbean countries had less stable macroeconomic situations compared to the East Asians countries, in terms of high inflation rates, larger fiscal deficits, and unsustainable balance of payments positions that led to debt servicing problems.

Third, the investment ratios between the two groups of countries were not that different. What seems different, however, was the high proportion of private investment in total investment in the East Asian countries. Savings in the Caribbean countries as a proportion of GDP was lower, with lower public savings.

Fourth, the Caribbean countries had much lower export growth rates compared to the East Asians countries. The concentration of exports in a few products, the bias against exports arising from the existing levels of import protection, uncompetitive real exchange rates, and their relative instability contributed to this slow export growth. Being small island economies, the Caribbean countries had high trade-to-GDP ratios like Hong Kong and Singapore. The latter, however, were open economies, and their domestic prices better reflected international prices, given the low rates of import protection and competitive exchange rates.

Fifth, educational achievement in the Caribbean was better than in almost all the East Asian countries on the eve of their rapid growth, and even today the educational achievements of Malaysia, Indonesia, and Thailand are not as good as the Caribbean for primary and secondary school enrollments. Tertiary and university education rates are lower in the Caribbean compared to Hong Kong and Singapore. Education quality is certainly lower in the Caribbean countries when compared to Hong Kong, Singapore, South Korea and probably Malaysia.

Sixth, labor markets are more rigid, less able to allocate labor efficiently in the Caribbean compared to the East Asian countries, and there is evidence of lower productivity in the Caribbean, in terms of lower growth in total factor productivity.[22]

Finally, the Caribbean countries had preferential access to the United States and the European Community, and were subject at least in part to a regional trading agreement, while East Asia had a looser arrangement under the ASEAN.

---

[22] A recent study has recorded low factor productivity growth for Dominica, St. Lucia, St. Vincent and Grenadines, Barbados, Jamaica, and Trinidad and Tobago (World Bank 1994).

The External Environment with Special Reference to NAFTA

In contrast to the East Asian countries, Caribbean countries depend on a number of preferential trading arrangements. First, these countries, with the exception of the Bahamas, are members of CARICOM, in which trade among the group is subject to the least restrictions and trade with the rest of the world is influenced by the common external tariff (CET) and other provisions. While many of the provisions have exemptions that are not closely followed or implemented, it is nevertheless an important factor in the trade relations among them and with the rest of the world.

In addition to CARICOM, there are preferential agreements, such as the preferential market for bananas in the United Kingdom and the European Union (EU). Then there is the Lomé agreement on sugar protocol, which provides guaranteed access to sugar for these countries. There are three U.S.-related preferences. Under sections 806/807 of customs regulations and the Caribbean Basin Initiative, garments and electronics enter the United States with low duties arising from the exemption on the use of U.S. inputs (only value added in the Caribbean countries is subject to import duties). The United States also provides guaranteed access through a sugar quota, as does the EU.

These various preferences increase the amount of exports to the European and U.S. markets. They involve a subsidy from the importing countries and reduce competition from other producers of similar products. These concessions, however, are not bound,[23] and the concessions and assistance granted under the CBI were at least partly offset by the reductions in the U.S. sugar quota.[24] These concessions help to preserve the pattern of exports and production and have contributed to the presence of inefficient producers, such as some banana producers, who could not have survived a regime of equal access of other producers to these markets. This was certainly not the case for the East Asian countries. To be sure, they had access to the U.S. and European markets to the same extent that other developing countries had, but there was no instance of preserving a part of the production for protected markets like that of bananas and sugar.

In the minds of Caribbean policymakers, the biggest concern appears to be NAFTA. This arises from a number of factors. The first is the fear of exclusion, which is related to the potential for being penalized from the rules of origin granted to Canada and Mexico and to other potential members. Second,

---

[23] The new banana regime in European market that came into effect on 1 July 1993 is nontransparent: quotas are to be set annually and cannot be transferred among the producing countries.

[24] This is noted by Krueger (1993).

there is the threat of the loss of preferential access in terms of reduced quotas and increased tariffs. Third, there is the concern about more administrative protection, with limited recourse to dispute settlement for those outside NAFTA.

Mitigating these concerns are the following. First, NAFTA does not lead to increases in explicit protection, and the agreement's implementation is spread over fifteen years: a likely erosion of preferential access will therefore not take place overnight. Second, the Caribbean countries have the opportunity to enter NAFTA according to its rules of accession. Third, there may be possibilities for preserving at least a part of the existing preferences by special bilateral concessions from the United States and Canada, given the existing agreements such as the CBI and CARIBCAN. Finally, general trade liberalization under the Uruguay Round could help the Caribbean countries with the planned reduction in tariffs under the Round, the phasing out of MFA, and a reduction in agriculture subsidies in the EU. But the Caribbean countries would have to produce textiles and garments and other manufacturing and agricultural goods at lower costs compared to competitors, and take advantage of their proximity to the northern markets.

What are the implications of NAFTA to the Caribbean countries given the above general considerations?[25] The two main unilateral preferences that are granted by the United States to the Caribbean are the GSP and the CBI. The changes in these arrangements related to NAFTA will have greater effect on countries that are exporting more to the North American and Mexican markets. Of the countries that are more likely to be affected by NAFTA, the Bahamas is in the lead, given the concentration of its trade in that region. The least affected would be Dominica, Grenada, and St. Lucia, since their exports are concentrated in Europe. It is also important to note that Caribbean exports themselves are concentrated. For example, Antigua and Barbuda exports only 67 tariff lines to the United States, compared to the total of some 8,700 tariff lines in the U.S. tariff code. There is even further concentration of exports receiving preferential treatment. For example, 82 percent of the exports from Antigua and Barbuda enter the United States duty-free. For the Caribbean countries as a group, on average some 58 percent of the tariff lines enter duty-free, but a country like the Bahamas has 92 percent of its tariff lines duty-free. When there are tariffs, they tend to be low compared to other exporting countries, due to the special status arising from CBI and related U.S. concessions. However, individual products carry higher duties, as is the case of footwear and textiles that are exempt from CBI.

The impact of NAFTA on the Caribbean countries will depend on the extent to which Caribbean exports are competitive with Canada and Mexico,

---

[25] This section of the paper draws on the work of Yates et al. (1994).

since these two countries will have duty-free access. Mexican textile and garment exports to the United States and Canada will not be subject to the MFA quotas, and these quotas will remain until the MFA is finally discontinued ten years down the road for countries outside NAFTA. Caribbean textiles and garments exports will be subject to MFA quotas, and any exports through Mexico will be subject to rules of origin. Trade displacement due to NAFTA would be highly concentrated in a few textile and clothing products and uppers of leather footwear: U.S. tariffs on footwear are already small, at some 3 percent, while those on textiles and garments are high. In the case of knitted and non-knitted clothing, some diversion could be expected, given that Mexico would have reduced tariffs and not be subject to a country quota. Thus, Caribbean clothing will have to compete more with Mexican, given the latter's low wages, rather than with U.S. and Canadian textile producers. This reinforces the analytical point that trade diversion will take place to the extent that potential Mexican exports are substituted for Caribbean exports.

The possible trade diversions from the Caribbean countries due to NAFTA are expected to be small. Static diversion measures based on partial equilibrium analysis put the diversion of Caribbean exports from the United States to be somewhat small, but static measures could understate the impact. However, even if it is assumed that a 3 percent diversion does takes place, the impact would still be small, some $120 million out of a total export figure of nearly $5 billion. Displacement by Mexican textiles would also be small, given that its share of the U.S. market is small, less than 3 percent. In addition, NAFTA has certain domestic content requirements that will also constrain Mexico's ability to increase its competitiveness in the U.S. market. Of course, these totals hide the individual impact of different Caribbean countries, and it is fair to conclude that NAFTA will erode a part of the unilateral preferences granted to the Caribbean countries.

The other concern about NAFTA is its likely impact on DFI, which is around 8 percent of total investment in the Caribbean countries. The issue is whether DFI that goes to the Caribbean countries from the United States and Canada will now be diverted to Mexico. To consider this issue, it is important to know the relative foreign investment regimes in Mexico and the Caribbean. One advantage Mexico has is that NAFTA binds its investment regime, which eventually will be harmonized with that in the United States and Canada. Assuming that this harmonization will take time to be achieved, it is the trade diversion factors that help to determine investment diversion.

The trade regime, investment climate, legal system, labor regulations, land titling, adequate infrastructure, and tax codes are the principal factors that would determine the relative DFI flows. For labor-seeking type DFI, it is necessary to have a well-trained labor force and transparent and reliable labor laws; for component outsourcing, rules of origin come into play. So, even if components can be produced at low costs in the Caribbean countries, only a part of the component's value added would have tariff-free status. NAFTA would apply rules of origin to textiles, clothing, and motor cars; Mexico's duty-free status would apply only to value added in that country. This has been designed to prevent others from using Mexico as an export platform.

The United States gives tax preference treatment for investments in the Caribbean countries under the CBI. Investments in the Caribbean qualify for tax exemption status in relation to section 936 of the U.S. tax code, however NAFTA does not provide similar tax treatment. Meanwhile, Mexico becomes more attractive, because the binding of the investment laws in Mexico with NAFTA gives Mexican laws more credibility to investors. To what extent a DFI diversion could take place due to NAFTA is difficult to predict. It will depend very much on the attractiveness of the climate for DFI in the Caribbean countries in relation to Mexico.

Lessons and Conclusions

The validity of inferring policy lessons from one experience to another depends on the particular political economy and institutional contexts. To infer lessons from the East Asian experience to the Caribbean context, one can note some similarities in the institutional arrangements, even though the political economy contexts are different. It is Hong Kong and Singapore that the Caribbean countries can relate to in the institutional context, given the British colonial experience shared by both groups of countries and the close affinities in laws and administrative systems. One feature that is dissimilar is the presence of strong unions in the Caribbean, compared to the two Asian countries. Policy formulation undoubtedly has to be influenced by this fact, given the strong democratic tradition in the Caribbean. This similarity also breaks down when it is noted that the Caribbean countries have significant agricultural activities; in fact, many are principally dependent on sugar or bananas.

The policy lessons from the East Asian countries relate to all countries. If anything, the clearest lesson that emerges from that experience is the importance of good policies for economic success. The other is that physical endowment is not as important as human capital. The Caribbean countries have good initial conditions in respect of human capital, with high literacy rates and school enrollment.

In the view of mainstream economists, the fundamental lessons are clear. Maintaining macroeconomic stability is essential for allowing incentive policies to work. It gives confidence to private sector agents to save and invest, and prevents the unproductive phenomenon of stop-and-go policies. The prime instrument to secure macroeconomic stability is good fiscal policy. To be sure, this is a challenge for small, open economies vulnerable to large external shocks. The antidote to external instability, however, is greater price flexibility, carrying sufficient reserves, and maintaining adequate borrowing capacity. At this juncture, the Caribbean countries need to consolidate the reforms of the mid-1980s and to preserve the stability they have achieved. Raising incentives for saving through stability and financial sector reform would be an important feature of the policy agenda. The corollary to this is to raise public savings. Proper exchange rate policies would help, too, by discouraging the flight of capital in search of high rates of return. The proper macroeconomic stance is more important for maintaining competitiveness than the type of exchange rate regime. This was the message of the different inflation outcomes related to the OECS and the other countries in the group.

On the incentive side, there is a good opportunity to increase productivity. It was noted that the investment rates between the two sets of countries were not all that different, but that there were considerable differences in GDP growth outcomes. Steadier public investment rates, a greater role for private investment, and complementary public investment in infrastructure should move in tandem with the incentive reforms needed in trade, regulatory environments, the tax system, and the treatment of DFI.

Completing the trade reform agenda will be crucial for increasing competitiveness. There are as yet many quantitative restrictions in operation; in some cases, the effective protection rates are as high as 100 percent. There is a significant bias against exports, on the order of 35 percent to 40 percent, that proffers a cost advantage to external competitors of the Caribbean countries. And there are many taxes and levies that have differential impacts on levels of protection within CARICOM, which increases variance in protection. In addition, many would consider the planned convergence of the CARICOM's CET to 5 to 20 percent over a five-year period somewhat slow and, as a consequence, undermining the transport cost advantage of the Caribbean to the NAFTA market. To exploit these trading opportunities, there must be adequate infrastructure such as port facilities, telecommunications, and transport to export and import points. There is a new regime for services opening up in the region with the completion of the Uruguay Round, and the Caribbean is well placed to benefit from it, if appropriate investment in communications and policy reforms in the services sector, ranging from tourism and insurance to data processing and health services, are undertaken.

Educational quality can be raised with proper policies to go up the technological ladder quickly. In the Caribbean, the number of trained graduates leaving college has declined, while expenditures per pupil have fallen. Meanwhile, the business sector is lacking trained staff for management, finance and technology jobs. This inhibits future technological advancement, a crucial ingredient for competition in emerging fields such as services.

Labor market issues have to be addressed in a number of dimensions. Public sector wages influence private wage settlement and introduce an upward bias on unskilled labor and a downward bias against skilled labor. Excess labor in the public sector has been put at 10 percent to 50 percent of the labor force, depending on the country. Labor management is dispute ridden and this increases the costs of labor, particularly in highly unionized countries. Adjustment to negative external shocks is made more difficult due to labor market rigidities, and unemployment rather than real wage adjustment is the result. There is thus a substantial agenda for labor market reforms. This would require a more consensual approach to resolution than has been the practice in the Caribbean.

In terms of the external environment, particularly in the context of NAFTA, few lessons and conclusions emerge. The Caribbean countries now face a more competitive world, where preferential access is eroding. Although preferential access has served national welfare, preferences have been a double-edged sword. They render at least some agricultural exports noncompetitive and there is a consequent need for adjustment. This is particularly true with bananas. The cost disadvantage in banana production has been offset by guaranteed access under the EU banana regime, which has weakened. It would seem advisable now to reduce the pass-through of the benefits of preferential access to the producers, inducing them to switch to alternative activities and invest those funds in high-return activities that will support export infrastructure.

Finally, while static estimates of NAFTA's impact are not large, it will have a strong impact on some countries with exports concentrated in the northern market. The adverse impact of reduction of preferences could be somewhat compensated by increased access from the Uruguay Round, particularly with respect to textiles and garments. Nevertheless, the Caribbean must remain ready to compete with the rest of the world as the MFN access increases. There is a strong rationale for the Caribbean countries to enter NAFTA individually or through the auspices of CARICOM or related arrangements, which will give the Caribbean countries access similar to Mexico's. NAFTA should be seen as an opportunity and not as a threat. It might help to rally domestic support for reform and to lock in the reforms through an accession agreement.

In sum, the growth of East Asian countries carries important lessons for the Caribbean region, lessons that are highly appropriate for its present state of development. The regions differ greatly in terms of political economy, however, particularly in union activity and power. Thus, some Caribbean institutions will need to adapt and reform, and for this purpose a consensual approach seems most fruitful.

Appendix:
Performance Indicators for East Asian and Caribbean Countries

Table 7A.1 GDP and Per Capita GDP Growth, East Asia
(Percent)

	GDP Growth Rate			Per Capita GDP Growth Rate		
	1966–92	1966–80	1980–92	1966–92	1966–80	1980–92
Hong Kong	7.6	8.5	6.8	5.7	6.3	5.4
Indonesia	6.3	6.7	5.9	4.1	4.3	4.0
South Korea	9.1	9.3	7.9	7.4	7.2	6.7
Malaysia	6.9	7.3	6.5	4.3	4.7	3.8
Singapore	8.7	10.2	7.2	6.8	8.4	5.1
Taiwan	8.9	9.9	7.6	6.8	7.4	6.1
Thailand	7.8	7.6	7.8	5.3	4.6	5.9
All Countries	7.9	8.5	7.1	5.8	6.1	5.3

Source: World Bank.

Table 7A.2 Inflation and Budget Deficit, East Asia
(Percent)

	Inflation			Fiscal Balance/GDP			Current Account Balance/GDP		
	1965–92	1965–80	1980–92	1965–92	1965–80	1980–92	1965–92	1965–80	1980–92
Hong Kong	7.5	6.8	9.0	-	-	-	3.3	3.8	2.1
Indonesia	30.7	47.3	9.3	-2.0	-2.6	-1.4	-2.2	-1.7	-2.3
South Korea	11.3	15.3	8.3	-1.1	-1.3	-1.0	-2.7	-5.1	-0.3
Malaysia	3.9	4.2	3.7	-8.0	-6.6	-10.7	-1.1	0.2	-2.6
Singapore	3.9	5.0	2.8	2.2	0.7	4.2	-5.3	-9.8	-0.4
Taiwan	6.1	8.3	4.5	1.1	-	1.0	4.9	1.4	8.6
Thailand	6.0	7.0	5.7	-2.0	-2.7	-1.4	-3.3	-3.0	-4.0
All countries	9.9	13.4	6.2	-1.6	-2.5	-1.5	-0.9	-2.0	0.2

Note: Fiscal balance figures for Taiwan relate to 1965 and 1991 only.
Source: World Bank.

Table 7A.3 Manufactured and Non-Manufactured Exports, East Asia
(Percent)

	Manufactured Exports/Total Exports			Non-Manufactured Exports/Total Exports		
	1965-92	1965-80	1980-92	1965-92	1965-80	1980-92
Hong Kong	98.1	98.0	98.4	1.9	2.0	1.6
Indonesia	9.3	1.4	19.3	90.7	98.6	80.7
South Korea	83.4	77.2	92.5	16.6	22.8	7.5
Malaysia	24.0	13.7	37.8	76.0	86.3	62.2
Singapore	47.8	32.3	70.2	52.2	67.7	29.8
Thailand	29.5	17.6	45.7	70.5	82.4	54.3
Taiwan	42.0	-	92.0	58.0	-	8.0
All Countries	47.7	40.0	65.1	52.3	60.0	34.9

Note: Taiwanese figures are for 1965 and 1991 only.
Source: World Bank.

Table 7A.4 Growth of Exports and Imports, East Asia
(Percent)

	Growth Rate of Exports			Growth Rate of Imports		
	1966-91	1966-80	1980-91	1966-91	1966-80	1980-91
Hong Kong	7.8	11.0	4.2	10.0	9.3	11.3
Indonesia	7.2	8.4	4.9	10.4	10.9	11.1
South Korea	19.8	25.6	11.8	15.3	17.9	10.0
Malaysia	7.9	5.7	10.0	6.8	4.4	10.8
Singapore	8.1	7.5	8.8	8.3	8.5	8.4
Thailand	11.4	8.5	14.8	9.0	7.3	11.3
Taiwan	15.4	19.0	11.0	12.9	15.1	10.1
All Countries	11.1	12.3	9.4	10.4	10.5	10.4

Source: World Bank.

Table 7A.5 Investment and Savings, East Asia
(Percent)

	GDI to GDP Ratio			GDFI-Public to GDP Ratio			GDS to GDP Ratio		
	1965-92	1965-80	1980-92	1965-92	1965-80	1980-92	1965-92	1965-80	1980-92
Hong Kong	27.1	26.2	28.9	3.6	3.3	4.0	28.3	26.2	31.0
Indonesia	23.6	18.0	30.5	-	-	-	24.8	19.0	33.0
South Korea	28.3	26.2	31.3	4.9	5.3	4.7	24.5	18.8	31.9
Malaysia	27.1	23.9	31.4	11.0	8.7	12.9	30.2	28.2	33.0
Singapore	38.3	35.7	42.1	9.5	8.2	11.3	32.7	24.8	42.8
Taiwan	25.7	28.0	23.6	11.1	12.4	10.4	30.0	28.5	32.0
Thailand	27.2	25.1	29.8	7.0	6.6	7.5	23.8	21.8	26.0
All Countries	28.2	26.1	31.1	7.9	7.4	8.5	27.8	23.9	32.8

Source: World Bank.

Table 7A.6 Performance Indicators for Caribbean Economies

	GNP (millions of US$) 1992	Average Inflation Rate 1985-92	GNP per Capita US$ 1992	Real Growth Rate 1985-92	Share of Agriculture in GDP 1992	Share of Exports in GDP 1992	Share of Investment in GDP 1992
Antigua and Barbuda	395	5.9	4870	1.1	-	-	-
Bahamas	3161	5.5	12020	-1.2	-	-	-
Barbados	1693	4.3	6530	0.6	-	63	19
Dominica	181	5.0	2520	5.1	26	54	27
Grenada	210	5.2	2310	4.4	15	53	33
Jamaica	3216	23.9	1340	2.9	5	64	20
St. Kitts and Nevis	181	8.8	3990	5.3	9	47	46
St. Lucia	453	3.6	2900	5.2	14	73	-
St. Vincent	217	4.3	1990	4.7	18	-	-
Trinidad and Tobago	4995	5.2	3940	-3.0	3	44	19

Source: The World Bank Atlas, 1994.

Bibliography

Amsden, Alice. 1989. *Asia's Next Giant: South Korea and the Late Industrialization.* London: Oxford Univ. Press.

Balassa, Bela. 1971. *The Structure of Protection in Developing Countries.* Baltimore: Johns Hopkins Press.

Beason, Richard, and David Weinstein. 1993. *Growth, Economics of Scale and Targeting in Japan: 1955–1990.* Discussion Paper #1644. Harvard Institute of Economic Research.

Bhagwati, Jagdish, V.K. Ramaswamy and T.N. Srinivasan. 1969. "Domestic Distortions, Tariffs and the Theory of the Optimum Subsidy." *Journal of Political Economy* 77(6).

Bhagwati, Jagdish. 1978. *Foreign Trade Regimes and Economic Development: Anatomy and Consequences of Exchange Control Regimes.* Cambridge, Mass.: Ballinger.

Birdsall, Nancy and Richard Sabot. 1993. *Virtuous Circles: Human Capital and Growth and Equity in East Asia.* World Bank.

Elias, Victor. 1990. *The Role of Total Factor Productivity in Growth.* Washington, D.C.: World Bank.

Ito, Takatoshi and Anne O. Krueger. 1993. *Trade and Protectionism.* Chicago: Univ. of Chicago Press.

Krause, Lawrence B. 1988. "Hong Kong and Singapore: Twins or Kissing Cousins?" *Economic Development and Cultural Change* 36(3): 45–67.

Krueger, Anne O. 1978. *Foreign Trade Regimes and Economic Development: Liberalization Attempts and Consequences.* Cambridge, MA: Ballinger.

Krueger, Anne O. 1993. *Economic Policies at Cross Purposes: The United States and Developing Countries.* Washington D.C.: Brookings Institution.

Lal, Deepak, and Sarath Rajapatirana. 1987. *Foreign Trade Regimes and Economic Growth in Developing Countries.* World Bank Research Observer 2:189–217.

Leipziger, Danny M., and Vinod Thomas. 1993. *Lessons of East Asia: An Overview of Country Experience.* Washington, D.C.: World Bank.

Little, I.M.D., Tibor Scitovsky, and Maurice Scott. 1970. *Industry and Trade in Some Developing Countries: A Comparative Study.* London: Oxford Univ. Press.

Little, I.M.D., Richard N. Cooper, W. Max Corden, and Sarath Rajapatirana. 1993. *Boom, Crises and Adjustment: The Macroeconomic Experience of Developing Countries.* London: Oxford Univ. Press.

Lucas, Robert E. Jr. 1993. "Making a Miracle." *Econometrica* 61(2): 251–272.

McCarthy, Desmond, and Giovanni Zanalda. 1994. *Caribbean Experience with External Shocks.* Washington, D.C.: World Bank.

Michaely, Michael, Demetris Papageorgiou, and Armeane Choksi. 1991. *Liberalizing Foreign Trade: Lessons of Experience in the Developing World.* Oxford: Basil Blackwell.

Petri, Peter. 1993. *The Lessons of East Asia: Common Foundations of East Asian Success.* Washington, D.C.: World Bank.

Riedel, James. 1987. *Myths and Realities of External Constraints on Development.* London: Gower Press.

Wade, Robert. 1990. *Governing the Market. Economic Theory and the Role of Government in East Asian Industrialization.* Princeton, N.J.: Princeton Univ. Press.

Woo, Wing Thye, Anwar Nasution, and Bruce Glassburner. 1994. *Macroeconomic Policies, Crises and Long-Term Growth in Indonesia: 1965–1990.* Washington D.C.: World Bank.

World Bank. 1993a. *The East Asian Miracle.* New York: Oxford Univ. Press.

———. 1993b. *Caribbean Region: Access, Quality and Efficiency in Education.* Washington D.C.: World Bank.

———. 1994. *Caribbean Region: Coping with Changes in the External Environment.* (March) Washington D.C.: World Bank.

Yang, Ya-Hwei. 1993. "Government Policy and Strategic Industries: The Case of Taiwan." In *Trade and Protectionism*, ed. Takatoshi Ito and Anne O. Krueger. Chicago: University of Chicago Press.

Yates, Alexander, Carlos A. Primo Braga, and Geoffrey Bannister. 1994. *The Impact of NAFTA on U.S. Preferences Towards Latin America and the Caribbean.* Washington, D.C.: World Bank.

Young, Alwyn. 1993. *Lessons from the East Asian NICS: A Contrarian View.* National Bureau of Economic Research Paper #4482 (October). Boston, MA: NBER.

Chapter 8

The Caribbean in Economic Transition

Elena M. Suárez

The Caribbean is facing a changing external environment. Preferential market access will be increasingly eroded by certain developments: the implementation of NAFTA, completion of the Uruguay Round, revised European policies on bananas and other commodities, the potential shift to a market-oriented Cuba, and forthcoming changes to Lomé 4 and the General System of Preferences. If some of these developments coincide, as seems likely, they will have a severe impact on the region.

This paper first reviews the Caribbean Basin Initiative (CBI), reflecting on the program's successes and shortcomings for trade and investment. Next, it considers the external challenges that affect the region's economic future and the need for a Caribbean response. The third section looks at the NAFTA parity issue and the need for a transition period to plan more reciprocal arrangements and prepare for the inevitable free trade environment. The fourth section examines the trend towards reduced levels of official assistance, providing data on the structure of financial flows moving into the region. With private flows exceeding official flows, these changes represent certain consequences and opportunities for the region. The paper then discusses the region's business environment, particularly the need for a private sector development strategy to attract foreign investment and meet the challenges of a changing global environment. The final section concentrates on regional integration developments and the approach to cross-Basin integration that will prepare the Caribbean for participation in the global economy.

Revisiting the Caribbean Basin Initiative

The Caribbean Basin Initiative has provided a unique impetus to the development of trade and investment between the U.S. and the Caribbean Basin. The result has been an increased flow of trade and investment both ways. According to the September 1993 International Trade Commission report on the Caribbean Basin Economic Recovery Act (CBERA), U.S. imports from countries in the Caribbean Basin totaled $9.5 billion in 1992, an increase of 14.3 percent over the 1991 level of $8.3 billion, the fourth consecutive year that U.S. imports increased. Caribbean Basin countries accounted for 1.8 percent of total U.S. imports in 1992, making the Caribbean Basin the 14th largest supplier of U.S. imports (USITC 1993, 1–2).

U.S. exports to countries in the Caribbean Basin totaled $11.3 billion in 1992, rising 11.4 percent over 1991. Accounting for 2.7 percent of total U.S. exports in 1992, the Caribbean Basin ranked tenth as an export market for the United States, ahead of such countries as Belgium and Singapore. Except for 1985, U.S. exports to the Caribbean Basin have increased annually since CBERA was implemented in 1984.

The United States has had a consistent trade surplus with the Caribbean Basin since 1986. In 1992, the U.S. trade surplus with the region amounted to $1.8 billion. One could easily argue that since the inception of the CBI, the United States has been the primary beneficiary of this program. One of the CBI's major shortcomings has been the disproportionate share of total benefits on a country or subregional basis. Trade figures for each of the various CBERA subgroupings show these uneven results. In 1992, Central America accounted for 42.3 percent of U.S. imports from the Caribbean Basin, followed by the central Caribbean countries (the Dominican Republic, Jamaica, and Haiti) accounting for 32.5 percent, and the oil-producing countries (comprised of Aruba, the Bahamas, Netherlands Antilles, and Trinidad and Tobago) with 23.1 percent. Eastern Caribbean countries accounted for only 2.1 percent of total U.S. imports from the Caribbean Basin.

The major Caribbean winners under the CBI are the Dominican Republic, Jamaica, Trinidad and Tobago, and the Bahamas. In 1992, the Dominican Republic was by far the largest source of U.S. imports, within the central Caribbean subgroup and among CBI countries. Imports from the Dominican Republic rose by 19.7 percent and from Jamaica by 5.7 percent. Imports from the Bahamas and Trinidad and Tobago also increased.

The eastern Caribbean is the only subgroup where U.S. trade has declined since the inception of the CBI program. Notwithstanding, in 1992, U.S. imports from that region increased to $194.8 million. Guyana and St. Kitts and Nevis were primarily responsible for this increase.

Traditional products are still a significant part of total U.S. imports from the region. However, less favorable terms of trade for these products have prompted CBERA countries to diversify their exports. Light manufactures account for an increasing share of U.S. imports from the region and are the fastest growing sector for new investments. Textile and apparel articles are the leading imports, followed by petroleum and petroleum products, bananas, coffee, aromatic drugs, sugar, aluminum ore and concentrates, shrimp, footwear uppers, beef, medical instruments, ammonia, and jewelry.

U.S. imports from the Caribbean Basin that are not eligible for CBI terms, such as textiles and apparel, attained a level of $4.5 billion in 1992, or nearly one-half of total U.S. imports from CBERA countries. This last point is particularly important with respect to the NAFTA parity issue.

Considering the investment trends, CBI has clearly been instrumental in encouraging expanded investment in the region. Most important, it has drawn investor interest and focus to the region. Since the CBI program began, certain countries (notably Jamaica, the Dominican Republic, and several Central American countries) have been very successful in drawing new investments. Some focused on the production of export-oriented products; other investments occurred in nonexport areas, such as tourism. A number of these investments were funded with 936 financing, which will be considered later.

Much of this new export-oriented investment was directed towards the production of articles not covered by the CBI. Textile and apparel production remained a leading sector during 1992. Many of these investment projects are in free trade zones: they assemble U.S.-made components that are then returned to the United States.

Despite some achievements, most countries still have difficulty drawing foreign investment. The obstacles to foreign investment include political instability, inconsistent reform processes and macroeconomic instability, deficient business environments, restrictions on foreign exchange and profit repatriation, and inadequate physical infrastructure. Finally, investment in the region in 1993 may have suffered due to the uncertainty surrounding NAFTA and its impact on the Caribbean.

In sum, in the area of trade and investment, some CBI beneficiary countries have made great strides as a result of the Caribbean Basin Initiative. Perhaps most significantly, new opportunities for trade and investment within the CBI framework have inspired creative, free market-oriented economic thinking in the region. However, the CBI has not attained all its goals of generating employment and private sector-led investment, and broadly based economic growth has not been realized. How governments view the private sector and shape more attractive business environments will greatly determine the region's future trade and investment. The Caribbean can no longer rely on preferential trade schemes that are becoming obsolete in the rapidly changing free trade environment.

The Erosion of Preferences

The region faces a difficult transition period from an environment of special trade treatment to one ruled by principles of free trade and reciprocity. Preferential market access is being eroded by the extension of U.S. trade preferences to the Andean nations, the implementation of NAFTA, and the successful completion of the Uruguay Round.

Looking towards Europe, the Caribbean countries face the same type of challenges—an existing regime of significant preferences and a long-term future without them. Many predict that when Lomé 4 expires, it will not be renewed in anything resembling its present form, giving way instead to a more reciprocal free trade arrangement. Many European officials have stated that European trade policy towards the Caribbean and Central America will increasingly converge, as the region itself pursues greater integration and preferential relations give way to reciprocal ones (Pearson 1994).

Another factor that could erode the region's competitiveness is the potential opening of Cuba. A market-oriented Cuba reintegrated into the Caribbean economy will have a substantial impact on other countries in the region. Some predict that "Cuban growth in trade and investment will either add to or displace levels elsewhere in the region. Trade-creating effects are more likely for tourism, trade-diverting effects for assembly industry, with nontraditional agricultural exports somewhere in between" (Preeg 1993, xv). Others believe that if Cuba re-establishes its economic links with industrialized economies, the Caribbean countries will face strong and direct competition for export of foods and services, especially in agriculture, apparel, and manufacturing.

Against this background, the Caribbean must take the necessary measures within its means to meet these irreversible challenges. Reciprocal trade agreements are inevitable, but reaching that stage will require a transition period while the Caribbean economies progress towards liberalization and integration.

Preparing for the Transition: NAFTA Parity

Caribbean Basin countries are worried that NAFTA will neutralize the current trade preferences they receive under the CBI and thus divert foreign investment. Of particular concern is how the region's apparel and textile sector will be impacted. This sector has become a critical component of the region's export profile. Since 1988, textiles and apparel have been the main U.S. imports from the region that are not eligible for CBI treatment. Imports of textiles and apparel doubled from $1.5 billion in 1988 to $3.0 billion in 1992, and were 17.1 percent higher than in 1991 (USITC 1993, 2–9). In the Caribbean, the textile and apparel sectors that NAFTA could harm significantly are in the Dominican Republic, Dominica, Haiti, Jamaica, St. Lucia, and St. Vincent and the Grenadines.

The Mexican manufacturing sector will be the greatest beneficiary of NAFTA's liberalized trade and investment rules. NAFTA allows Mexican manufacturers to gain substantial international orders that would previously have gone to third countries. For the Caribbean Basin, the NAFTA challenge is nowhere greater or more dangerous than in the competition for apparel orders from U.S. firms. Formerly, apparel exported from Mexico was subject to relatively high import duties and incurred further indirect costs arising from U.S. government–imposed quantitative restrictions; that is, quotas limiting the amount Mexico could export to the United States in specific products (Marsh 1994). Under NAFTA, import duties were removed immediately on a very high proportion of Mexico's current apparel trade with the United States—probably in excess of 80 percent. Mexican apparel that did not become duty-free on 1 January 1994 will benefit from an accelerated implementation of free trade, with annual duty cuts and quota liberalization beginning on 1 January 1994 and ending by the beginning of the year 2001. Furthermore, documentation requirements and other enforcement measures are to be simplified or eliminated (USITC 1993).

NAFTA will make the Mexican manufacturer more competitive in other ways. Under NAFTA, transportation bottlenecks will disappear as discriminatory government regulations are removed. Furthermore, the United States and Mexican governments are committed to subsidizing improvements in the border infrastructure, which will enable goods to move faster and more cheaply.

Altogether, these NAFTA benefits will dramatically tilt the playing field in Mexico's favor. In other words, the Caribbean Basin will find itself with an overriding and immediate threat of trade and investment diversion due to NAFTA. NAFTA provides a reduced rate and generous quota for Mexican apparel made from Asian fabric, for which CBI countries have no preferential access. Furthermore, in the critical competition in the assembly industry for 807A goods (garments assembled from U.S.-manufactured fabric pieces), Mexican exports will be entering duty-free, while CBI exports will still pay duty on their value-added portion.

In response to the urgent concerns of CBI countries, the Clinton administration is considering attaching CBI–NAFTA parity legislation to the Uruguay Round implementing bill. The CBI parity bill introduced in 1993 by Congressman Sam Gibbons, which would have extended certain NAFTA benefits received by Mexico to CBI beneficiaries for three years, is no longer an alternative. As it appears now, the proposed legislation would involve the following:

- Extending a limited form of NAFTA parity in apparel for CBI countries. This is different from the CBI Parity bill introduced by Congressman Gibbons, which proposed similar treatment with respect to tariffs and quotas as received by Mexico for all U.S. imports from the Caribbean Basin not eligible for CBI treatment.

- Criteria will involve some reciprocal concessions by the countries, for instance in the area of bilateral investment treaties, intellectual property rights, and local market access for apparel and textile products. If these commitments are not kept, the parity benefits would expire at the end of three years.
- Application of parity would not be automatic, but parity would be applied to countries meeting certain criteria, similar to the CBI designation process in 1984.

Ideally, this "nominal parity" in apparel will allow CBI countries to negotiate for specific tariff and quota liberalization in products assembled from: U.S.-formed and -cut fabric; products whose fabric is imported from third countries, cut-to-shape in the United States and assembled in the Basin; products made entirely in the Caribbean Basin from fabrics formed in the region or in the United States that meet the NAFTA-origin test; and products made entirely in the Caribbean Basin of fabrics from third countries. The latter concession will be the hardest to obtain.

This legislation would have support from the Congressional Friends of the Caribbean Basin and the group's co-chairmen, Congressmen Sam Gibbons and Phil Crane. Additional support might come from Senator Graham of Florida and members of the Black Caucus; furthermore, the legislative initiative is gaining support in the Hispanic Caucus. Although no official commitment at the political level of the U.S. administration has been made, parity could be introduced with the Uruguay Round implementing bill in 1994.

Reduced Assistance

The economic challenges facing the region are even more daunting, considering the trend towards reduced levels of assistance. According to a 1994 World Bank report, the sources of external finance available to the Caribbean region have drastically changed. Net capital flows[1] from bilateral and multilateral sources have decreased considerably, from an annual average of $70 per capita during 1980–82 to an average $31 per capita for 1990–92. Net lending from multilateral sources amounted to only $72 million in 1992, compared with $546 million in 1982. Net bilateral lending actually turned negative in 1992, amounting to –$32 million, compared with $603 million ten years earlier (World Bank 1994a, xiv).

---

[1] Net external capital flows equal grants, plus disbursements, less amortization of medium- and long-term debt, plus net use of IMF credits. These figures include Antigua and Barbuda, the Bahamas, Barbados, Belize, Dominica, the Dominican Republic, Grenada, Guyana, Haiti, Jamaica, St. Kitts and Nevis, St. Lucia, St. Vincent and the Grenadines, Suriname, and Trinidad and Tobago.

The World Bank study reports that this downward trend will prevail, because the donor community perceives that Caribbean countries as a whole have now reached a level of development where their needs are less urgent than those of Africa and Eastern and Central Europe. Efforts to alleviate deep-rooted poverty in Africa will continue to absorb a large share of concessional development finance; furthermore, the dissolution of the former Soviet Union, the changes in Eastern Europe, and recent moves towards peace in the Middle East will lead to major new claims upon the resources of development agencies (ibid.).

Regarding U.S. assistance trends in the Caribbean, the news is even more dramatic. U.S. Agency for International Development levels in the Caribbean were reduced from $217 million in 1992 to an approximate $180 million in 1993, while total U.S. assistance to the region has dropped even more substantially (USAID 1992, 29). To provide some examples, total U.S. assistance to Jamaica was $133 million in 1992, but only about $68 million in 1993. U.S. assistance to St. Kitts, St. Lucia, and St. Vincent was approximately $1 million in 1989, compared to zero funds allocated in 1993.[2] USAID plans to close a number of missions in the Caribbean over the next few years, including the regional office in Barbados. These trends are not likely to change in the foreseeable future, as the United States continues to focus on other parts of the world, in particular Russia and the Middle East.

Furthermore, a GAO report released in February 1994 reopened the 1992 election-year dispute over Washington's support for the Caribbean Basin program. The report alleged that USAID has facilitated the shifting of U.S. manufacturing jobs overseas. The damage imparted in 1992 by the CBS news program *60 Minutes* and the ensuing controversy were considerable. These developments are highly worrisome, but there are also some positive changes. According to the World Bank, private financial flows to the region now exceed official ones. In particular, massive flows of direct foreign investment (DFI) are taking place in the world. Direct foreign investment has rebounded from earlier low levels and is now an important source of foreign capital to many countries. In 1993, approximately $60 billion of DFI flowed into developing countries, of which $13 billion went to Latin America and the Caribbean. Given that multilateral and bilateral aid flows to the Caribbean are expected to decrease even further, it is critical that the Caribbean region tap into these direct foreign investment flows (World Bank 1994a, 2).

In the Caribbean itself, the World Bank reports that DFI has increased significantly. "Whereas, in the mid-1980's DFI to the Caribbean countries amounted to U.S. $100–200 million per year, with much of it destined for the

---

[2] This does not include funds from the U.S./Caribbean Regional program, which amounted to approximately $30 million for both years, 1989 and 1993.

Trinidadian petroleum and petrochemical sectors, the Caribbean countries have attracted U.S. $500–600 million in each of the last three years" (ibid., 37). The DFI level in the Caribbean reached $656 million in 1992. Trinidad and Tobago is no longer the main recipient, as the Dominican Republic, Jamaica, and St. Lucia are attracting increased foreign investment.

Much of that investment is partly linked to offshore assembly provisions of the U.S. tariff code 9802, for which the Dominican Republic, Jamaica, and Haiti are the main exporters. The other main source has been section 936 funds, which have also influenced the degree of direct foreign investment in the Caribbean. In 1986, the U.S. Congress added a new component to section 936, which allows U.S. corporations operating in Puerto Rico to invest their profits to promote economic development in the Caribbean Basin. In order to access 936 funds, the Caribbean Basin country must sign a Tax Information Exchange Agreement (TIEA).[3]

To date, a total of ten nations have signed TIEAs, including eight Caribbean countries: Barbados, Dominica, the Dominican Republic, Grenada, Guyana, Jamaica, St. Lucia, and Trinidad and Tobago. Since beginning in 1985, the Caribbean 936 lending program has had impressive results, funding over $850 million worth of investments. In 1993 alone, over $200 million was disbursed to the region, a total exceeding the previous year's, and an 83 percent increase in the total number of projects promoted. These projects provide substantial benefits to the Caribbean Basin economies by creating new jobs (an estimated 20,000 jobs have been created in the Caribbean Basin as a result of these projects), direct investment, technology transfer, foreign exchange earnings, and other gains in the form of indirect employment and related businesses.

Given the reduction in net official flows to the region, efforts should be stepped up to promote DFI and to enhance programs that spur investment and development, such as the 936 Caribbean lending program. The primary economic challenge to Caribbean countries is to reposition themselves to take advantage of new market realities: to reduce trade barriers and increase private investment flows to the region.

Towards a Private Sector Development Strategy

Private finance and direct foreign investment will flourish if an attractive institutional, regulatory, and policy environment is established that is conducive to economic prosperity. More than ever, the region will have to rely on its private sector as the engine of growth. The Caribbean governments should continue

---

[3] A TIEA is a mutual and reciprocal obligation to exchange information relating to the enforcement of tax laws.

to empower the private sector and forge ahead with sustainable private sector development strategies.

Significant progress has been achieved in monetary reform, privatization, modernization of business codes, reduction of tariff barriers, fostering of new capital markets, and other key elements of an export-driven, private sector–oriented free market economy. However, these important policy reforms should be buttressed by additional reforms to ensure economic development.

Private–public sector collaboration is now more important than ever. Although the business environment in the Caribbean has improved significantly, many obstacles remain to increasing investment and expanding production. These include delays in processing investor applications, administrative requirements, discretionary public sector interventions and taxation levels, as well as other factors related to exchange rates, currency convertibility, company laws, and banking regulations. Together, these constraints contribute to uncertainty regarding the rules of doing business (World Bank 1994b, ii). On the one hand, the Caribbean governments must convince the private sector that they are serious about reform; on the other hand, the private sector needs to support the governments in helping them to adopt and maintain sound macroeconomic policies that will foster a more competitive business environment.

The private sector in Caribbean countries is comprised of four main groups: local, small-scale entrepreneurs; local, small- and medium-sized enterprises; locally established and resident entrepreneurs with non-Caribbean origins; and non-Caribbean, nonresident foreign businesses. The small-scale sector employs by far the largest number of people. Its contribution in the region as a whole is important, and it is gaining economic strength, as small entrepreneurs organize themselves into self-help groups, such as savings and credit associations, producer groups, cooperatives, and indigenous business associations (ibid., 3–4).

In the end, economic prosperity will depend on Caribbean countries improving their production and their competitiveness. This calls for advances in worker training, management quality, and all areas linked to the production of goods and services. The foreign sector has an important role, working closely with the indigenous private sector, to infuse capital, and introduce modern technologies and managerial methods.

Developments in Regional Integration

Another critical factor that will allow the region's private sector to cooperate and prosper is the substantial progress made towards integration among regional and subregional trading groups. During 1993, Latin America and the Caribbean Basin expanded their network of free trade agreements (FTAs), aiming to implement free market reforms and to liberalize trade and investment on a regional basis.

CARICOM is consolidating its internal cooperation and looking outward to increase its regional competitiveness, while proceeding with internal harmonization and tariff-reduction plans. A crucial challenge for CARICOM is to speed up its integration process and to move promptly towards a single market. The sooner this occurs, the better its position to negotiate with other subregional groups and expand trade and investment relations throughout the hemisphere.

The decision of CARICOM and other Caribbean nations in July 1994 to join with Mexico, Venezuela, Columbia and the Central American countries in a new Association of Caribbean States, was aimed at furthering economic integration and cooperation. CARICOM clearly recognizes that a market of only five million people cannot enable it to prosper and compete in the rapidly changing global environment (Bryan 1993, 35). Major challenges for the ACS include the implications of Cuba's membership; how to overcome linguistic differences; staffing and funding levels; first priorities; the precise trade and investment relations among members and externally; the modus operandi; guarantees of national economic sovereignty; and the private sector's role.

Meanwhile, the Caribbean and Central America have cooperated more closely through ministerial meetings and by establishing a consultative forum to analyze opportunities for intraregional trade and information exchange. In 1992, Venezuela signed a trade agreement with CARICOM, under which CARICOM members will enjoy nonreciprocal trade access for ten years in certain product areas. CARICOM is seeking a similar arrangement with Colombia, which has recently expressed a willingness to pursue the matter of reciprocity along similar lines of the CARICOM–Venezuela agreement. Colombia, however, would request preferences for a list of Colombian products from CARICOM after an initial period. In sum, the prevailing commitment to integration throughout the Caribbean Basin will deepen subregional trade, and holds encouraging prospects for the long-term goal of hemispheric integration.

Conclusions

The Caribbean Basin Initiative has resulted in an increased flow of trade and investment between the United States and the Caribbean. However, the program is not broad enough in scope, and some countries have benefitted more than others. One-way, duty-free trade schemes are quickly becoming obsolete and will be replaced by reciprocal trade agreements. The Caribbean should welcome this as an inescapable, long-term reality, although reaching it will require a transition period. NAFTA parity would not only safeguard the future of the region's textile and apparel industry, but also aid the region in making the difficult transition to a free trade, post–NAFTA era.

Economic prosperity in the Caribbean has been closely tied to the proximity of the U.S. market, access to preferential markets, and concessional official assistance. Net aid flows to the Caribbean have been rapidly dwindling in recent years, yet increased flows of private capital provide a window of opportunity for the region. Success will depend in part on how the Caribbean repositions itself to attract a share of these flows. How far Caribbean governments continue to implement reform agendas with the private sector as the engine of growth will determine the degree of their economic prosperity. This is a time for transition and opportunity, a time for renewed private–public sector commitment, and most importantly, a time for action.

Bibliography

Bryan, Anthony T. December 1993. *Beyond NAFTA: The Caribbean Community and the Proposed Western Hemisphere Trade Area.* IDB-ECLAC Working Papers on Trade in the Western Hemisphere.

Marsh, Ben. March 1994. *Communication Regarding NAFTA Parity & Caribbean Basin Economic Security.* Washington, D.C.: Caribbean/Latin American Action.

Pearson, Cathy. February 1994. *The 17th Annual Miami Conference on the Caribbean Communiqué.* Washington, D.C.: Caribbean/Latin American Action.

Preeg, Ernest H. 1993. *Cuba and the New Caribbean Economic Order.* Washington, D.C.: The Center for Strategic and International Studies.

USAID (U.S. Agency for International Development). April 1992. *Latin America and the Caribbean: Selected Economic and Social Data.* Washington, D.C.

USITC (U.S. International Trade Commission). September 1993. *Impact of the Caribbean Basin Economic Recovery Act on U.S. Industries and Consumers: Eighth Report 1992.* Washington, D.C.

World Bank. April 1994a. *Caribbean Region: Coping with Changes in the External Environment.* Sector Report 12821, Latin America and the Caribbean Region. Washington, D.C.

———. April 1994b. *Caribbean Countries: Policies for Private Sector Development.* Sector Report 12617, Latin America and the Caribbean Region. Washington, D.C.

Chapter 9

Political Management of Conflict in a Multicultural Society

Ramesh Deosaran

Since Trinidad and Tobago (hereafter "Trinidad") became politically independent in 1962, contests over representation and socioeconomic equality in this multiethnic society have generally been negotiated within an ethnic frame of reference. The noisy linkages between politics and cultural identity remain a central part of social discourse. As in many other areas of the world, this leads to intellectual and political emphasis upon ethnic consciousness.

In Trinidad today, there is constant debate about the role of ethnicity in politics—a far cry from the 1970s, when social class was the pivotal and more respectable lever. Whatever the issue—victims of crime, cultural festivals, election campaigns, socioeconomic opportunities, or beauty contests—race becomes a conceptual lever in the controversy.

Trinidad is one of thirteen CARICOM countries surrounded by a few Spanish- and French-speaking countries, notably Cuba and Haiti. How to define the Caribbean region is fraught with political and cultural problems. Furthermore, even CARICOM's viability is now seriously questioned by the emergence of NAFTA. Some of its member countries have attempted to enter NAFTA and taken other initiatives toward southbound Latin American trade.

Politics, Psychology, and Culture

With a small but ethnically mixed population of 1.2 million, Trinidad provides a Caribbean example of how the political system responds to challenges based on cultural identity and conflict. Africans and East Indians each form approximately 40 percent of the population; Whites, Chinese, and Syrian-Lebanese form about 4 percent; and the mixed group is 16 percent. As to religion, Christians (mainly Catholics) constitute over 60 percent of the population, Hindus 25 percent, and Muslims 6 percent. These challenges and consequent adaptations emerge from a mixture of objective and subjective factors. For example, although we record statistics on the ethnic distribution of government jobs, complaints of relative deprivation by different ethnic groups continue to hinder any policy adjustments in this regard.

The staging of cultural conflict has become a functional mechanism for political mobilization. It sometimes appears that if reasons for engaging in cultural conflict cannot be discovered, we will simply invent them. Apart from policy construction, this tendency presents serious problems for social science measurement. While we can measure the consequences of cultural conflict, the motivations for it are difficult for an observer to uncover. Further, the attendant controversies depend not only on the issues of contention, but also how the participants define themselves. For example, they may define themselves by their citizenship in one instance, and by their racial or religious status in another.

This paper notes some difficulties faced by the political system and the state in particular when dealing with issues of ethnic conflict. Given its historical linkages and its many intangible motivations, cultural identity and its role in political conflict are matters from which the state should remove itself as far as possible. Given the historical linkages and current tensions that flow from ethnic consciousness in Trinidad, its government should adopt a policy of secular neutrality. The state should not appear to be an accomplice for one or the other ethnic group. Culture, race, and ethnicity are not necessarily the same, of course: persons of similar racial background, for example, may have different cultural preferences. In the broad outlines of this paper, however, the terms culture, race, and ethnicity are used interchangeably for ease of discussion.

In ethnic relations or ethnic conflict, the external validity of symbolic cultural objects is generally less important than the social consequences flowing from the use of these objects. In the postcolonial era, Trinidad's major public institutions (e.g., parliament, judiciary, public service) were built to function upon universalistic assumptions (e.g., without regard to race, culture, or religion). Yet certain energies that challenge and even threaten these institutions have emerged from feelings of ethnic deprivation. The fact is that current assumptions of universality or ethnic neutrality did not apply in the stratification order that existed in the colonial era. This is evident especially in the public service. Therefore, current assumptions of ethnic neutrality are inevitably contradicted by the visible historical legacy. So we have the assumptions on one side, and the visible legacy on the other.

All political parties in the country base their support upon ethnic groups in varying degrees. Once in power, however, a party formally disclaims but informally nurses its ethnic roots. Therefore, the central problem today for democracy in this island-state is how to make the formal political system more accommodating to ethnic appeals, without itself becoming irretrievably fragmented or divisive. Let us review some early comments on this situation.

In 1978, Sir Ellis Clarke, the president of the country and the major architect of its republican constitution, was quoted as saying: "What worries me is what seems to be an attitude of disenchantment with the political process, something that could easily degenerate into a feeling of hopelessness or helplessness" (*Guardian*, 27 August 1978).

Arguing for a economic strategy to unlock ethnic enclaves, La Guerre stated: "Economic development and the re-allocation of economic resources between and among groups will erode the traditional relationships." (La Guerre 1974, 106)

Putting that hope aside, Winston Dookeran saw the situation this way: "An economic system that creates the need for a trade-off between cultural persistence and economic betterment accepts implicitly a strategy for the absorption of the sub-culture into the dominant culture." (Dookeran 1974, 80)

The nation's constitution forbids discrimination on grounds of race, color, religion, or sex. But these guarantees are assured only in public bodies, and there is as yet no supporting legal machinery to apply in private business. The Industrial Relations Act of the country does forbid discrimination or unfair treatment to workers on the grounds of race, color, religion, or sex, but that only concerns work conditions. In the private sector, the right to private property is sometimes in direct competition with the right to equal treatment. For example, a landlord could rent or eject on grounds of race, color, or religion. He cannot be required to defend himself in court, at least not until some human rights mechanism is legislated that redefines private property so as to prohibit acts of discrimination.

In an early attempt to construct a psychological link between culture and opportunity, this researcher framed two hypotheses for Caribbean society:

- The further removed a cultural group is from the source of socioeconomic rewards, the greater the stress factors in that group's attempt to compete and gain access to such rewards.
- The further removed a cultural group is from the source of socioeconomic rewards, the greater the pressures for deculturalization, and the greater the likelihood that negative stereotyping would be used to justify that group's exclusion from social and economic rewards. (Deosaran 1981)

Of course, one's position in the socioeconomic ladder is not framed on objective considerations alone, but perhaps more functionally upon subjective feelings, especially of relative deprivation. One or another ethnic group may obtain some political mileage and mobilization by claiming socioeconomic deprivation: therefore one finds developed in Trinidad the classic notion of "equality in inequality." For example, political folklore has it that "Indians have economic power and Africans have political power." In each claim is some measure of myth and reality, reflecting the overall cultural conflict in the country.

Such parallel claims are used to maintain political equilibrium and ethnic boundaries. Assuming this power dichotomy to be true, some attention should be given to economic power as being more of a private exercise and political power as a public exercise. However, the fact that both are linked through bureaucracy and state policy creates areas for political discretion in private sector endeavors, and vice versa. In these circumstances, and given the sociological roots of political power, socioeconomic adjustments through limited state resources may be necessary, but are certainly not enough for interethnic harmony. The use of state resources to neutralize ethnic conflict is a very short term and counterproductive mission. Ethnic deprivations carry an insatiable appetite, and the state is not a bottomless pit of resources.

This dilemma between cultural conflict and state intervention has been allowed to simmer, mainly because for years, expressions for nationalism and cultural integration have been accorded more respect than ethnic diversity and a policy of ethnic representation. The former, it appears, reflect national norms; the latter, ethnocentrism. On one hand, there is a clear recognition of the nation's formal agenda. On the other hand, there are underlying, even threatening currents of ethnic consciousness and subordinated appeals for political, social, and economic policies that would flow from such a consciousness. The People's National Movement (PNM) government once proposed the secondary school system as the cradle of social integration. At the same time, religious bodies are allowed to operate primary and secondary schools, with student populations largely of one or another religion. The dilemma over unity in diversity arises from the need for a political system that is viable and integrated enough to govern effectively, without being pulled and tugged by competing ethnic interests.

Lodged in the Western Hemisphere and influenced by British political traditions, Trinidad—and in fact the entire Commonwealth Caribbean—have inherited a superstructure that presumes cultural homogeneity and political interests free from ethnic differences. Simply put, it is a superstructure built for the people, but not by the people. This *theory* of Caribbean politics has therefore been under strain and unrelenting challenge from the *practice* of Caribbean politics. The question of cultural identity in Caribbean countries, particularly Trinidad and Guyana, has been inextricably linked to the country's political structure, with important social and economic consequences.

Two and a half years after he led a violent insurrection against the government of Trinidad, Muslimeen leader Abu Bakr said in an interview:

> In Trinidad you cannot talk about the population generally. You have to talk about the groups, the interests, the sectors in the society. When there is a pie to be shared everybody does not get. It is groups still fighting on the explanation for their survival. A great deal of the motivation in this society is based on racism. This is a Christian society. The highest order is the Trinity Cross. This has nothing to do with any Hindu or Muslim. (Deosaran 1993)

Bakr's comment is important, not because of his skills in political theory, but because these feelings led him and his Muslimeen to commit the most violent political attack the country has ever witnessed. In 1970, another group, the Black Power movement, protested in the streets, smashing some business places. This caused the government to embark immediately upon policies to hire more blacks within the public sector and private banks. While the government made political and economic concessions, the Black Power protest was itself energized by feelings of ethnic deprivation. In other words, the thousands of black youths who formed the protest were mobilized first by the rhetoric of alienation and dispossession. East Indians, while expressing similar feelings of deprivation, did not participate significantly in the Black Power protests of 1970. According to one observer, the East Indians saw the Black Power protest as a "family quarrel."

A troublesome feature of this problem is that a significant number of East Indians in fact show visible wealth, while a significant number of Africans command political power. But in the political marketplace, arguments over power and wealth do not include these intraethnic variations. Expressions of conflict have been generalized, conveniently embracing all Indians on one side and all Africans on the other. The fact is that the arithmetic of cultural conflict cannot truly represent the psychology underlying it. As they say in Trinidad, "There is always more in the mortar than the pestle."

Ethnic identity itself has been linked to membership in political parties. For example, both of the two major parties in parliament in 1994—the ruling People's National Movement (PNM) and the opposition United National Congress (UNC)—are ethnically linked, though each struggles to dislodge the links. Only three of the twenty elected PNM representatives are of Indian descent: sixteen are African, while one is White. On the other hand, thirteen of the fourteen elected UNC representatives are of East Indian descent (the other is a local White). Thus, the PNM is effectively seen as the African party, and the UNC as the Indian party. Both parties have organized efforts to attract a more mixed membership. Just after the general elections of 1991, for example, the PNM's political leader made a public appeal for "more Indians in his cabinet and party," while the UNC leader became less belligerent in pursuit of East Indian rights and made repeated gestures to attract Africans to the party.

When the National Alliance for Reconstruction (NAR) formed the government from 1986 to 1991, ten of its thirty-three elected representatives were of East Indian descent. About one year after assuming office, the NAR experienced a severe ethnic split from its cabinet down to base membership. Key members from the East Indian–based United Labour Force (ULF), one of four parties forming the NAR, were removed from the cabinet. Just after the 1987 split, the ULF leader publicly branded the prime minister a "racist," and he called those few East Indian parliamentarians who remained with the NAR "traitors." The NAR gradually took on a core African profile with strategic support from the business community. Eventually it lost the 1991 elections, with East Indian support largely going to the newly formed UNC, and African support to the PNM. The NAR's attempt to construct a political machine on a viable multiethnic base was tragically short lived, and the sleeping giant of ethnic consciousness once again awoke to dominate the election results.

This short summary reveals how deeply ethnic identity runs in the stream of national politics. With such a background, it is difficult to see in the short term how either the PNM or the UNC can become a multiethnic political party. While the African-based PNM is now in its seventh consecutive run of political power, no Indian-based party has ever won a general election on its own. Considering this trend within the context of population distribution, the strain upon the political system is evident. To a large extent, East Indian spokesmen have called for political reform on this distribution, especially as, in Trinidad's first-past-the-post voting system, only the winner in a given constituency gets into power: no matter how close the runner-up comes, he is effectively left out. The adversarial Westminster-based parliament has at times comprised a government without a clear majority of the nation's *voters*, even though it has won a majority of the *seats*. This has been another reason advanced for political reform.

All major political parties except the PNM have called for proportional representation or some variant of it, to give added legitimacy to each citizen's vote and, by implication, to ethnic votes. The most vociferous appeals have come from East Indian–based parties. But proportional representation does not in itself cater exclusively to ethnic voting. Even in areas where the PNM has won, significant numbers of African votes have gone to other parties. The same situation exists with the UNC. However, one apprehension regarding proportional representation is that it might institutionalize ethnic divisions across the society. Implicit in this fear is that ethnic diversity should not be reflected in parliament, for that, it is feared, would destabilize the concept of nationhood.

The price for such nationhood is therefore clearly evident in the number of people whose votes are not directly counted in the corridors of power. Antagonists have pointed to nearby Guyana, where proportional representation has been alleged to cause ethnic strife. Proportional representation in itself cannot democratize the electorate. Other kinds of political reforms are needed, at least in the case of Trinidad. For example, apart from the voting system, the structure of parliament will have to be changed in order to accommodate interests that may contain but also exceed ethnic considerations. Specifically, there should be a system of open committees that accommodate the presence and views of the nation's interest groups. While the pros and cons of proportional representation are well known, the test for Trinidad was clearly put on the national agenda when the NAR came into power. Before coming together as the NAR, the four political parties (ULF, ONR, Tapia, and DAC), while functioning as opposition parties, had called for proportional representation. But once in power as the consolidated NAR, their commitment weakened: incumbency seemed to dull the thirst for proportional representation. Although establishing a Constitution Reform Commission in 1987, the NAR failed to implement the Commission's recommendations.

Earlier, in 1974, a Constitution Commission set up by the PNM had given full attention to proportional representation as a viable alternative to the first-past-the-post system. This Commission was established as a substantial response to ethnic pressures upon the political system. After concluding that "race is perhaps one of the most significant of political behaviours in Trinidad," the Commission recommended, as a comprise, a mixed system of voting to include both proportional representation and a first-past-the-post system (Commission Report, 1974). Parties would be afforded additional seats depending on their success at the first-past-the-post elections. This was a compromise between the need for a "stable, effective" parliament and the accommodation of ethnic diversity. The PNM rejected its report, however. It is perhaps worth noting that Trinidad's national anthem includes the verse: "Where every creed and race finds an equal place."

The State and Culture

Any democratic regime for this island-state must come to terms with the demands of ethnic diversity on one hand, and effective, overall governance on the other. The shortcut taken through engineered cultural assimilation in the present circumstances is constantly challenged by expressions of ethnic differences. A wide public discussion on ethnic rights and cultural identity is required. For example, the distinction between cultural assimilation and integration should be understood, so as to clarify the boundaries of political power and influence.

Such progress toward democracy must include a certain degree of manageable cultural tension. It is fruitless to assume, in the context of scarce resources, that there will be no cultural conflict in Trinidad and Tobago. Political reform or economic adjustments alone will not lead to ethnic peace and harmony. As long as government is framed upon ethnic constituencies, there will be ethnic tensions. This is especially true of Trinidad, where government takes responsibility for developing cultural policy and allocates resources accordingly. The question is how to minimize and manage such tension while sustaining the political legitimacy of the state.

In Trinidad and the Caribbean generally, cultural integration has been a disguised form of cultural assimilation. It could be no other way. There has been no equivalence, no equal exchange among different ethnic values and customs. With a stratification order based on Eurocentric values at the top, the net effect of colonial socialization was predetermined. Linked as it still is to socioeconomic and political power, cultural identity is exchanged or sustained on the basis of social values representing the political and cultural elite. Even within different ethnic groups, a stratification order exists, based on social and economic values. The educational system, the work place, and television are some of the leveling forces. In such circumstances, social class converges with race to confuse the examination of political behavior.

In this large sense, in contemporary Trinidad, the pressures for both assimilation and integration fall more heavily upon the East Indian community, whose ancestors came as indentured laborers. These pressures, relatively speaking, had formerly been laid upon the African population, given their earlier arrival as slave labor. Creolization became a mechanism of adaptation for them. The struggle for cultural space and integrity are therefore naturally played out from two different ethnic perspectives, but the experience of psychological dissonance today would be greater for the East Indian community as a whole.

Notwithstanding a significant degree of Westernization (more precisely, Americanization) within both the African and East Indian communities, the process of cultural identification still rests on vague stimuli and myths. In Trinidad, the authenticity of ancestral origins matters less than the current beliefs that lead to self-distinctions. The quest for difference, for group solidarity, is a functional part of the adversarial system in post-colonial, ethnically mixed societies. Persons from various ethnic groups often exaggerate their ethnicity in order to consolidate their political constituencies, but that is lost or suspended when such persons attain national office: here they preach ethnic unity and nationalism. The problem is then to keep ethnic constituents privately loyal, while publicly appearing to be free from ethnic favoritism. This is yet another feature of the dynamic conditions that surround ethnic consciousness in the country's political system. Cultural negotiations and debates are thus based upon these psychological paradigms, rather than upon questions of economic equality.

Cultural integration is not a neutral process. With the history of labor and colonialism in the Caribbean, the process was more one of assimilation than integration. Wherever cultural persistence remained, it was a feature of dissonance in an unfriendly cultural environment. The inequity of material rewards does attract assimilation, but it also creates resistance through cultural persistence. According to the *Oxford Dictionary*, to integrate means "to bring into equal membership of society especially without regard to race or religion," and, indeed, the formal criteria for membership in Trinidadian society rule out race and religion (see, for example, the constitution of Trinidad). But in the informal agenda of living and mixing, race and religion are part and parcel of our feelings of equity or deprivation. Today there is a mounting call for an Equal Opportunities Commission, to provide a formal mechanism for attaining equal citizenship.

Assimilation carries with it processes of psychological coercion and other implications, such as shame or stress. Cultural integration, on the other hand, presumes a neutral process, a willingness to share, mix, and mingle in groups with an equivalence of psychological comfort. But can this ever be so in a culturally stratified society? Cultural coercion to assimilate is not necessarily physical, in the sense of a forced change of religion or eating habits. It arises due to centrifugal forces established by the values and living styles of the cultural elite, which are propagated by the mass media and other social institutions. At some critical point, the culturally subordinate group gives up more than the culturally dominant group. Put another way, resistance to cultural change may carry a price that ranges from the material (lack of social membership) to the psychological (shame or alienation). And it is an existential disaster when someone becomes culturally assimilated, yet enjoys little or nothing of the promised rewards of the dominant value system. Such a person, culturally orphaned, will seek other modes of resolving the dilemma.

How then can cultural assimilation, which is really the more realistic alternative, become a pleasant process for social harmony in Trinidad? I would advance two positions: the first concerns social adjustment and cultural diversity. Assimilation does not necessarily mean a total divestment of one's native cultural preferences. Rather, it means that when assimilation is needed, activities within the public domain should be part of a fair exchange process. The one who assimilates should become an equal partner in the competition for opportunity, goods, and services in the public domain, especially since assimilation does not mean a complete disappearance of ethnic physiognomy.

In other words, since activities in the public domain require a good measure of universal values, some cultural divestment will occur; but it should take place within a framework of equal opportunity and a fair reward structure. The process is therefore both individually and socially determined. This is the benevolent process of social/psychological assimilation.

The second position concerns "psychological space" and the state as a source of conflict in cultural diversity. In the public sphere (e.g., voting, employment, legal rights) there is a necessary integration of values and objectives. In the private sphere (e.g., religion, festivals, food and dress customs) cultural parallelism or diversity could exist. Cultural conflict arises when these values from the private sphere become politically patronized or functionally correlated with values in the public sphere. To help avoid this conflict, the formal state apparatus and its operations must be explicitly secular.

A state like Trinidad, which adopts secularism yet uses its resources in ways that influence the private cultural sphere, is bound to be caught in the web of cultural conflict between the constituent groups. Given the intrinsic linkage between ethnicity and politics in this country, much of the cultural conflict experienced in Trinidad is linked to the state's direct political role, through patronage, in cultural matters. For instance, there has long been a National Cultural Council, a government agency responsible for cultural policy. Both this council and the Ministry of Culture have come under repeated fire from the East Indian community and, to a lesser extent, from non-Indian groups.

The state itself thus becomes a politically divisive point for cultural controversy. If integration is to mean integration of public-centered values, then the state's role should be confined to these, leaving the private values of religion and culture to private preferences and resources. State support of cultural activities has naturally become politics in disguise.

Ethnic diversity does not monopolize political conflict in the country. Pressures for resources naturally arise from other sources; the business community, for example. However, ethnic conflict over state resources has taken on wider dimensions, and the government has also been criticized by non-Indian groups. Through the National Carnival Commission, for example, the state has control over Carnival and its related activities. On several occasions, the Carnival bandleaders, calypsonians, and masqueraders have criticized government for its neglect, inefficiency, and politically partisan attitudes.

As calypso singing itself has gained private sponsorship, so too should the entire Carnival festival be left to private preference and resources. Let the true owners take it over and operate it as a business for both local enthusiasts and tourists. With private support and participation, Carnival could become a more effective cultural catalyst for social interaction. This proposal aspires neither to ban Carnival or to diminish its importance: to the contrary. It seeks to place Carnival as an element of private preference with support from private resources, so as to bring greater benefit to participants, while also serving as a smoothing mechanism for social integration.

The state can legitimately defend its role in public-centered values and institutions. Here integration can be correctly defined as "equal membership without regard to race or religion." But the state's direct involvement in cultural policy or cultural celebrations inevitably makes such membership conditional upon race and religion, especially where political support is inextricably related one way or another to cultural identity. The legitimacy of state power rests on its undertaking tax-supported activities framed upon wide public consensus. The Muslim community and several Christian communities have issued strong objections to the Carnival celebrations, sometimes seriously questioning whether the Afro-dominated Carnival is worthy of its status as a national festival. Notwithstanding the passion of Carnival enthusiasts and the fact that it fills a cultural gap in the lives of the African population, this cultural arithmetic cannot be ignored.

Even if the state removes itself from the center-stage of culture, this will not wipe out the dilemmas of cultural relations in a multiethnic society. However, it would help create a clearer understanding of cultural rights as private rights and a more manageable, justifiable arrangement for cultural diversity. Furthermore, wherever cultural assimilation did occur, it would be less a matter of state coercion, but rather of private preferences and private resources.

Conclusion

The relationship between culture, politics, and governance in Trinidad could be summarized as follows:

- Given the state's role in developing cultural policy and distributing resources to cultural groups, culture is not independent of politics. This has made the state a continuing focus of cultural conflict in this multiethnic nation. If the government lessens its role in directing and supporting culture in this multiethnic society, ethnic expectations in the political process would be lessened, as would ethnic pressures upon the government.
- Given the history of African and then East Indian labor, and the socioeconomic consequences of entry, the degree of assimilation by the African population exceeds that of the East Indian population. This difference in assimilation has helped institutionalize differential access to political power.
- The psychological distance from Westernization and its surrogate Creolization is different for each group, with the East Indians, on average, further placed from the cultural mainstream. Thus the potential for cultural dissonance is greater in the East Indian community than in the African community. The Africans have experienced much cultural dissonance and are more advanced in their modes of dissonance reduction. Manifestations of cultural conflict therefore reflect these historical differences.

- Effective cultural assimilation depends upon the structure and implementation of the socioeconomic reward system, especially that in the hands of the state apparatus.
- The practice of using ethnic mobilization for election campaigns has helped institutionalize ethnic antagonism in the adversarial political system.
- There are layers of cultural antagonisms in the society. When the higher layers becoming activated, they are spontaneously drawn down to agitate lower levels. This is the "condensation effect."
- Cultural conflict is part of wider social conflict. There are also different degrees and kinds of cultural conflict. One type is manifested during elections; another is experienced by students in school. The nature of cultural conflict depends upon several factors, such as how a situation is structured.
- Cultural conflict sometimes produces creative social and psychological tensions, which can in turn lead to positive modes of understanding and cultural innovation. In the arena of private rights, cultural conflict is sometimes necessary for growth in citizenship, since it gives rise to situations of choice that can force adjustments in the social and economic environment.
- Cultural conflict, in varying degrees, is here to stay. Various community and quasi-judicial mechanisms are needed to referee such conflict in ways that lead to a better arrangement of socioeconomic resources and privileges.

Bibliography

Crowley, D. 1960. "Cultural Assimilation in a Multi-Cultural Society." In *Social and Cultural Pluralism in the Caribbean* (Annals of the New York Academy of Sciences), ed. V. Rubin. New York: Kraus Reprint Co.

Deosaran, R. 1981. "Some Issues in Multi-Culturalism: The Case of Trinidad and Tobago in the Post-Colonial Era." *Plural Societies* 12(1–2).

———. 1981. "Multiculturalism in Trinidad and Tobago: A Political and Psychological Analysis." *Ethnic Studies: An International Journal of Ethnic Studies* 3(3).

———. 1986. "Political Reporting in a Multi-Party State." *Indian Journal of Political Science* 47 (2).

———. 1987. "The Social Psychology of Cultural Pluralism: Updating the Old." *Plural Societies* 17 (1).

———. 1988. "The Politics of Information in the Caribbean: Beyond the New World Information Order." *Indian Journal of Political Science* 49 (2).

———. 1992. *Social Psychology in the Caribbean: Directions for Theory and Research*. Trinidad: Longman Limited.

———. 1993. *A Society Under Siege: A Study of Political Confusion and Legal Mysticism*. Trinidad and Tobago: The McAL Psychological Research Centre, The University of the West Indies, St. Augustine Campus.

Dookeran, W. 1974. "East Indians and the Economy of Trinidad and Tobago." In *Calcutta to Caroni*, ed. J. La Guerre. London: Longman Limited.

La Guerre, J. 1974. *Calcutta to Caroni*. London: Longman Limited.

Nettleford, R. 1978. *Caribbean Cultural Identity*. Jamaica: Institute of Jamaica.

Smith, M. G. 1960. "Social and Cultural Pluralism." In *Social and Cultural Pluralism in the Caribbean* (Annals of the New York Academy of Sciences), ed. V. Rubin. New York: Kraus Reprint Co.

Chapter 10

In Search of Caribbean Basin Sociocentric Self-Interest

Karen S. Walch

The 1994 Miami Conference on the Caribbean and Latin America, sponsored by Caribbean/Latin America Action, was placed at the center of a bold vision for the twenty-first century. Following the historic Summit of the Americas, the Conference served as a forum to cultivate commitments toward Western Hemispheric economic integration. The summit's declaration of principles—a pledge in favor of democracy, free markets, expanded trade, and greater regional economic integration—was accepted by every democratically elected government in the Western Hemisphere. Its goal of "no barriers within 10 years" will have dramatic consequences for public- and private-sector interests in the Caribbean Basin and the United States. In particular, Caribbean Basin identity, political sovereignty, and post-structural adjustment policies will be challenged, as these nations are required to meet hemispheric obligations. This process will require a more critical dialogue of regional governments and business interests, in order to recognize and comprehend the various interests at stake.

The problem-solving and dialogue that now characterize Caribbean Basin–U.S. relations exemplify broader international trade issues and government-business activities, in a context of increasing economic interdependency and discord. In general, various Caribbean Basin and U.S. economic and political interdependencies have altered the way states and policymakers define their self-interest in international relations. Narrow definitions of self-interest have long been considered fundamental, rational, and functional in international relations (IR) theory. However, more sociocentric (versus egocentric) definitions are now emerging, as governments acknowledge that each state is a part of a greater social, political, and economic whole.[1]

As public- and private-sector actors acknowledge their connectedness with others in the region, their world view becomes increasingly sociocentric. Furthermore, through the interactive problem-solving dialogues developing in the Caribbean Basin, a view concerning self-interest that reflects the struc-

---

[1] Sociocentrism is not altruism, wherein the actor sacrifices the self for the other; rather, it conceptualizes the self as interdependent with the other.

tural reality of interdependence is emerging. This view takes into account the perspectives of others and how one government's actions affect others. Thus there are significant efforts to pursue "reciprocity in relations" (Piaget 1965, 66), where all relevant views are considered in coordinating policy. Individual governments realize they cannot independently solve the region's diverse economic and security problems and that the private sector increasingly influences the course of government policies. Ultimately, these combined forces will broaden the definitions of self-interest.

This article explores some of the dialogue and problem-solving processes that have developed through Caribbean Basin–U.S. government-business relations, and how they encourage interdependent and sociocentric notions of self-interest. The article concludes that institutionalized joint agenda setting, problem-solving, and transgovernmental efforts to manage foreign economic trade are critical to future governance in the Caribbean Basin and the Western Hemisphere.

What Are the National Interests?

The U.S. State Department has primarily defined national interests regarding the Caribbean Basin in security terms: concern for the region's political stability. A stable Caribbean Basin is a crucial U.S. security issue, because the area's shipping lanes are vital to U.S. defense and prosperity: one-half of all U.S. trade and two-thirds of all imported oil and strategic materials pass through the Panama Canal and the Gulf of Mexico. In addition, natural resources such as bauxite, oil and gas reserves, and local minerals from the Caribbean are important to U.S. economic prosperity (Payne and Sutton 1984, 193-194). Since the formulation of the Caribbean Basin Initiative (CBI-I) in the 1980s, the U.S. government has generally viewed both Central America and the insular Caribbean as a single unit. In this, the U.S. government was motivated, not so much to control the region, but to keep out others viewed as hostile (Pastor 1982, 1042).

The Caribbean Basin countries, on the other hand, have determined their national interest in terms of the international economy. International trade, including tourism, represents a high proportion of most Caribbean Basin countries' GNP. Most of them depend on a narrow range of markets for agricultural products, bauxite, petroleum, and tourism. Since World War II, North American transnational corporations have been involved in almost every sector of Caribbean economies, including banking, insurance, transportation, construction, mining, manufacturing, and tourism. In foreign aid, Caribbean Basin countries continue to receive significant amounts of financial, technical, and material assistance for poverty reduction, private sector development, diversification of international integration, environmental protection, and public sector reform.

CBI-I Dialogue

While CBI-I became official policy during the Reagan administration, its ideas originated in the Carter years. Following brief consultations with the U.S. Congress and other governments in the region, the Reagan administration designed a package of investment, tax, trade, and aid concessions. The idea behind this plan was to tackle the region's chronic problems of underdevelopment with a market-oriented approach. The Caribbean Basin Economic Recovery Act (CBERA) of 1 January 1984, however, was a "pale reflection of the original plan of action." (CBI Embassy Group 1989, 1). Many of the provisions that would have enabled the beneficiary countries to make full use of their comparative advantage on specific products were either removed or "watered down" (ibid.), largely due to fear of import competition on the part of U.S. domestic interests.

In the CBI-I policy, the U.S. government attempted to provide an economic component to its Caribbean foreign policy. For the sake of U.S. national self-interest, the CBI was to shape and influence the economic policies of the countries in the region. Its key elements included one-way, duty-free treatment of exports for twelve years; allocation of $350 million in emergency aid for some countries; and tax incentives for U.S. investments. In order to receive duty-free access, however, eligible countries had to meet certain political requirements. They could not, for instance, be communist; they could not nationalize industries; they could not provide preferential treatment that would adversely affect the United States. Further, they had to provide equitable and reasonable access to U.S. markets and resources, and to observe certain limits that would not distort international trade (Pantojas-Garcia 1985, 105–108).

Criticisms of CBI-I

By 1986, CBI-I was considered minimally successful at best, with new investment figures disappointingly low and imports to the U.S. actually having declined since 1984. Critics stated that the Caribbean Basin's economic problems were related to inadequate infrastructure; lack of affordable financing and U.S. distribution and marketing techniques; and investor perceptions regarding political and social instability. Caribbean countries were small domestic markets, with uncertainties regarding continuation of tax preferences, and regulatory obstacles. In addition, CBI-I was unable to liberalize Caribbean Basin preference for products denied duty-free treatment, or to reduce tariffs on textiles and apparel, for example. All Caribbean Basin countries had already received Generalized System of Preferences benefits, which represented 80% of Caribbean Basin export products (*Caribbean Business* 15 November 1989, 30); CBI-I did little to improve the existing economic trade situation.

Much criticism was directed at deficiencies in the CBI-I policy process. For example, some analysts pointed out that the U.S. should have gained more regional support and consulted with Mexico, Canada and Venezuela. Others suggested that the U.S. government take a more collaborative effort to advance regional progress. Indeed, the U.S. did not attempt to promote regional economic integration and did not consult any regional organizations in designing CBI-I. Pastor also asserted that, by excluding Nicaragua and Cuba, the CBI-I policy process and U.S. political efforts in Central America were regionally divisive. He maintained that CBI-I encouraged development strategies with a priority on industry, and neglected agricultural diversification, which led to increased migration from the region. (Pastor 1982, 1040).

Other analysts asserted that summits of regional leaders and consultations with Caribbean Basin regional organizations should have been conducted during the CBI-I policy development phase. These might have addressed such issues as population-planning programs, increased investment in agriculture, new linkages for resource supplies and markets for new investments, encouragement of joint ventures and labor-intensive projects, and improvement of middle- and upper-management skills. Such consultations would have helped to define the interdependencies of national interests in the region and to solve problems of unemployment, migration, development, political change, and security.

Critics also suggested that broader participation of various regional private and public sector actors in the development of CBI-I should have been practiced. This could have "replaced bilateralism with a broader regional approach, a balancing of interests between the private and public sector in the region, a shift of investment toward labor intensive, agricultural, integrated industry strategies rather than just assembly plants, and a shift away from the exclusive preoccupation with anticommunist confrontation" (ibid., 1051, 1058). Many analysts asserted that neither CBI-I's implementation nor its narrow process of policy formation were viable alternatives to a policy or process that would have utilized the regional institutions carefully established during the 1960s and 1970s (Polanyi-Levitt 1985, 238). Finally, many humanitarian and religious groups contended that by delaying urgently needed political and economic reforms, CBI policy actually increased political tensions and violence within the region (Wilber 1984, 12).

CBI-II Dialogue

The dissatisfaction of various political and economic analysts with the CBI-I policy process led to various study missions in 1986, and, ultimately, the proposal of CBI-II in 1987. CBI-II policy development officially began in January 1986 with a visit by the Subcommittee on Western Hemisphere Affairs to the Caribbean region, which was organized subsequent to the various reports provided by the International Trade Commission and the Department of Labor concerning the limited successes of CBI implementation (Report of Congressional Study Mission on CBI, September 1987, 4).

The delegation's trip to the region marked the beginning of interactive problem-solving and consultation. The subcommittee staff visited six Caribbean Basin countries and met with several government and private sector leaders. It also enlisted the assistance of The Development Group for Alternative Policies in arranging visits with representatives of a wide range of Caribbean Basin "social sector" organizations (ibid.).

The policy development process also included a January 1987 delegation visit to the Caribbean region led by Congressional Representatives J. J. Pickle and Sam Gibbons, which investigated the economic impact of CBI-I trade provisions and held discussions with various government and private sector leaders. The unsatisfactory findings from these consultations led to Representative Gibbons' proposal of H.R. 3101 (CBI-II), which was to extend CBI benefits for another twelve years and remove or reduce trade barriers to sugar and other goods (ibid., 5).

The CBI-II policy process became a regional dialogue concerning the proposals of H.R. 3101. Both the Caribbean Basin and the United States were beginning to realize that CBI-I would not slow the region's deteriorating economic situation. The chairman of the Subcommittee on Western Hemisphere Affairs, Representative George W. Crockett, Jr., determined that a thorough review of the CBI was needed—of its implementation, the assumptions underlying it, and proposals for alternative approaches. Thus, the CBI-II process became a dialogue and problem-solving process that involved various government and private sector leaders knowledgeable in a broad range of regional economic and social sectors (ibid., 4).

These consultative activities included a September 1987 symposium organized under the joint sponsorship of the Subcommittee on Western Hemisphere Affairs and the Subcommittee on International Economic Policy and Trade, which provided an interactive forum for members of Congress and various Caribbean Basin public and private sector leaders. Included in the dialogue were U.S. congressional representatives from the Subcommittee on International Economic Policy and Trade, three Caribbean Basin government ministers, the president of the Caribbean Development Bank, the leader of the Economic Division of the Caribbean Common Market (CARICOM), and the director general of the Organization of Eastern Caribbean States (OECS). Also attending were representatives of development organizations, academia, the private sector, trade unions, churches, small business and farmers' organizations, and opposition political parties. The aim of the symposium was to establish a precedent for ongoing, broad-based consultations on CBI-II and other related policies (ibid., 5).

Symposium participants unanimously agreed that CBI's effectiveness had been limited. It had been based on the assumption that an emphasis on export production, without strong links with local economies, would yield self-sustaining growth and a broad sharing of development benefits; in fact, the emphasis on exports had diverted resources from Caribbean Basin producers, namely, regional food systems (ibid., 1). There was also consensus that the CBI should provide greater access to the U.S. market for Caribbean Basin goods, while promoting regional approaches to economic self-reliance and greater control by the poor over their own development. Participants also agreed that the CBI could be improved by directing resources to small producers' organizations, and to development of the infrastructure required by these groups, larger businesses, and by the region's public and private financial institutions (ibid., 2).

In addition, U.S. government representatives were urged to shift CBI's primary focus from the assembly of imported components, to efforts that would promote and increase regional self-reliance: for example, strengthening Caribbean Basin capacity to transform its raw materials into processed goods for local consumption, and diversifying exports. Caribbean Basin participants also pointed out that the United States rarely committed resources to the employment of Caribbean area consultants, or to the training of Caribbean personnel (ibid., 2). All tariffs on Caribbean products should be phased out, they believed, and a fund should be established to help stabilize commodity prices. In order to eliminate uncertainties and confusion among Caribbean Basin exporters, the U.S. Department of Agriculture and U.S. Customs Service were asked to make detailed information available regarding import requirements. Conferees also suggested that current U.S. trade barriers constrained Caribbean tourism, one of the region's largest industries (ibid., 2).

Certain shortcomings in the formulation and implementation of CBI-I were attributed to insufficient consultation in the region. The mission's report concluded that regular communication should be implemented between U.S. and Caribbean Basin government and private sector actors. The conferees suggested that the United States work with existing regional organizations, such as the Caribbean Common Market, the Caribbean Development Bank, and Caribbean

Food Corporation, as well as regional nongovernmental organizations, to avoid duplicating existing programs (ibid., 2).

In addition to symposia and conferences, hearings were conducted throughout the CBI-II policy development process, which facilitated the integration of various U.S. and Caribbean Basin government and private sector points of view. The Subcommittee on Trade of the Committee on Ways and Means held hearings on H.R. 3101 in December 1987, March 1988, and September 1988, to improve the operation of CBI-II. These included representatives from various U.S. government agencies (e.g., the U.S. Trade Representative, the U.S. Department of Agriculture, and the State Department–Trade Division), who also participated in reviewing CBI-II proposals.

At these hearings, various U.S. public and private sector interests were represented, as well as Caribbean Basin public and private sector viewpoints. Throughout the process it was clear that a conflict existed between U.S. administration desires to maintain an open global trading system and congressional concerns for protecting constituent markets and domestic employment. As a result, much of the dialogue involved the expression of Caribbean Basin public and private sector concerns regarding greater U.S. market access through the elimination of duties and quotas, specifically for footwear, leather, tuna, textiles, and sugar: interests that conflicted with concerns expressed by U.S. manufacturing groups. Trade association representatives expressed concerns regarding import issues where "lobbying and self-interest were strong" (American Textile Manufacturers personal interview, 14 July 1990).

In addition to official hearings, various informal consultations on CBI-II proposals were held. In 1987, the CBI Embassy Working Group was organized and held various meetings with U.S. administration and congressional representatives. It also met on occasion with various domestic interests concerning the CBI proposals, and there were assertions by Group members that there was a definite need and willingness to participate in multilateral consultations. They also recognized that all the "vital concerns of the [Caribbean] region may not be addressed in the CBI-II legislation" (Embassy Working Group 1989).

The Embassy Working Group also held numerous meetings with potential CBI-beneficiary embassy trade representatives, which led to position and resource papers that represented the Group in various discussions with U.S. administration and legislative members concerning CBI-II (H.R. 3101 in the 100th Congress, and H.R. 1233 in the 101st Congress). The Group worked on issues that went beyond the CBI-II legislation, but became most involved in ongoing dialogue and consultations with the U.S. administration and Congress regarding CBI-II (Embassy Working Group 1989).

On 20 August 1990, the Caribbean Basin Economic Recovery Expansion Act of 1990, or CBI-II (Title II of the Customs and Trade Act of 1990), was signed by President Reagan. However, the enacted CBI-II omitted two major provisions of the original legislation: one allowing duty-free quotas for nontextile import-sensitive articles, and the other providing a minimum annual sugar import quota for CBERA beneficiaries (CRS 1990: 2). Despite significant dialogue and consultation, the U.S. government appeared to be "more generous in promise than in delivery" (Economist 1990). However, various Caribbean Basin public and private sector actors were instrumental in NAFTA parity legislation (H.R. 1403, The Caribbean Basin Free Trade Agreements Act) introduced in 1993.

Other Dialogue and Problem-Solving Processes

In addition to formal CBI and NAFTA parity initiatives, interaction among public and private sector actors has continued through the Caribbean–Latin American Action (C/LAA) promotion of the annual Miami conference. In the 1980s, when it was known as Caribbean/Central American Action, C/LAA facilitated dialogues between the public and private sector in the Caribbean Basin concerning trade, investment, competitiveness, and the promotion of efforts to increase a prosperous North American and hemispheric economic and trading system. Since then, the Miami conference has become a "town meeting" (C/LAA 1994), promoting dialogue and interactive problem-solving in the Caribbean Basin beyond formal trade negotiation activities. The notions of self-interest have been reformulated through these dialogues, as topics of economic integration, business development, quality and competitiveness have been discussed by government and business sector decision makers.

The 1994 Miami conference was a significant conduit between the vision of the Summit of the Americas and the practice of economic integration, by providing a forum to extend the public and private sector dialogue established through CBI and other policy activities. In particular, the working sessions, expositions, task forces and seminars promoted interactive problem-solving dialogues that will be critical to the formulation of interests and policy initiatives. The interdependent interests of the public and private sectors concerning telecommunications, energy, the environment, transportation, Caribbean development programs, investment, and financing are under continual re-evaluation throughout this discourse and will be critical to future commitments to economic integration.

Self-Interest in the Caribbean Basin

A recent study[2] evaluated the quality and type of dialogue which encourages reciprocal exchange, the integration of viewpoints, the search for alternative ways to handle the Caribbean's economic problems, as well as how this dialogue is related to decision makers' definitions of self-interest. Based on the study's results, this article concludes that those decision makers in the Caribbean and United States who participated in transgovernmental reconceptualization of interests through agenda setting, diagnosis of regional economic options and solutions, and collaboration in dialogue and problem-solving activities, defined their self-interest in sociocentric ways.[3] Irrespective of whether decision makers represented the U.S. government (executive or legislative branch), Central American or Caribbean governments, or the private sector, sociocentric definitions of self-interest were perceived by those with extensive dialogue participation, involving transgovernmental diagnosis and consultation.[4]

In sum, regardless of who the participants represented, reciprocal exchange and integration of viewpoints facilitated an assessment of their own welfare in association with—not in isolation from—others' economic preferences. A participant's official role was in this sense unimportant, but the acts of participation were apparently more salient.

The evidence of sociocentrism in CB–U.S. policymaking has implications for the emergence and durability of the cooperation necessary for economic integration in the Caribbean Basin and the Western Hemisphere. If egoism is overcome, then CB–U.S. decision makers can better comprehend situations of real economic and political interdependency, mutual vulnerabilities, and cooperative solutions. Furthermore, social and political relationships, including international relations, need not be in persistent contention, making coopera-

---

[2] For research design and instruments, see Walch, in *Caribbean Affairs* (Trinidad and Tobago), forthcoming 1996.

[3] In this study, evaluations of self-interest by Caribbean Basin and U.S. public- and private-sector actors ranged from egoistic to sociocentric. The definition of sociocentric interest primarily pertains to perceptions of the "self" within a larger social system, including attention to both public- and private-sector awareness of the need to accommodate to the critical interdependent relationships in the region, and support of policy proposals which coordinate the realities of various relevant Caribbean Basin interests. Where extensive CB–U.S. public- and private-sector dialogue and communication assisted to "stretch the human imagination so individual self-interest was reconceptualized and reconstituted as the We" (Barber 1984, 92), self-interest is defined as sociocentric. Therefore, self-interest is not considered to be static, but is socially constructed by the relevant decision makers through dialogue and problem-solving processes.

[4] The U.S. Trade Representative, U.S. Embassy representatives in the Caribbean Basin region, legislative committees, Caribbean Basin governments, U.S. consumer groups, and Caribbean Basin region stockholder actors, all fall into this category.

tion difficult or impossible to generate and maintain, as most IR theories would predict.

This research concludes that a problem-solving orientation provides a supportive dialogue climate where there is planning with one another rather than for the other (Nierenberg 1973). This orientation encourages decision makers to pay attention to the differences between conflicting parties, rather than ignoring them. This process encourages decision makers to treat the conflict as a joint problem, and incites efforts by decision makers to "stop fighting over their positions and start concentrating on their underlying interests" (Fisher 1981). These institutional processes encourage a step closer to a regional management of the area's burdens, by addressing conflict as problems in relationships, rather than as competition over resources in an anarchic environment, as generally defined by IR theory.

While transgovernmental reciprocal exchange, dialogue, problem-solving, and integration of viewpoints are fragile enterprises, such activities deserve critical attention for CB–U.S. relations in particular, and for IR in general. On the other hand, if the Caribbean Basin and the United States pursue institutionalized dialogue and problem-solving practices that foster conflict in legalistic, factual terms, they only advance the inevitability and endurance of conflict wherein the irreconcilable opposition of basic egoistic interests cannot be resolved (Rothman 1991).

Implications for Future U.S.–Caribbean Basin Relations

The future of Caribbean Basin and Western Hemispheric trade, investment, and financial arrangements will significantly influence national economies, as it becomes increasingly more difficult for national leaders to ensure stable and predictable commercial environments on their own. But economic instability and unpredictability incite the crucial participation of relevant public and private sector decision makers in efforts to understand the realities of economic integration; and this interdependence increasingly necessitates policy outcomes that are more inclusive and representative of interdependent public and private sector interests. This, however, requires institutional processes which facilitate a quality reciprocal exchange, and integration of transnational viewpoints in foreign economic policymaking. But while the benefits of liberal international trade and the coordination of trade agreements to promote economic stability and certainty appear to be widely accepted by national leaders, they do come into conflict with the short-term goal of protecting narrowly defined domestic interests.

Nevertheless, as Caribbean Basin and U.S. governments work more effectively with the private sector, and with regional and international organizations, governments become important strategic brokers (Nettleford 1992), and an appropriate agenda will emerge through the interaction between the public and private sector in order to construct an effective business environment. Conferences, consultations, and dialogues that encourage the facilitation of joint agenda setting, diagnosis, and problem-solving will be critical in the areas of health, education, science and technology, labor, agriculture, transportation, environment, and trade and investment issues. The challenges for the Caribbean Basin countries to enter the global markets and enhance their economies will require strategies that enhance shared definitions of self-interest, and institutionalized processes which encourage the sharing and transferring of knowledge will be critical in this endeavor.

As the foundations of sociocentric conceptualizations are further defined, the process can be utilized in identifying services or manufacturing options, foreign investment and training programs, and business-government partnerships with vocational schools and businesses which encourage the win-win solutions that are critical in and to the context of interdependency. In this, the Caribbean Basin and the United States need to continue to build on the foundations of interactive problem-solving processes which have developed in this area. Caribbean Basin, United States, and Western Hemispheric collective security may depend upon it.

Bibliography

Barber, Benjamin. 1984. *Strong Democracy: Participatory Politics for a New Age.* Berkeley: Univ. of California Press.

Caribbean/Latin American Action. 1994. *Caribbean Basin Commercial Profile, 1994.* Washington, D.C.: Caribbean Publishing Company, Ltd.

Caribbean Basin Initiative Embassy Group. 1989. Economic Development in the Caribbean Basin Region. (January) Washington, D.C.

CRS (Congressional Research Services). 1990. *CBI-II: Expanding the Caribbean Basin Economic Recovery Act.* (December) Washington, D.C.

Economist Staff. 1990. *The Economist.* 25 August 1990.

Fisher, Roger, and William Ury. 1981. *Getting to Yes: Negotiating Agreement Without Giving In.* Boston: Houghton Mifflin.

Nettleford, R.M., et al. 1992. *Report of the Committee of Advisors on Government Structure.* Kingston, Jamaica: Ministry of the Public Service.

Nierenberg, Gerald I. 1973. *Fundamentals of Negotiating.* New York: Hawthorne Books.

Pantojas-Garcia, Emilio. 1985. "The U.S. Caribbean Basin Initiative and the Puerto Rican Experience." *Latin American Perspectives* (fall): 105–128.

Pastor, Robert. 1982. Sinking in the Caribbean Basin (Analysis of President Reagan's CBI). *Foreign Affairs* (summer): 1038–1058.

Payne, Anthony and Paul Sutton. 1984. *Dependency under challenge: the political economy of the Commonwealth Caribbean.* Dover and Manchester: Manchester Univ. Press.

Piaget, Jean. 1965. *The Moral Judgement of the Child.* New York: Free Press.

Polanyi-Levitt, Kari. 1985. "The Origins and Implications of the Caribbean Basin Initiative: Mortgaging Sovereignty?" *International Journal* (spring): 229–281.

Rothman, Jay. 1991. "Introduction: Prenegotiation as a Merging of Theory and Practice." *The Jerusalem Journal of International Relations* 13 (March): 1–21.

U.S. House Committee on Foreign Affairs. 1987. *The Caribbean Basin Initiative: Caribbean Views. Report of a Congressional Study Mission and Symposium on the Caribbean Basin Initiative.* 100th Cong., 1st sess., 18–19 September.

U.S. House Subcommittee on Trade of Committee on Ways and Means. 1988. *Caribbean Basin Economic Recovery Expansion Act of 1987.* 100th Cong., 1st sess., 14 December 1987d, 28 March and 15 September.

Wilber, Vincent. 1984. "The CBI: A Plan That Won't Work." *Multinational Monitor* (March): 12–13.

Chapter 11

The United States, Democracy, and the Caribbean

Richard J. Bloomfield

For much of its history, the United States has regarded the Caribbean as of great strategic importance because of its proximity. This will always be true, of course, but with the end of the Cold War, strategic considerations have receded from the forefront of U.S.–Caribbean relations. That being so, does it make sense to analyze U.S. policy towards the Caribbean? Is there an overarching theme that informs current U.S. policies and programs in the region? If we take the Clinton administration at its word, there is. It is not, however, a concept designed exclusively for the Caribbean, but rather the same theme that the administration says is the basis for U.S. foreign policy in world at large, namely, the promotion of democracy.

In September 1993, the entire Clinton foreign policy team made a series of speeches defending itself from the charge that it had no foreign policy to defend. One of those who spoke in September was the national security advisor, Anthony Lake. His assignment was to outline what one of his predecessors, Henry Kissinger, used to call "the conceptual framework" of U.S. foreign policy. According to Lake, this framework is now to be the "enlargement of the world's free community of market democracies." Lake made it clear that the U.S. preference was to carry out this pro-democracy policy with other like-minded nations, rather than unilaterally. He said that the United States would pursue this effort by building upon the core of "major market democracies," by which he presumably meant the countries of the North Atlantic Treaty Organization and Japan. He singled out Eastern Europe and the former Soviet Union as the most immediate candidates for the application of this policy.

Lake also mentioned the "Western Hemisphere community of democracies," but only in passing. Be that as it may, in this hemisphere the administration's pro-democracy policy has come up against the hard realities associated with trying to nourish democracy from the outside. I refer, of course, to Haiti. And, true to its desire to act in concert with others, the administration has been trying to achieve its objectives in Haiti by working with other democracies through multilateral organizations.

What stake do the Caribbean nations have in the Haiti crisis? After all, Haiti has been the odd man out, even in its own neighborhood. All the governments of the area, except those of Cuba and the Cedras regime in Haiti, are the product of elections, and the Commonwealth Caribbean has an enviable record of respect for democratic institutions. That is true, but these should not be reasons for complacency. The Caribbean nations are, after all, small, vulnerable, and mostly poor states facing grave social and economic problems. Their democracies are under great stresses and strains, and their traditions do not make them immune from anti-democratic eruptions, just as Uruguay and Chile, also countries with long democratic traditions, were not immune from authoritarian takeovers in the 1970s. The Caribbean is especially vulnerable to the machinations of the international drug mafia, which has shown it is not afraid of attempting to immobilize an entire state, if necessary.

There are also historic grounds for concern when the neighboring superpower proclaims an ideal as noble and as abstract as democracy to be the *raison d'être* of its foreign policy. The promotion of democracy, especially in this hemisphere, periodically comes to the fore as the rationale for U.S. policies and programs. One remembers in this regard Woodrow Wilson and John F. Kennedy and, more recently, Ronald Reagan. The pursuit of democracy can cover a multitude of sins, or at least a multitude of policies and programs that presidents and bureaucracies wish to undertake for their own purposes. So it behooves the Caribbean nations to pay careful attention to this latest manifestation of the "democracy as foreign policy" syndrome.

The latest version of this syndrome did not start with President Clinton, but with his predecessor. It was the Bush administration that not only used "democracy" and "free markets" as the catchwords to describe the objectives of U.S. policy in this hemisphere (as did Reagan), but attempted to pursue those objectives through multilateral means; that is, through the Organization of American States.

By the time the Clinton administration took office, the Organization of American States had already laid the groundwork for a multilateral pro-democracy regime. Almost three years ago, in June 1991, the OAS, at its annual general assembly meeting in Santiago, Chile, agreed to what might be called a charter for an international regime to promote and defend democracy in the Americas. One resolution, which has become known as "the Santiago Commitment," pledged the OAS members to take "efficacious, timely, and expeditious procedures to ensure the promotion and defense of democracy." The first part of that pledge, that referring to promotion, has so far evoked from the foreign ministers broadly worded commitments to address those problems that are thought to undermine democracy, such as extreme poverty, official corruption, and the lack of civilian authority over the military. Clearly, such grand goals can become operational only over a long period of time, and by themselves can hardly be said to constitute a full-fledged international regime at this time.[1]

The ministers followed up on the second part of the Santiago Commitment—to defend democracy—by approving Resolution No. 1080. This resolution provides that, in the event "of any sudden or irregular interruption of the democratic institutional process" in a member state, an emergency meeting of OAS foreign ministers can be convoked within ten days to decide on collective action.

Because it contemplates the possibility of collective intervention in a region in which, for most countries, nonintervention has long been sacred dogma, the approval of Resolution 1080 was a remarkable event. The ministers did not have long to wait for their new mechanism to be put to the test. Barely three months after the Santiago meeting, President Aristide was overthrown. Seven months after that, President Fujimori of Peru carried out his *autogolpe*, or self-administered coup, by which he closed down the legislature and the courts and took full power unto himself. A third test occurred in May 1993, when the then-president of Guatemala, Jorge Serrano, attempted to imitate Fujimori. Having miscalculated the extent of the opposition his action would provoke both internally and abroad, however, Serrano was himself ejected within less than two weeks.

The Case of Haiti

The recent history of Haiti is well known, especially to people from the Caribbean. What the OAS attempted to accomplish in Haiti, the restoration of President Aristide, was seen by Aristide's enemies as a total surrender on their part, with grave consequences for their well-being and in some cases no doubt for their lives. In such circumstances, they would yield to OAS demands only if the consequences of not giving in were more painful than refusal. The instrument chosen to apply the requisite pain, a trade embargo, proved to be fatally flawed, as it included only the members of the OAS (and even then was not binding). In fact, the most essential commodities for the survival of the usurper regime, oil and guns, were easily obtained from outside the hemisphere. Certain European states, for example, refused to abide by the embargo. Clearly, more than

---

[1] International regimes are "sets of implicit or explicit principles, norms, rules, and decision-making procedures around which actors' expectations converge in a given area of international relations" (Krasner 1983). International regimes can be formal organizations like the International Postal Convention or the United Nations or informal networks like Western central banks.

a leaky embargo was needed, but the Bush administration was divided internally as to whether it was in the best interests of the United States for Aristide to be returned to the presidency. As a result, it dithered over Haiti for the remainder of its term.

The Clinton administration entered office determined to take a tougher line toward Haiti.[2] After obtaining a binding embargo on oil and arms from the UN Security Council, the U.S. government undertook to enforce it by a naval blockade. Haitian assets in the United States were frozen and visas were denied to complicit Haitians. These moves helped those U.S. and UN diplomats who were negotiating with General Cedras to convey the new president's determination to achieve an agreement for Aristide's return. No doubt, Cedras and company were reminded of the fate of another Caribbean general who had personally challenged the credibility of a U.S. president, and who has since languished in a U.S. prison. Fearing that the United States might intervene, either unilaterally or with the blessing of the Security Council, Cedras agreed (in negotiations held on Governor's Island, New York) to Aristide's return by the end of October 1993, and to eventual reform of the army and police under international supervision.

This might have been the happy ending of the story, had not the debacle in Somalia intervened, setting off a panic in the U.S. Congress that coincided with a planned landing in Haiti of a UN contingent of advisers, including U.S. soldiers. With U.S. senators declaiming that the return of Aristide was "not worth the life of one U.S. soldier," the threat of an invasion, Panama-style, collapsed, and so did the Governor's Island agreement. After that the policy of the Clinton administration came to eerily resemble that of George Bush, indecisive and ambivalent toward Aristide.

What lessons, then, can be drawn from the Haiti experience? First, that under certain conditions, nothing short of armed force will be sufficient to dislodge a usurper regime. These conditions are:

- That the economy and social structure of the country in question be primitive. By this I mean that, although foreign trade may be significant, the economy is not highly integrated into the network of international financial, technological, and commercial relationships that are the lifeblood of most modern economies; the usurper regime, therefore, and the small upper class that

---

[2] The reason for the Clinton administration's concern about Haiti was quite obvious: candidate Clinton had sharply criticized the Bush policy of having the Coast Guard return Haitian boat people to the island. During the transition, President-elect Clinton had to eat his words and agree to continue the repatriation policy for fear that thousands of refugees would set sail for Florida the minute he took the oath of office. This embarrassing about-face made Clinton a strong proponent of restoring Aristide and thereby avoiding the refugee problem.

supports it, can survive by drawing down their foreign bank accounts and smuggling in a few essential commodities, like oil.
- That the usurper regime is willing and able to use a high degree of repression in order to force the majority to accept the suffering imposed by international sanctions and to prevent its opponents from mounting an insurgency against it. Once Cedras' regime thought the new U.S. administration might use force to dislodge it, he signed an agreement by which Aristide would return; as soon as it became apparent that the Clinton administration was unwilling to use force, Cedras reneged on the agreement.

A multilateral expeditionary force under OAS auspices to restore President Aristide would be very unlikely. The opponents of the use of force in the OAS are many, and strong enough to prevent that body from approving an armed invasion of a member country for whatever purpose. If the recently announced, more comprehensive UN sanctions fail to budge the Cedras regime, and they might well do so, the Clinton administration will be faced with the same unpalatable choices it faced in October 1993, when the *Harlan County* was turned away by an angry mob in Port-au-Prince; that is, to be humiliated, or to use armed force, either unilaterally or under the aegis of a Security Council resolution.

The Case of Peru

Unlike Haiti, Peru's society and economy are sufficiently complex and integrated into the international system that economic sanctions do provide the outside world with substantial leverage. In Peru's case, foreign donors cut off bilateral aid and the United States threatened to scuttle a large, pending international aid package. This induced President Fujimori to accede to OAS demands that his proposed political reforms be accomplished in a democratic fashion. Fujimori agreed to hold OAS-monitored elections for a congress to write a new constitution and to work out the terms of the process with the traditional political parties.

Subsequently, however, Fujimori succeeded in manipulating events to his advantage. The political parties and the government made only a halfhearted effort to negotiate a mutually agreeable process. In the end, Fujimori took matters into his own hands and dictated the powers of the constituent congress and the timing of the elections. The two largest parties refused to participate, and the result was a congress dominated by Fujimori supporters. Inevitably, the outcome has been a powerful presidential regime, which some call authoritarian in democratic disguise.

Whether the OAS could have prevented this outcome is a matter of hot debate in Peru. Some critics of the OAS charge that it made a serious mistake in officially closing the Peru case in early 1993. This was just after elections for the constituent congress but before congress was underway, so the OAS was unable to monitor the constitution-drafting process that would determine whether the new charter would be truly democratic. Others say that, given the circumstances, the OAS did about all that could have been expected. These observers credit the OAS with at least preventing Fujimori from going as far as he had originally intended in weakening democratic institutions and curtailing human rights.[3] They argue that interrupting the loan package Peru needed to support its economic adjustment program would have risked plunging the country into an economic crisis, thereby helping the Shining Path.

The lessons of the Peru case are that, under the right circumstances, economic sanctions can be effective in inducing a usurper regime to agree to restoring some form of democracy. The right circumstances include that the target country be well integrated into the international system and that the entrepreneurial and middle classes have a considerable stake in maintaining that integration. In addition, the timing must be right—that is, sanctions must threaten at a moment when foreign assistance is badly needed. Most importantly, the OAS should be willing to compromise: the usurpers need to achieve some of their original objectives.

There are significant caveats as well. If, as in Peru, the usurper regime has the support of the majority of the populace, probably the most the OAS can achieve is to ameliorate the situation; that is, to get the regime to allow opposition participation in whatever electoral process is established and to promise to adhere to minimum safeguards of political and human rights. A second caveat is that a majority of OAS countries may not wish to resort to extreme measures, such as indefinite sanctions, because to do so might jeopardize their own interests in the country concerned. That was the case in Peru, as well as in Haiti.

Structural Inhibitions

Beyond the lessons of Haiti and Peru, there is what I call a structural obstacle to a strong OAS defense-of-democracy regime: a number of Latin American nations fear that too much collective oversight of internal affairs, in Haiti or elsewhere, could create precedents that might someday be used against them. In the Haiti case, for example, by the fall of 1992, when it had become clear that the OAS sanctions were not working, several OAS members proposed taking the case to the United Nations Security Council. This proposal was rejected

---

[3] For a detailed account of the coup and its aftermath, see Costa (1993).

by some of the leading Latin American members, however, on the grounds that the situation in Haiti, no matter how deplorable, did not constitute a threat to international peace and security under Chapter VII of the UN Charter, and the Security Council, therefore, had no jurisdiction in the matter. Leading proponents of this view were Mexico, Brazil, and Colombia.

Why this touching concern for international law? Because each of these nations feels itself vulnerable to international criticism on various issues, such as human rights, drug trafficking, environmental degradation, and, in some cases, their own lack of democratic practices. These countries are very wary of creating precedents that might legitimize collective intervention by international bodies in their internal affairs. This camp, which I call "the noninterventionists," includes more than the three countries named. They can be counted on to resist any proposals to toughen the regime's enforcement powers, such as automatic escalation of sanctions, giving the Security Council a role, and, of course, the use of force.[4]

Implications for the Caribbean

What are the implications of the limitations on the OAS defense-of-democracy regime that I have described for the Caribbean? I would say there are at least two.

The first is the old saw, that an ounce of prevention is worth a pound of cure. By now it should be obvious that reversing a coup is more problematical than preventing one. More attention should be paid to what can be done to consolidate and deepen democracies so that coups will not occur. The OAS can and should play a leading role in this regard. For example:

- The OAS should develop norms and standards by which democracies can be judged. What is representative democracy? How essential is the separation of powers? What characterizes a democratic judicial system?
- The OAS should devote more of its limited resources to helping countries strengthen their democratic institutions, such as legislatures and courts, which are often dominated by the executive.
- The OAS should help to legitimize democratically elected governments by making international observation of elections a common practice among its members.
- The OAS should seek ways of helping democratic governments strengthen their ability to bridge the gap that exists between the civil authorities and the military in many countries.

---

[4] For more discussion of the structural obstacles, see Bloomfield (1994).

- The OAS should engage in preventive diplomacy to deter coups.
- The OAS needs to strengthen its human rights regime. In spite of the triumph of democratic governments throughout the region, the Inter-American Human Rights Commission has lately come under sharp attack from several members of the OAS.

These precepts, of course, do not apply only to Caribbean members of the OAS, but by virtue of their number and the one-country one-vote rule, they play a key role in OAS decisionmaking. Many of the larger nations in the OAS, as I have said, are themselves vulnerable to criticism on their performance on human rights and other issues. They do not wish to legitimize the intrusion of the international community in their internal affairs, and they will be lukewarm at best towards strengthening the ability of the OAS to undertake the kinds of proactive programs mentioned here. The Caribbean should therefore use its voting power in favor of a more robust OAS role in democracy and human rights.

The second implication for the Caribbean regarding limitations on the OAS defence-of-democracy regime is that there is a link between democracy and security in regions made up of small, vulnerable states. This link has been particularly obvious in Central America, and it was demonstrated again in the 1980s, when internal civil wars in the region spilled over national boundaries. It also appears to be the case in the eastern Caribbean, if the events leading up to the invasion of Grenada are any indication. It has been true on the island of Hispaniola, where the Dominican Republic is a key factor in the Cedras regime's ability to survive. Added to this is the possibility that the United States could, under circumstances not too difficult to imagine, define for itself a threat to democracy in the Caribbean that required intervention.

The security of states of the area can, in fact, be affected by internal political developments in other states. Therefore, should not the small states of the Caribbean Basin join together in security arrangements that explicitly recognize their interdependence? That would allow them to deal collectively with threats to democracy in one of their number, while better controlling any outside intervention that might be contemplated in such a case by the OAS, the UN, or the United States.

The Esquipulas Agreements provide a precedent.[5] Only when the countries of Central America agreed that their security depended on democratic

---

[5] The Esquipulas Agreements take their name from from the site in Guatemala of a meeting of Central American presidents held on 6-7 August 1987, in which the presidents assumed full responsibility for reaching a settlement of the Central America crisis, thereby supplanting mediation efforts by outside powers, such as those of the Contadora Group.

reforms, were the wars in Central America brought to a close. Esquipulas also provided the framework for inviting the UN and the OAS to mediate peace, to assist in implementing the peace agreements, and to organize and monitor elections. The Esquipulas model needs to be taken a step further, to guarantee that external intervention will be available when needed and that the region's countries will control whether, and in what manner, such interventions occur.

Bibliography

Bloomfield, Richard J. 1994. "Making the Western Hemisphere Safe for Democracy." *The Washington Quarterly* 17(2).

Costa, Eduardo Ferrero. 1993. "Peru's Presidential Coup." *Journal of Democracy* (January) 4(1).

Krasner, Stephen, ed. 1983. *International Regimes.* Ithaca: Cornell Univ. Press.

Chapter 12

The Group of Three: Political Concertation, Trade Liberalization, and Regionalism in the Caribbean Basin

Andrés Serbin

During the Fifth Meeting of Foreign Ministers of the Group of Eight held in Puerto Ordaz, Venezuela on 3 March 1989, Mexico, Colombia, and Venezuela founded the Group of Three (G-3). Their specific aims were to promote the economic integration of the three member countries and stimulate cooperation with Central America and the Caribbean (Serbin 1991b). This initiative gave rise to a series of top-level meetings among the presidents of the three countries, as well as numerous consultations at the ministerial level and among the respective technical commissions. Then, on 6 June 1994, in Cartagena de Indias, Colombia, the three countries signed a free trade agreement.

The foundation and consolidation of the G-3 is part of the development of subregional integration schemes in Latin America and the Caribbean that has taken place since the late 1980s. Among these are the reactivation of the Andean Group and CARICOM, and the creation of the G-3 and of MERCOSUR (CEPAL 1991a, 1992b; SELA 1991; Bouzas and Lustig 1992; Beckerman 1992; Serbin et al. 1992b). This increasing trend towards integration is a response to both exogenous and endogenous factors.

Among the exogenous factors are the end of the Cold War, accelerated globalization and interdependence of the world economy, the growing priority of economic and commercial issues in the global agenda, and the tendency towards the consolidation of three economic blocs: the EU, NAFTA, and ASEAN (Moneta 1992a; Quenan 1991). The endogenous factors include the obvious influence of the debt problem and its consequences, most notably the economic crisis that characterized the 1980s as the "lost decade" in Latin America and the Caribbean. That crisis culminated in the current policies of economic adjustment based on attempts to promote an export-led development strategy, so as to achieve more competitive integration within the world economy. Meanwhile the region is experiencing the social and political results of economic policies that carry significant social costs, while there is a parallel attempt to renew and consolidate democratic regimes.

These characteristics of the integration process now being promoted in the region are quite different from those that inspired Latin American and Caribbean integration initiatives in the 1960s and 1970s. Current integration strategies emphasize trade liberalization, the stimulation and diversification of nontraditional exports, and a more relevant role for the private sector in the context of an outward-looking process of development (CEPAL 1991a, 1992b; Rodriguez 1993).

Nevertheless, current attempts to stimulate regionalism in Latin America and the Caribbean are not merely responses to the imperatives of the new conditions imposed by the world economy. They differ substantially from similar processes in other parts of the world. First, especially in the case of the G-3, there is a previous history of political concertation and economic cooperation underlying the different initiatives, a history that must considered in order to gauge their prospects (Frohman 1990; Moneta 1992b; Hurrell 1992). Second, these initiatives respond not just to more global and contradictory tendencies of economic globalization and regionalism, but also to the recently established North American Free Trade Agreement between the United States, Canada, and Mexico. The Latin American and Caribbean initiatives reflected growing concern in the region about its eventual marginalization within the world economy, and were under way before the United States initiatives were significantly advanced (Weintraub 1991). Thus the G-3 agreement has distinctive features that reflect an attempt to graft a new economic dimension onto a previously successful experience of political concertation and regional cooperation, within the framework of particular regional problems generated by the new economic and geopolitical realities of the world order.

Political Concertation and Subregional Cooperation

The process of political concertation among the three countries has roots as far back as the mid-1970s, and must be understood as a response to the general hemispheric context and the increasing political instability of the Caribbean Basin. By then, the proliferation of military regimes in the continent had left Mexico, Colombia, and Venezuela as the only major Latin American countries firmly committed to maintaining civilian rule, and thus relatively isolated. At that time, dramatic increases in oil prices on the world market and favorable markets for other raw materials enabled the three to pursue a more active and autonomous foreign policy as "middle-regional powers" (Maira 1983; Grabendorf 1984).

Their search for allies led to growing cooperation between the three countries and to greater involvement in Caribbean Basin affairs, both in Central America and toward the recently independent states of the non-Hispanic Caribbean (Serbin 1991a). The concern for Third World problems encouraged South-South cooperation—expressed in such initiatives as the creation of the Latin American Economic System (SELA), which included Cuba; the incorporation of Mexico, Colombia, and Venezuela as donors to the Caribbean Development Bank (CDB); and the first initiatives to implement what became the San José Pact, by which Mexico and Venezuela offered smaller Caribbean countries preferential access to their oil (Serbin 1991b). Meanwhile, there was an evident increase in the diplomatic convergence between the three countries, and a growing awareness of the existence of common interests, especially with regard to regional problems (Serbin 1993a).

This convergence of political interests increased due to the Central American crisis in the late 1970s. The three countries all initially supported the Nassau Initiative, which would later culminate in the Caribbean Basin Initiative launched by President Reagan in 1983 (although the three Latin American countries and Canada did not participate in the CBI). The same year, Mexico, Colombia and Venezuela, together with Panama (which for the time being had developed closer relations with the three, particularly after they supported the Torrijos-Carter treaty in 1977), would launch the Contadora Group. Contadora was to play a crucial role in the Central American crisis: on the one hand, limiting the possibilities of direct United States intervention, and on the other, contributing decisively to the regional pacification process through Esquipulas II in 1986 (Díaz Callejas 1985; Cepeda and Pardo 1985; Rojas Aravena and Solís 1988).

Thus, despite different priorities traditionally sustained by their respective foreign policies, from the 1970s on the three succeeded in gradually consolidating an experience of joint diplomatic initiatives and of political concertation that was of fundamental importance for the stability and the geopolitical evolution of Central America and of the Caribbean Basin as a whole (Serbin 1991a, 1993a). The Contadora experience was also part of a general process of "re-learning" political concertation in Latin America, as Frohman points out, leading first to the creation of the Support Group to Contadora, then the Group of Eight, and finally the Rio Group (Frohman 1990). This process, despite its ups and downs, reaffirmed democratic values and the traditional Latin American foreign policy principles of nonintervention, self-determination, and the peaceful resolution of regional conflicts (ibid.).

Furthermore, the Contadora Group illustrated the potential for cooperation among the middle-regional powers of the Caribbean Basin (Grabendorf 1984). These powers cooperated as a result of their profound concerns regarding the stability of the region and the regional effects of East-West antagonism. For Mexico, the intervention of extraregional actors and the dimensions of the crisis underscored possible threats to its own national security and political stability, particularly in the Central American area (Bagley 1990; Jauberth et al. 1992). The same potential problems faced Colombia (Drekonja 1982; Pardo and Tokatlian 1988) and Venezuela (Josko 1992), though in varying degrees, according to their respective domestic situations and regional priorities. For Venezuela, the crisis between the United States and Cuba meant a real threat to the stability of the insular Caribbean, regarded as vitally important to its national interests (Serbin 1993b).

Cooperation among the Caribbean Basin countries thus became a key instrument for contributing to the region's political stability, not simply a means for increasing political leverage. This cooperation also reflected a common approach to the roots of the regional crisis that emphasized its social and domestic political dimensions, an approach that clearly differed from the eminently geostrategic focus of United States policy. The converging interests of the three countries, along with similar perceptions of the main causes for the crisis, eventually encouraged closer collaboration in the Caribbean Basin.

Cooperation and Regionalism in the Nineties

The above picture explains the contemporary importance attributed by the G-3 to cooperation with Central America and the Caribbean from the very outset. In the inaugural meeting of the Group, a high-level commission was appointed to deal exclusively with this aspect (Grupo de los Tres 1991). This emphasis on cooperation reflected the new geopolitical situation in 1989, which required a greater involvement of the three countries in regional affairs. As a consequence of the end of the Cold War, the gradual retreat and disengagement of extraregional powers has resulted in a geopolitical vacuum in the Caribbean Basin. Beyond the inertial effects of the confrontation with Cuba, the new security agenda of the major powers, particularly the United States, was no longer dominated by the aim of containing Cuban-Soviet influence. The new U.S. security priorities for the region in the early 1990s emphasized issues such as control of drug trafficking, migration flows to the north, and environmental threats. These problems are not necessarily as important to the regional powers, and their impact on the region differs from that of the Cold War confrontation (Serbin 1992a).

Given the traditional economic and political vulnerability of Caribbean Basin states, the region's middle powers have increased their interest in regional security and stability. The positions assumed by Mexico, Colombia, and Venezuela regarding Cuba's current domestic crisis illustrate this. An abrupt political change in Cuba would clearly threaten regional stability: Thus G-3 members have attempted to facilitate the reincorporation of Cuba into the Latin American and Caribbean community, as was clear when they invited Fidel Castro to the 1991 presidential meeting in Cozumel (Serbin 1993a). Both Venezuelan President Carlos Andrés Pérez, before his impeachment, and Colombian President Gaviria attempted unsuccessfully to develop a personal diplomacy with Fidel Castro, to mediate in re-establishing relations between Cuba and the United States. However, Venezuela's domestic political situation, the Torricelli Amendment, and the pressure of Cuban exiles on the Clinton administration hindered these attempts. Nevertheless, Colombia and Cuba have re-established diplomatic relations and their trade links are increasing. President Gaviria's personal efforts (notwithstanding some impasses regarding Cuban government relations with Colombian guerrillas groups), were oriented to consolidate this initiative by the Colombian government, and should eventually be followed up by subsequent administrations.

Concern for the Caribbean is also evident in steps the G-3 have taken towards trade liberalization and closer regional economic ties during recent years. They entered CARICOM as observers in 1990, and in the same year a draft agreement of free trade was signed by Mexico and the Central American countries. A similar initiative toward Central America was signed by Venezuela in June 1991; a nonreciprocal free trade agreement has been in force between Venezuela and the CARICOM states since January 1993, and Venezuela applied to become a full member of this organization in 1991. Colombia joined Venezuela in cooperative gestures toward Central America and the English-speaking Caribbean. A top-level meeting was held among G-3 presidents and their Central American counterparts (Caracas, February 1993), leading to the signing of a free trade agreement and pledges to advance towards the creation of a subregional free trade zone. October 1993 saw the Port of Spain summit between the CARICOM and Suriname heads of state and the G-3 presidents; and in July 1994, the accord creating an Association of Caribbean States was signed.

The negotiations leading to these agreements have inevitably confronted many difficult problems, and the process still faces important obstacles. For example, Costa Rica has been reluctant to sign a nonreciprocal trade agreement with Colombia and Venezuela of the type accepted by the other Central American countries. There are also difficulties in the way of a free trade agreement between Mexico, on the one hand, and Colombia and Venezuela, on the other (*El Diario de Caracas* 1993a, 27-29; *Economía Hoy* 1993a, 22-26; 1993b, 18-19).

Nevertheless, these problems have not prevented significant advances towards trade liberalization in the region during the past five years. The initiative to create an Association of Caribbean States including the Three, as recommended by the West Indian Commission (West Indian Commission 1992) and formally assumed during the Port of Spain CARICOM summit, consolidates this process and underscores the particular dynamics of regionalism in the Caribbean Basin.

The Group of Three and the Caribbean: An Assessment

Despite the apparent success of recent G-3 initiatives in the region and the optimism provoked by exercising greater influence in regional affairs, expectations of transforming the G-3 into a genuine free trade area or the nucleus of a profound process of regional integration may be exaggerated. We need to analyze more carefully the difficulties that remain.

The major obstacle to a transition toward effective economic integration among G-3 members is related to the asymmetries among their respective economies, especially their different paces of economic reform and adjustment to the demands of the international economic system. While preparing for the Caracas February 1993 meeting and during its deliberations, Colombia and Venezuela acknowledged these asymmetries, particularly those related to specific economic sectors, such as the automotive industry and petrochemicals, when implementing the free trade agreement and the corresponding schedule of tariff reductions. To answer problems posed by the larger size of the Mexican economy, they suggested an arrangement similar to that achieved by Mexico in negotiations with the United States and Canada within the NAFTA (*El Diario de Caracas* 1993a, 26; *El Universal* 1993, 2–1; *Economía Hoy* 1993a, 23). On the other hand, Mexico is concerned by Venezuela's (and to a lesser degree, Colombia's) support to different sectors, such as mining, steel, cement, aluminum and petrochemicals, through subsidies in energy and water (*El Financiero* 1993, 3A). Mexico is also particularly concerned that negotiations include such issues as services and the ownership of intellectual property rights.

At the same time, Venezuela and Colombia have advanced rapidly in their bilateral agreements on economic integration (Romero 1993). In contrast, Mexico conceives economic links among the three countries basically in terms of a free trade agreement without, in the short run, contemplating a more far-reaching integration. Further trade liberalization is conditioned by these different expectations, by the different paces of their respective adjustment programs, and the obvious difficulties in harmonizing macroeconomic policies. With regard to the latter, there are differences not only in the design of development strategies and subsequent foreign policy priorities, but in the rhythms with which they are implemented. They also have varying consequences for deregulation and tariff policies, industrial reconversion and diversification programs, and technological development strategies, which assume particular characteristics in each case.

These economic asymmetries are further reinforced by significant differences in attempts to reform and modernize the respective political systems, and have had different political and social impacts. In Mexico, President Salinas de Gortari's government had succeeded until 1993 in maintaining an atmosphere of political stability, despite the social costs implicit in the adjustment program and integration into NAFTA. An important spectrum of interest groups had mobilized in support of the reform and modernization measures, especially in the case of the private sector. However, the Chiapas crisis and the murder of the PRI's presidential candidate at the beginning of 1994 significantly jeopardized this process, notwithstanding the PRI's successful performance in the August presidential elections.

At the same time, violence associated with the drug cartels and the guerrilla groups has hindered President Gaviria's attempts to implement similar policies in Colombia. In Venezuela, the policies pursued by President Carlos Andrés Pérez were stymied by popular resistance and discontent within the armed forces, as evidenced in the *caracazo* (27 February 1989), two unsuccessful military coups in 1992, and impeachment of the president in April 1993 (Serbin et al. 1993). In Colombia, President Samper's administration may still follow the economic program promoted by the former government; but in Venezuela, President Caldera's response to social and political pressure during the first six months of his administration sent mixed signals regarding economic policy and trade liberalization.

Even in the bilateral negotiations between Colombia and Venezuela, which apart from their relevance for the G-3, are a key element in reactivating the Andean Pact (Rojas 1992), discussions were influenced by border problems continually brought to public attention by both countries' nationalist and military sectors (Muller Rojas 1992). These were reinforced by tension arising from the attempt by Venezuela's minister of foreign affairs to compete with Colombia's former president for the secretary-general appointment to the Organization of American States.

Nevertheless, in the long run, the prospects of advances of the G-3 are conditioned above all by their general hemispheric context and by their relationship with the United States and NAFTA. For most Latin American and Caribbean countries, economic relations with the United States—their main market and trading partner, main creditor and source of technology and capital—are decisive in defining the general parameters of their foreign policy, and even more so for any subregional project. NAFTA has become a basic point of reference and model for negotiating similar free trade agreements. Notwithstanding the early endogenous attempts to advance the subregional integration process in Latin America and the Caribbean, any subregional initiative must now consider the potential (or explicit) interest of its participants in joining the

North American scheme on relatively favorable terms. Other issues include the further evolution of NAFTA under the Clinton administration, and new environmental and labor conditions introduced in agreements with Mexico. The Caribbean basin countries are also closely following certain adhesion clauses that might widen the spectrum of future NAFTA participants beyond the hemispheric context, and the implementation of new free trade agreements with Latin American partners (Gill and Serbin 1993).

This situation affects the G-3 members in different ways. Mexico, already incorporated into NAFTA, sees the G-3 primarily as a political counterweight to its North American bloc association, and especially to the United States, with no particular economic or political threats to its main priorities. For Colombia and Venezuela, however, the association with Mexico raises hopes (not necessarily well founded) of simultaneously expanding their economic space and improving their bargaining position vis-a-vis NAFTA (Serbin 1993d).

For Mexico, regional strategic and economic concerns are oriented mainly towards Central America, a particularly sensitive area for Mexican economic and geopolitical interests in the framework of the region's pacification process. For Venezuela, the insular Caribbean is a crucial strategic area, whose stability could be undermined by changes in Cuba and by destabilization processes in the non-Hispanic Caribbean countries; it is also an increasingly important market for Venezuela's nontraditional exports. Colombia's main regional concerns are the economic potential of the Caribbean Basin market and the destabilizing links of drug traffickers and guerrillas.

Finally, all three members of G-3 have common concerns for the consolidation of democracy in the Caribbean Basin, but their approaches and emphases differ in terms of principles and positions. While Mexico still strongly adheres to the principles of nonintervention and self-determination, Venezuela has accepted more external pressures to promote and deepen democratization in the region, though somewhat less under Caldera's administration. Furthermore, during Carlos Andrés Pérez's administration, Venezuela advanced this approach in the OAS, particularly in the cases of Haiti and Suriname, to an extent not shared by Mexico.

These concerns and interests are matched by the growing disposition of the Central American and insular Caribbean countries to diversify and deepen their economic and political links with the G-3, vis-a-vis their eventual marginalization from NAFTA and their decreasing strategic relevance for extraregional actors, with significant impacts on the nonreciprocal agreements such as the CBI, Lomé, and CARIBCAN. Despite the distinctive priorities of Mexico, Venezuela and Colombia, the G-3 has significantly increased its members' influence in the Caribbean Basin. In the face of the gradual disengagement of external powers, the G-3 has transformed the three regional middle powers into a crucial point of reference for regional affairs. Indeed, the G-3, together with CARICOM and the Central American states, are the most active protagonists in the progressive articulation of a regional economic and political bloc.[1] They have succeeded despite political, linguistic, and cultural differences; despite the varying vulnerability and asymmetrical magnitudes of their respective economies; and despite domestic difficulties they are experiencing due to economic adjustment policies.

From this perspective, distinctive perceptions about the G-3's importance and its relations with NAFTA are associated with different foreign policies priorities on the subregional level and contrasting expectations concerning their respective economic and political performances. Notwithstanding the progress in political concertation and subregional cooperation evidenced by the Group of Three members, significant questions remain regarding its further evolution as a free trade agreement and an economic and geopolitical focus for regionalism in the Caribbean Basin. This is particularly true with regard to the role that the Group and its members can perform in the creation and consolidation of the Association of Caribbean States as a regional response to the changing international environment.

---

[1] Relations among these three groups of actors have not always been easy, especially for Central America and the CARICOM countries. A recent case of conflicting interests concerns banana exports to the EU. A meeting to promote closer links between the two groups of countries, initiated in February 1992 by President Callejas of Honduras and Prime Minister Manley from Jamaica, proved unsuccessful. On the other hand, along with collaboration there is also growing competition between the G-3 and CARICOM for leadership in the region, which will probably become increasingly evident through the Association of Caribbean States. Additionally, the traditional rift between the English-speaking Caribbean and Dominican Republic has led to a Dominican initiative to establish closer links with Central America.

Bibliography

Bagley, Bruce. 1990. "Los intereses de seguridad de México y de Estados Unidos en Centroamérica." In: *En busca de la seguridad perdida*, eds. Sergio Aguayo and Bruce Bagley. Mexico: Siglo XXI, 315-339.

Beckerman, M., ed. 1992. *Mercosur: oportunidad y desafío*. Buenos Aires: Legasa.

Bouzas, R., and Nora Lustig, eds. 1992. *Liberalización comercial e integración regional*. De NAFTA a MERCOSUR. Buenos Aires: FLACSO/Grupo Editor Latinoamericano.

CEPAL (Comisión Económica para América Latina). 1991a. La integración económica en los años 90: perspectivas y opciones. Doc. LC/R 1024, Santiago, Chile, 24 August.

———. 1991b. "Coordinación de políticas macroeconómicas en la integración latinoamericana: una necesidad o una utopía?" Doc. LC/R 1064, 23 October.

———. 1992a. "Los nuevos proyectos de integración en América Latina y el Caribe y la dinámica de la inversión," Doc. LC/R 1145, 20 May.

———. 1992b. "Convergencia de los esquemas de integración," Doc. LC/R 1192, 2 October.

Cepeda, Fernando y Rodrigo Pardo. 1985. *Contadora: desafío a la diplomacia regional*. Bogotá: Oveja Negra.

(El) Diario de Caracas. 1993a. 12 February, 27-29.

———. 1993b. 13 February, 27-29.

Díaz Callejas, Apolinar. 1985. *Contadora: desafío al imperio*. Bogotá: Oveja Negra.

Drekonja, Gerhard. 1983. *Retos de la política exterior Colombiana*. Bogotá: CERC.

Economía Hoy (Caracas). 1993a. 11 February, 22-26.

———. 1993b. 12 February, 18-19.

———. 1993c. 13 February, 28-29.

(El) Financiero (Mexico). 1993. 25 March, 3-A.

Frohman, Alicia. 1990. Puentes sobre la turbulencia. *La concertación política latinoamericana en los ochenta*. Santiago: FLACSO.

Gill, Henry and Andrés Serbin. 1993. "El Caribe de habla inglesa y la Iniciativa para las Américas." In *América Latina y la Iniciativa para las Américas*, ed. F. Rojas Aravena. Santiago: FLACSO.

Grabendorf, Wolf. 1984. "Las potencias regionales en la crisis centroamericana: una comparación de las políticas de México, Venezuela, Cuba y Colombia," In *Entre la autonomía y la subordinación*, eds. H. Muñoz and J.Tulchin. Buenos Aires: Grupo Editor Latinoamericano, 267-296.

Grupo de los Tres. 1991. "Coordinar las acciones de cooperación e integración." *Comercio Exterior* (Mexico) 1(41):125-126.

Hurrell, Andrew. 1992. "Latin America in the New World Order: A regional bloc for Latin America?" *International Affairs* (London) 68(1): 121-139.

Jauberth, Rodrigo et al. 1992. *The Difficult Triangle. Mexico, Central America and the United States*. Boulder, CO: Westview/PACCA.

Josko, Eva. 1992. "Cambio y continuidad en la política exterior de Venezuela: una revisión." In *Reforma y política exterior en Venezuela*, ed. C. Romero. Caracas: COPRE/INVESP/Nueva Sociedad: 41-76.

Maira, Luis. 1983. "Caribbean State Systems and Middle-Status Powers: The Cases of Mexico, Venezuela and Cuba." In *The Newer Caribbean. Decolonization, Democracy and Development*, eds. Henry Paget and Carl Stone, 177-204. Philadelphia: Institute for the Study of Human Issues.

Moneta, Carlos. 1992a. "El sistema internacional en la década del noventa." In *Reforma y política exterior de Venezuela*, ed. Carlos Romero, 19-40. Caracas: COPRE/INVESP/Nueva Sociedad.

———. 1992b. "Los espacios de intercambio económico regional." *Capítulos del SELA* (Caracas) 31 (enero-marzo): 10-23.

Muller Rojas, Alberto. 1992. Venezuela y la seguridad en el Caribe. Paper for workshop, La Nueva Agenda de Seguridad en el Caribe, INVESP, Caracas, July.

Pardo, Rodrigo and Juan Tokatlian. 1988. *Política exterior Colombiana*. Bogotá: Tercer Mundo/Uniandes.

Quenan, Carlos. 1991. Impacto de los procesos internacionales en la realidad latinoamericana: América Latina y la economía de los grandes bloques. Report for COPRE, Caracas, June.

Rodriguez, Miguel. 1993. Apertura económica e integración en América Latina: la experiencia Venezolana. Paper for workshop, La democracia bajo presión: política y mercado en Venezuela, INVESP/North-South Center, Caracas, November.

Rojas Aravena, F. and Luis Guillermo Solís. 1988. *Súbditos o aliados?* San José: Porvenir/FLACSO.

Rojas Aravena, F., ed. 1993. *América Latina y la Iniciativa para las Américas.* Santiago: FLACSO.

Rojas, Laura. 1992. "Aspectos económicos de la política exterior de Venezuela." In *Reforma y política exterior en Venezuela*, ed. C. Romero. Caracas: COPRE/INVESP/Nueva Sociedad.

Romero, Carlos, ed. 1992. *Reforma y política exterior en Venezuela.* Caracas: COPRE/INVESP/Nueva Sociedad.

———. 1993. "Venezuela y la dimensión económica del Grupo de los Tres." *Excelencia* (Caracas), March: 6.

SELA (Sistema Económico Latinoamericano). 1991. "Apertura comercial e integración regional en América Latina. Diagnóstico y escenarios alternativos." ED/17, July.

———. 1992. *La nueva etapa de la integración regional.* Mexico: SELA/Fondo de Cultura Económica.

Serbin, Andrés. 1990. *Caribbean Geopolitics: Toward Security Through Peace?* Boulder, CO: Lynne Rienner.

———. 1991a. "El Caribe: mitos, realidades y desafíos para el año 2000." In *El Caribe hacia el año 2000*, A. Serbin and Anthony Bryan, eds., 13-34. Caracas: Nueva Sociedad/INVESP.

———. 1991b. "The CARICOM States and the Group of Three: A New Partnership Between Latin America and the Non-Hispanic Caribbean?" *Journal of Interamerican Studies and World Affairs* (Miami) 33(2): 53-80.

———. 1992a. "Cooperación para la paz en el Caribe: utopías, realidades y obstáculos." In CLADDE-FLACSO: *Seguridad, paz y desarme. Propuestas de concertación pacífica en América Latina*, 183-196. Santiago: CLADDE-FLACSO.

———. 1992b. "Venezuela y el Grupo de los Tres en el marco de las transformaciones globales y hemisféricas." In *El Grupo de los Tres. Políticas de integración*, A. Serbin et al., 13-28. Bogotá: FESCOL.

———. 1993a. "Las transformaciones globales y hemisféricas y la proyección subregional del Grupo de los Tres." In *El Grupo de los Tres: Evaluación y prospectiva*, eds. A Serbin and C. Romero. Caracas: Nueva Sociedad/INVESP/FESCOL.

———. 1993b. Venezuela y el Caribe: un reto persistente? Paper for workshop, El Grupo de los Tres y la cooperación con la Cuenca del Caribe, Ministry of Foreign Affairs and FESCOL, Bogotá, January.

———. 1993c. Medidas de confianza mutua, paz y cooperación en el Caribe. Report for the project, Hemispheric Security in the Nineties, Woodrow Wilson Center/ FLACSO-Santiago.

———. 1993d. Venezuela, el gran viraje y las opciones regionales. Paper presented to the 34th International Studies Association (ISA) Conference, Acapulco, March.

Serbin, A., A. Stambouli, J. McCoy, and Bill Smith, eds.: *Venezuela: la democracia bajo presión.* Caracas: INVESP/North-South Center/Nueva Sociedad.

(El) Universal (Caracas). 1993. 12 February, sec. 2-1.

West Indian Commission. 1992. *Time for Action,* Barbados: WIC.

Weintraub, Sidney. 1991. "The New United States Economic Initiative Toward Latin America." *Journal of Interamerican Studies and World Affairs* (Miami) 33(1): 1-18.

Chapter 13

The European Union and the Caribbean: Challenges Ahead

Amos Tincani

In the short span of a decade, the European Union (EU) has changed considerably, and so have its relations with an array of developing countries of the South and the East.[1] New rules of the economic game have been established internationally, particularly by the Uruguay Round (UR) and NAFTA. While Caribbean countries have responded to these changes in varying degrees, their willingness and capacity to respond are somewhat mixed. The political economy of change remains a difficult issue in the Caribbean.

The Evolving European Architecture

Over the last ten years, the European Union embarked on a deepening and widening path that, while bumpy at times, advanced forward. Two steps deepening the alliance were establishment of the single European market and the European Union; two steps widening it were the creation of the European Economic Area and the inclusion of Austria, Finland and Sweden.[2]

The first step was the achievement of the single European market. Between 1985 and 1992, the EU embarked on establishing a barrier-free single market, based on four freedoms: the free movement of people, goods, services, and capital. The huge legislative program that achieved this replaced some three thousand diverse national laws with about three hundred common EU provisions. The introduction of weighted majority voting among member states to implement the single market program made this legislative effort possible.

---

[1] The Maastricht Treaty in 1993 replaced the term "European Community" with "European Union." The latter term is used here, even for the period prior to 1993.

[2] See in particular the European Commission publications, *From Single Market to European Union*, and *European Union*, published in 1992.

This is the beginning of a federalist structure, since no individual country in the Union, however big, can veto legislation on its own.

To suppress physical and administrative barriers to the free flow of goods, services, capital and people, the EU had to achieve regulatory convergence in all fields affecting such flows, by setting either a common rule, or a range within which national rules could be established. For instance, competition rules were harmonized, educational standards were set for skilled labor, and VAT rates were brought within a narrow range, as were technical standards for goods. Regulatory convergence was the underlying principle that ensured a level playing field, or common rules for all.

Freedom of movement among the twelve EU countries is not dissimilar today from freedom of movement within the United States, with one notable exception: we do not have a common currency.

The second step was creation of the European Union between 1991 and 1993, as we negotiated and ratified the Maastricht Treaty. The Union is built on three pillars: the European Community proper; the Common Foreign and Security Policy (CFSP), or intergovernmental cooperation in foreign policy, based on unanimity; and Home Affairs and Justice, which is akin to the CFSP. The EU treaty also contains provisions for an eventual economic and monetary union. The Maastricht negotiators, admitting that the treaty did not go far enough, foresaw a new intergovernmental negotiating conference in 1996.

As the twelve member countries were achieving a single European market, the EU negotiated its extension to European Free Trade Area (EFTA) countries. Following a negative referendum in December 1992, Switzerland withdrew, but on 1 January 1994 Austria, Finland, Iceland, Norway, and Sweden became members of the European Economic Area (EEA). They became de facto nonvoting members of the pre-Maastricht EU, with the four freedoms of the single market.

The EEA was not yet operational when the EU started negotiating with Austria, Finland, Norway, and Sweden for full membership. Negotiations concluded in the spring of 1994, and in a cliff-hanging referendum, Norway eventually voted against entry, but the others joined the EU in January 1995.

In summary, one could say that the European house grew four times over the past decade. Clearly there were setbacks—one applicant to the EEA and one to the EU were lost on the road, key controversial decisions were postponed, there is still potential conflict between deepening and widening—yet in a relatively short period the European house has changed considerably. While politically driven, these developments are based on sound economic considerations: Today the EU is more efficient and much better able to compete in the world's post-Uruguay Round (UR) markets.

EU Relations with Developing and Transforming Countries

Over the years, the EU has established a set of economic and trade relationships with developing countries of the South and the transforming economies of the East. These relationships can be grouped in three main categories (see Appendix): NAFTA-type reciprocal free trade arrangements, nonreciprocal contractual preferences, and nonreciprocal unilateral preferences. Of the three, reciprocal FTA schemes are clearly on the rise.[3]

The EU is pursuing agreements in various stages with thirteen middle-income countries that foresee reciprocal free trade as the final goal. Four of these agreements are with Mediterranean countries (Israel, Turkey, Malta, Cyprus) and nine are in Central Europe (Bulgaria, Czech Republic, Estonia, Hungary, Latvia, Lithuania, Poland, Romania, Slovakia). Negotiations on similar agreements are underway with several North African countries, and the beginning of a free trade agreement between the EU and MERCOSUR is on the political agenda.

As for nonreciprocal preferences, the EU extends contractual preferences to the African, Caribbean, and Pacific (ACP) countries that are party to the Lomé Convention, and to North African countries through bilateral Mediterranean Agreements. Developing countries in Asia and Latin America receive unilateral preferences through the EU General System of Preferences (GSP); these terms are improved for Andean and Central American countries, to acknowledge their role in the anti-drug fight.

While some of these arrangements have existed for several years, reciprocal free trade schemes have recently predominated, particularly with Central European countries. These countries represent a top priority in EU foreign policy; their eventual eligibility to join the EU has been recognized, and EU current efforts are focused on a pre-accession strategy.

Challenges Facing the Caribbean Today

Caribbean countries have been relatively open economies, vulnerable to shocks arising from changes in the external environment. Over the past twenty years, the Caribbean, like many other developing regions, faced several external challenges and opportunities. Some were unfavorable, such as oil shocks, the debt crisis, falling terms of trade, high interest rates, and natural disasters. Favorable opportunities included the commodity boom of the 1970s, nonreciprocal

---

[3] See "The European Community as a World Trade Partner," published in *European Economy* (52) 1993.

trade preferences from the EU for some twenty years, and preferential access and proximity to the large North American market.

The capacity and willingness of Caribbean countries to adapt to unfavorable external circumstances, or profit from favorable ones, has varied. In the past two decades, the Caribbean countries and the so-called Asian Tigers have differed not so much in resource endowments, but rather in their attitudes and reactions to similar external circumstances. In fact, the Caribbean has historical advantages over Asian developing countries in terms of preferential access and proximity to the major markets of North America and Europe. As I have said, the political economy of change remains a difficult issue in the Caribbean.[4]

At present, Caribbean economies face several challenges that must be constructively addressed, including the following:

- Erosion of preferential market access, due to NAFTA, the UR, and the globalization of goods, services, and capital markets
- Potential for investment diversion, more than trade diversion, due to NAFTA
- High cost of certain exports, such as sugar and bananas, that are nonviable without preferential access
- Reduction of aid flows, particularly from the United States
- Cuba's potential challenge as a regional power.

External challenges can be favorable or unfavorable, depending on the way the Caribbean plays them. For instance, the UR is the single most important worldwide job creation and growth scheme that our leaders have delivered. The Caribbean countries (and all UR signatories) ought to adapt their policies appropriately to transform these potential gains into actual exports. Open international trade is a positive-sum game in which each country can gain. Likewise, a NAFTA-type scheme with North America and Europe would be in the long-term interest of Caribbean countries, if the transition is handled appropriately and their economies are strengthened to withstand tougher competition.

Except for Cuba, Suriname, and Haiti, Caribbean economies are now at various points on a curve of adjustment and liberalization. Fortunately for them,

---

[4] Market preferences for Caribbean exports into the EU and U.S. markets, although they facilitated access, at the same time locked Caribbean countries into certain productions and prevented a dynamic use of comparative advantage. The extreme case of dependency on preferential arrangements has been the banana sector of the OECS countries, which clearly needs an adjustment strategy.

the issue is no more whether, but how to adjust and liberalize. There seems to be broad consensus on what the next steps should be:

- Strengthening the role of the state in its regulatory and supervisory role in order to avoid monopolies and rents, whether by labor or capital
- Accelerating the state's withdrawal from production, and strengthening an incentives framework for private sector development (both domestic and international) to compensate for the sharp decline in official financial flows[5]
- Increasing the efficiency of public expenditures in the social sector, to ensure human resource development and a competitive labor force, as well as a social safety policy that caters for the transition in adjustment
- Pursuing fundamental principals of macroeconomics.

A recurring question of Caribbean countries concerns size: Does the size of an economy or a country matter? Can a small country carve specialty niches in the global marketplace, or should it join regional schemes to protect itself? The issue of size should be put in the context of the starting point and the objectives pursued. For a country like Chile, where a healthy and fit economy has resulted from a successful policy of unilateral liberalization towards the rest of the world, regionalism brings no advantages. For the Caribbean economies, placed somewhere in the middle of the adjustment and liberalization curves, regional alliances could enable them to adjust and liberalize concurrently—a stepping-stone to wider liberalization of trade with North America and Europe. Indeed, regional adjustment and regional integration can be mutually supportive.[6]

Just as Europe has moved from a common to a single market, CARICOM could be the venue for regulatory convergence among its members, to allow for gradual and total liberalization of the movement of goods, services, labor, and capital within the Caribbean Community. Various techniques are possible, such as CARICOM legal instruments defining Community-wide normative ranges on labor, investment, intellectual property, environmental standards, competition rules, coordination of macroeconomic and fiscal policies, and so on. As the ranges narrow, liberalization would ensue. Once a single market is created, say in investments, then CARICOM could be empowered to negotiate investment treaties with third countries.

---

[5] According to a World Bank study for the June 1994 Consultative Group meeting on the Caribbean, official financial flows to the region had decreased in the preceding ten years from $1.5 billion to $200 million, while direct foreign investment had grown from $270 million to $660 million.

[6] This point was made by the European Commission at a meeting of the World Bank–led Special Program of Assistance to Africa, in October 1990. See Commission staff paper, *The Regional Dimension of Adjustment in Sub-Sahara Africa*.

These examples are more illustrative than normative. The bottom line is that the Caribbean has a preferential scheme with the EU, the Lomé Convention, that runs until the end of the century. It is hoped that the United States will soon grant its Interim Trade Program until the end of the century, as well. However, it is not too early for the Caribbean to prepare the analytical groundwork and launch a public debate concerning reciprocal relations with North America and Europe for the next century.

Regarding the specific EU–Caribbean relationship after the year 2000, several new avenues can be explored:

- Reframe the relationship outside the Lomé context. The Lomé Convention is mainly Africa-centered in its objectives and instruments, and is not necessarily suited for more sophisticated, liberalizing, middle-income economies. Restructuring the partnership with Europe as Caribbean or Caribbean Basin countries would allow for more tailor-made policies.
- Develop a new economic partnership in terms of the themes emerging from NAFTA and the various FTA schemes being negotiated by the EU with other middle-income countries: reciprocal liberalization of trade and investment with an asymmetrical timetable; a decreased reliance on aid, and a more focused use of it for the reform of the state.
- Work on a true region-to-region agreement, in which each side negotiates and implements as one. This would imply that CARICOM proceeds in its integration drive and negotiates as a unit: for instance, an EU–CARICOM trade and investment treaty.

The EU is gradually becoming a global player with interests in and policies for most areas of the world, the Caribbean included. For years to come, however, Eastern Europe and North Africa will be at the top of its foreign policy agenda. By the end of the decade, the EU will negotiate concurrently with Central European countries for their admission into the EU, and with its Lomé partners for a successor agreement. In my view, this illustrates why the Caribbean countries should launch a public debate in earnest on a new set of relations with Europe and submit proposals to their European partners—the sooner the better.

Conclusions

This paper submits that the international environment and the rules of economic interchange are undergoing rapid transformation. Whether these changes are positive or negative for individual countries and regions, depends much on how they react and adapt to them. Historically, the Caribbean's capacity and willingness to adapt has been somewhat mixed. The UR, NAFTA, and globalization of the world economy are the new challenges for the region. How the Caribbean countries play their cards over the next few years will define their place in the wider scheme of things.

Appendix: Economic and Trade Relationships of the European Union

European Economic Area (EEA)

After the United Kingdom and Denmark left the European Free Trade Area (EFTA) to join the European Community in 1973, free trade agreements were negotiated with the remaining EFTA countries. These agreements, fully implemented by 1984, eased the impact of Britain and Denmark adopting the Community's external tariff.

Formal negotiations for a European Economic Area (EEA) were launched in 1990, as the EU was approaching its post-1992 single European market. Since January 1994, the EEA has extended the single market to Austria, Sweden, Finland, Norway, and Iceland, enabling them to benefit from the EU's four fundamental freedoms. These EFTA members have in turn adopted relevant EU legislation, subject to specific adaptations and transitional periods. The EEA represents an economic area of some 380 million customers. Switzerland also negotiated the EEA, but a national referendum in December 1992 stopped the process. Recently it began negotiating a bilateral free trade agreement with the EU, and has indicated interest in the option of negotiating for entry into the EEA and the EU in the future. Liechtenstein joined the EEA in January 1995. For Austria, Finland, and Sweden, who joined the EU as of January 1995, the EEA was a preparatory prelude to full membership.

Reciprocal Free Trade Agreements

Israel. After several agreements signed with Israel since 1964, in 1975 the EU concluded a comprehensive trade agreement with Israel that called for the reciprocal abolition of trade barriers. As of 1977, the EU granted duty-free access to Israeli industrial exports, and reciprocal free trade in industrial goods was implemented in 1989. The EU also grants Israel tariff preferences for almost all agricultural exports. In light of the Middle Eastern peace process, in

February 1994 the EU presented Israel with a negotiating mandate for an Association Agreement, which would extend free trade into services, liberalize public procurement, include a more comprehensive and structured political dialogue, and a wide range of other cooperation provisions in such areas as research, energy, and the environment.

Eastern Europe. In order to promote economic and political reforms in Eastern Europe, the EU concluded general Trade and Cooperation Agreements with its Eastern neighbors. These were followed by Association Agreements, so far signed with the former Czechoslovakia, Hungary, and Poland in December 1991, with Romania in February 1993, and Bulgaria in March 1993.

Also called "Europe Agreements," these call for the gradual establishment of a free trade area. Trade concessions will be reciprocal, but implemented in an asymmetrical fashion, with the EU's concessions introduced sooner (the Copenhagen summit of 1993 led to an accelerated timetable for opening the EU market). While many EU trade barriers have already been abolished, remaining barriers on industrial goods will be abolished by the beginning of 1995, whereas the elimination of quantitative restrictions will be linked to the Uruguay Round. The EU steel sector will be liberalized by 1996, and EU textile tariff barriers will be removed by 1998. Poland will meet the same objectives in seven years, the other countries in ten. Further concessions for the trade of agricultural goods (in addition to the temporary EU concessions, GSP status and suspension of quantitative restrictions) will be applied on a reciprocal basis, as well. Specific provisions will determine trade in processed agricultural and fishery products.

In addition to the trade provisions, the Europe Agreements include provisions for competition rules; economic, financial, and institutional cooperation; as well as political dialogue. As mixed agreements (article 238), they require ratification by all member states and the assent of the European Parliament. The agreements with Poland and Hungary went into effect on 1 February 1994. For the other associated countries, the trade liberalizing provisions of the Europe Agreements are being implemented through Interim Agreements. Both the Europe and the Interim Agreements were renegotiated with the Czech Republic and Slovakia. Europe Agreements with the Baltic states were signed in 1995.

The European Council agreed in June 1993 that associated countries who wish to become members of the EU may do so once they are able to meet the required economic and political conditions. Both Hungary and Poland have formally applied for EU membership and negotiations are likely to begin in 1997 or 1998. In the meantime, the EU will help applicant countries prepare for EU membership. The December 1994 European Council in Essen agreed on a so-called pre-accession strategy for signatories of Europe Agreements, which focuses on a structured political dialogue and harmonization towards internal market standards.

Turkey. The EU concluded an Association Agreement with Turkey in 1963, which foresaw a customs union and eventual EU membership. Relations suffered after the military coup d'etat in 1980, but have been normalizing since 1986. As of January 1987, all industrial and most agricultural goods (some retain timetable and reference prices) have duty-free access to the EU, whereas Turkey's tariff reduction is a more gradual process.

In November 1993, momentum towards a customs union was stepped up, as the EU and Turkey agreed on a program to achieve a customs union by 1995. Included in the program are the free movement of industrial goods, preferential access for farm products, trade-related services, intellectual property rights, and social and financial aid.

Morocco and Tunisia. Limited Association Agreements were signed with these two countries in 1969, giving practically all their industrial exports duty-free access, while giving limited tariff privileges to a few of their agricultural exports. The EU signed a Cooperation Agreement with Tunisia in 1976, providing for trade and labor, economic, financial, and technical cooperation. Trade relations were further strengthened with a protocol to the Cooperation Agreement (CAP) in 1987. The EU grants all Tunisian industrial exports and all non-CAP agricultural exports free access to its markets, whereas products covered by the CAP receive some privileges. Accords for a wider association, financial aid, and fisheries were signed with Morocco in 1988. The follow-up agreements with both countries were signed in order to allay the impact of Spain and Portugal entering the EU in 1986. The EU has negotiated reciprocal free trade agreements with both countries that aim at the gradual creation of a free trade area, and include provisions for political dialogue and economic and financial cooperation.

Nonreciprocal Contractual Concessions

ACP Countries. The EU grants its most generous preferences (as of Lomé IV) to sixty-nine African, Caribbean, and Pacific countries. These nonreciprocal preferences include virtually duty- and quota-free entry of industrial goods and agricultural goods, although several of the latter are subject to quantitative limits or calendar restrictions. There are also a number of commodity protocols, the most important of which is the Sugar Protocol (sugar is a CAP-competing product), which enables the ACP countries to export guaranteed amounts of cane sugar at the CAP equivalent price. The Lomé Convention also provides for EU financial support in order to stabilize ACP export earnings, as well as for financial and technical assistance.

The Mediterranean Countries. The EU has numerous economic and commercial agreements with the countries of southern Europe and the southern and eastern Mediterranean. While trade preferences for agricultural products are less than those extended to the ACP states, most industrial goods have duty-free access. The December 1994 European Council in Essen agreed that a future Euro-Mediterranean partnership as proposed by the European Commission, building upon the EU's existing global Mediterranean policy, should be pursued. Envisaged for such a partnership is a Euro-Mediterranean free trade area.

Most-Favored-Nation Status

The EU follows the GATT principle of MFN treatment, which ensures that imports from third countries be afforded equal treatment. This applies to the non-European OECD countries as well as the countries of the former Soviet Union.

Unilateral GSP Concessions

Under the Generalized System of Preferences, the EU grants duty-free access for all processed and semi-processed industrial goods subject to fixed amounts, or flexible ceilings for more sensitive products, as well as reduced preferential duties for some agricultural products subject to a safeguard clause, and quantitative limitations for five items. The GSP is granted on a yearly basis within a ten-year scheme, which is presently being revised. Since the ACP and the Mediterranean countries enjoy greater preferences than GSP recipients, the EU's GSP scheme has mostly benefitted Asian and Latin American countries. As of 1990, the Andean countries (Bolivia, Colombia, Ecuador, and Peru) enjoy an improved GSP, an exceptional and temporary preferential regime, which grants them duty-free access for all industrial goods (with no quantitative limitations) and for a much larger number of agricultural goods. This exceptional GSP regime was extended to Central American countries (Costa Rica, El Salvador, Guatemala, Honduras, Nicaragua, and Panama) in 1992 for a period of three years.

Chapter 14

The United States, the Caribbean Basin, and the Post–Cold War International Order

Alan K. Henrikson

When five leaders from the Commonwealth Caribbean visited the United States in 1993, President Clinton reassured them that the end of the Cold War "altered the nature, but not the depth of our interest in the Caribbean." American concern for the region, he explained, is firmly rooted in geographic proximity and in the resultant flows of people, commodities, and culture. Indeed, the specific issues he mentioned—control of drug trafficking, protection of economic interests, preservation of fragile ecosystems—had little to do with previous East-West conflict. "U.S.-Caribbean relations demonstrate the absolute inseparability of foreign and domestic issues," stated President Clinton, adding: "More than ever before, our nation is a Caribbean nation" (Clinton 1993).[1] This essay explores the meaning of that proposition.

In the post-Cold War world, the United States may be able to address the problems of the Caribbean region on their own terms—directly, and with practical intent, rather than with ulterior geopolitical or ideological purposes in mind. Such a development is not certain, however.

Some argue that a new geopolitics is now forming, one that emphasizes "the defense of democracy and markets" and possibly protective action to safeguard the physical environment (Talbott 1994a, emphasis added). This could increase the likelihood of U.S. political and military intervention in the Caribbean area, though probably in collaboration with other countries. Some analysts stress the need for "collective responses" (Kaysen et al. 1994; Downes 1994; Bloomfield and Treverton 1990). Such responses might include, for ex-

---

[1] The five visiting leaders were President Cheddi Jagan of Guyana, Prime Minister Erskine Sandiford of Barbados, Prime Minister Patrick Manning of Trinidad and Tobago, Prime Minister P. J. Patterson of Jamaica, and Prime Minister Hubert Ingraham of the Bahamas.

ample, the UN Security Council–authorized multinational force, including personnel from Caribbean Community (CARICOM) countries and other regions, that restored Haitian president Jean-Bertrand Aristide to office in October 1994.[2]

The range of possible cooperative relationships between the United States and countries of the Caribbean—by this we mean the whole Caribbean area, including Central America and the northern coast of South America as well as the West Indian islands—is today wider than ever before. Joint action for economic development, for environmental preservation, and for maintaining law and order can be contemplated. The area is no longer the cockpit of superpower rivalry (de Madariaga 1962; Blasier 1983; Henrikson 1986).[3] Instead of being the focus of a bipolarized international structure, a tense area of confrontation with the American eagle and Russian bear glaring at each other "eyeball to eyeball" as during the 1962 Cuban missile crisis (Rusk 1990, 237), the Caribbean of the post–Cold War era could, conceivably, become an exemplary sea of peace, a model for the rest of the hemisphere and indeed for the world.

In such an optimistic view, the New World as a whole might actually set the global pattern. "The Americas are and will be the bridge between Europe and Asia and between the North and South of our planet," declares a former president of Costa Rica, Rafael Angel Calderón Fournier. "The Americas will be a great trade area involved in dialogue and interchange with the other continents, a macroarea of development open to all the citizens of the world." In short: "The next century will be the Century of the Americas" (Calderón Fournier 1994). Admittedly grandiloquent, and probably unrealistic, this visionary expression—inspired by the Summit of the Americas meeting held in Miami in December 1994—is not wholly without political logic or some basis in geoeconomic fact. As was frequently noted during the Miami summit, to be discussed further below, the American leaders' principal project—a liberal trading order extending throughout the Western Hemisphere—would be unmatched

---

[2] After meeting in August 1994 to discuss multilateral action toward Haiti, four of the CARICOM nations that have armed forces—Jamaica, Trinidad and Tobago, Barbados, and Belize—agreed to contribute a token number of 266 troops to an American-led invasion force of 10,000. "What was very significant," observed Strobe Talbott, then Acting U.S. Secretary of State, "was that the CARICOM countries committed themselves as a group to support [UN Security Council] Resolution 940 and, very specifically, to the 'all necessary means' provision" (Talbott 1994b). The Caribbean troops were not to be in the invasion vanguard but were, rather, to help monitor police activities (Schmitt 1994). This "collective response" did not extend throughout the entire Organization of American States (OAS), some of whose members were critical of the U.S.-led operation in Haiti. A hemispheric will to intervene in more collective fashion does exist, but consensus within the OAS and with other organizations is often difficult to achieve. There remains a need, widely recognized if not welcomed, for decisive leadership and action by one country, most likely the United States.

[3] The origins of the conflict of great powers in the Caribbean is a subject magisterially treated by Max Savelle (1967).

in physical scope as well as unprecedented in history. "When our work is done," as President Clinton said at Miami, "the free trade area of the Americas will stretch from Alaska to Argentina. In less than a decade, if current trends continue, this hemisphere will be the world's largest market" (Brooke 1994c).

What will be the place of the Caribbean countries, and of U.S.-Caribbean relations, in such a scheme? The answer may lie in the organization of the Caribbean itself, with the major complicating factor of Cuba, and the further complication that the United States is increasingly a Caribbean nation. As yet, however, the U.S. government is remaining politically aloof from the Caribbean countries. Newly grouped in an Association of Caribbean States (ACS), founded at Cartagena, Colombia on 24 July 1994, the participating 25 sovereign members and 12 non-sovereign members of the Caribbean world[4] have a promising "framework" for closer economic, political, and other kinds of cooperation among themselves. Taken together, as it has been pointed out, the ACS countries constitute potentially "the world's fourth largest regional grouping"—after the European Union (EU), the North American Free Trade Agreement (NAFTA), and the Association of Southeast Asian Nations (ASEAN) markets.[5]

Whether the new ACS formation will consolidate further, taking advantage of the Caribbean area's full measure and mass, is open to serious question, if only because it includes the nonmarket, communist-led Cuba. The ACS will probably need to institutionalize further to unite the region and to become an effective interlocutor with the United States or with other regional entities. Without a strong corporate identity to bind its very different individual members, the ACS ensemble of nations cannot be dealt with by other partners in a unified, consistent way. The problem is circular. The U.S. government, for instance, needs a single address to send mail to—an established ACS headquarters.[6] As one specialist on Caribbean affairs, Anthony Bryan, frankly acknowledges, "The political and economic diversity of the Caribbean does not now provide the United States with any possibility of devising a single comprehensive foreign policy toward the region."

---

[4] The Republic of Cuba (in the person of Fidel Castro) was present, and the Commonwealth of Puerto Rico notably absent.

[5] The size of the ACS market would be approximately 200 million people, with a combined Gross Domestic Product of $500 billion and with total exports of $80 billion and imports of $100 billion (Bryan 1994, 41). In actuality, the ACS probably would be the fifth largest grouping, coming after the Southern Cone Common Market (MERCOSUR)—Argentina, Uruguay, Paraguay, and Brazil, being joined by Chile and Bolivia and probably other South American countries through free-trade treaties.

[6] Three countries—the Dominican Republic, Trinidad and Tobago, and Venezuela—originally contended for the regional headquarters, Belize being ruled out because of infrastructural weaknesses, and Jamaica seen as having its hands full as the site of the International Seabed Authority. The CARICOM members generally favored Trinidad.

The United States, for its part, probably also will need to achieve greater internal coherence to plan a well-concerted U.S. policy regarding the larger Caribbean zone. The potential is there, and there are also "agendas of opportunity," as Bryan points out. The "most immediate" opportunity for U.S.-Caribbean cooperation is "in the areas of trade and development, where the regional objectives of the Caribbean converge with the domestic concerns of the United States" (Bryan 1994, 41).

Despite the long-term and growing importance of the domestic sources of U.S. government policy toward the Caribbean, the region has repeatedly been viewed by U.S. leaders as a strategic area, or danger zone, in which foreign interests of the United States should, if the test comes, predominate. Especially after the Panama Canal was completed in 1914, international events in that region have been able to affect the whole Atlantic-Pacific equilibrium, and thereby the world political balance. "In short," as one historian recently epitomized past U.S.-Caribbean strategic relations, "the nation that controls the Caribbean controls the United States" (R. F. Smith 1994, xiv). Conversely, by dominating the Caribbean, the United States could influence the world.

The Caribbean exposure of North America opens out onto global issues. Three critical junctures will illustrate the point. The 1898 Spanish-American War, a watershed in the history of the United States in the Caribbean, did not result merely from movements of opinion inside America regarding dramatic events on the island of Cuba, but also from imaginative calculations and projections of "world power" (May 1961). The 1962 Cuban missile crisis, though locally centered and involving American governmental decisionmaking structures (Allison 1971), was fundamentally a problem of regional and global security, with the nuclear balance of the world palpably at stake. Cuban-American issues, including that of the compensation owed by the Castro regime because of U.S. business property seized, were a distinctly secondary concern.

Even the U.S. military landing in Grenada in October 1983, though launched by the Reagan administration to rescue American medical students and to preclude another Iran hostage crisis, had a higher-level international political and strategic rationale—even a relation to Star Wars, or the Strategic Defense Initiative (SDI). Officials in Washington had been concerned about the large Cuban-built airfield at Point Salines in Grenada which, they surmised, could be used by the Soviet Union and Cuba for reconnaissance flights, secret weapons deliveries, and relaying troops to Angola. President Reagan, in his 23 March 1983 SDI speech, showed an aerial photograph of the mysterious 10,000-foot runway at Point Salines to demonstrate the kind of strategic penetration of the American security sphere that he was up against (Reagan 1983). Furthermore, the U.S. invasion of Grenada on 24 October was also seen to be a warning to the Sandinista regime in Nicaragua and even to distant Syria, suspected of having had a hand in the bombing of the U.S. Marine barracks in

Beirut the day before. Even though not "an East-West confrontation," the Grenada move was, as former Secretary of State George Shultz has emphasized, "a shot heard round the world" (Shultz 1993, ch. 20; McNeil 1988, 172–176).

U.S. interests in dealing with the states of the Caribbean region, therefore, have been and probably will continue to be extrinsically linked, a matter of global politics. Yet President Clinton is surely right to note that the end of the Cold War has "altered the nature" of the U.S.-Caribbean relationship. Exactly how and to what extent, of course, remain questions. Nonetheless, it is clear that the two aspects of the two-level game, domestic and foreign, of U.S.-Caribbean transactions now can be brought closer together, even if not easily integrated.[7] The particular problems President Clinton cited—eradicating the drug traffic, protecting economic interests, and preserving the neighborhood's environment, not to mention fostering the tourist trade or coping with refugee problems—are indeed almost inseparably both internal and external to the United States. The domestic and foreign sides of these policy questions are like Siamese twins, conjoined even if not necessarily congenial.

Thus the fact that the United States increasingly is a Caribbean nation will more and more determine the U.S.-Caribbean relationship, on every scale of conflict, competition, or cooperation. The condition and outlook of the Caribbean states themselves will be profoundly affected, perhaps making them less able or willing to unite in dealing with the United States. And it may also influence in a negative way the disposition of the United States to address the countries of the still-loosely formed ACS group as a whole.

The U.S.-Caribbean Relationship: Continental, Global, or Regional?

What basic shape might the U.S.-Caribbean relationship take? There seem to be three possibilities. One is for the United States to handle Caribbean issues, in effect, as an extension of the North American, or continental, management system—through incorporation of all or nearly all the Caribbean countries into NAFTA, for example. This process and its outcome might be termed "continentalization."[8] The second, opposite, schematization would be to assume that the economies and political systems of Caribbean countries would be assimilated to wider international norms and multilateral procedures. These would include both the disciplines of the world marketplace and the universal-

---

[7] For a theoretical exposition of the "two-level game" of the management of international relations, focusing on economic policy, see Putnam (1988).

[8] To date, mainly Canadians have discerned and critically analyzed the continentalizing effects of U.S. policy and behavior. For the recent historiography, see Stuart (1994).

izing rules of the General Agreement on Tariffs and Trade, now more fully institutionalized as the World Trade Organization (WTO). This may be referred to as "globalization."

Third is a theoretical possibility that is the most desirable for most ACS members. That would be for the Caribbean islands, Central America, and northern South America to develop a somewhat autonomous regional integration system. While perhaps not optimal in operational efficiency or empirical results, such an organized Caribbean entity might shield them from the overweening power of the United States (continentalization) and from the tyranny of intercontinental and planetary forces (globalization). Being small or middle-sized countries, they are especially susceptible to the possible damage wrought by the shifting winds of U.S. policymaking, the turbulent dynamics of the world economy, and an increasingly disorderly post–Cold War political system. The internal Caribbean solution—the self-conscious concerting of outlooks of the governments of the area, and of some joint action in the realm of planning and external diplomatic representations—will here be termed, simply, "regionalization" or, more precisely, "Caribbeanization."

Caribbean regional cooperation, tempered by the idea of open regionalism, is an agenda that can now be presented by the Caribbean countries to the world (Dookeran 1994). An intermediate, somewhat indeterminate program, it would be a cross between Caribbean developmentalism, aimed at internal integration, and economic liberalism, aimed at wider transactions—to be a zone "open to all the citizens of the world" (Calderón Fournier 1994). What open regionalism essentially means, in perhaps the most straightforward definition, is "economic integration behind low import barriers" (Weintraub 1994, 31–32).[9] The term further implies that participation in one bilateral or regional trading arrangement does not preclude participation in others. On whatever scale open regionalism is pursued by the Caribbean countries—i.e., only within the CARICOM Common Market, among the participants of the wider ACS, in conjunction with the continents of North America or South America, or inclusively throughout all the whole hemisphere—the dilemma they face is much the same: too much openness, leading to too many outside relationships, could destroy the inner solidity needed for tight decisionmaking and bargaining with others. Yet, without such outside relationships, the Caribbean states might not secure the wherewithal to survive as a regional entity.

Regionalization, along with continentalization and globalization, as notional possibilities and, to some degree, actual policy options for all countries

---

[9] Weintraub refers to the 1994 United Nations Economic Commission for Latin America and the Caribbean (ECLAC) document, *Open Regionalism in Latin America and the Caribbean II* (LC/G.1801, SES.25/4, Santiago, Chile).

of the widest Caribbean zone (marginally including the United States itself), will be subthemes present in the following sections. The central question posed, to reiterate, is that of achieving Caribbean unity and of whether the United States, insofar as it is a Caribbean nation, can in some way harmoniously combine with a Caribbean regional entity. The broader, more speculative issue, raised by former President Calderón, is whether North American/Caribbean–Central American/South American cooperation could make the whole Western Hemisphere an exemplar of a "new world order" in international relations.

In attempting to predict the outcome of the interplay of continentalism, globalism, and regionalism with regard to the Caribbean area, one needs some grounding in the Caribbean international-political structure, which has been rapidly changing, as the unprecedented formation of the ACS attests. Also needed is a basic awareness of the changing involvement of the U.S. government in the region, including recent adjustments in policies and programs. Finally, current trends and tendencies in the international political system that may hold particular relevance for Caribbean affairs and for the U.S.-Caribbean relationship should be noted. These three factors—Caribbean polity, U.S. policy, and world politics, as they may summarily be called—will be discussed below in sequence.

Caribbean Polity:
From Subregional Federation to Regional Association

The Caribbean is both the Western Hemisphere's oldest and newest region, the first to be encountered by Columbus and his men (Judge and Stanfield 1986), and the last region to be shaped politically, by the founders of the new Association of Caribbean States. To some extent, the recent self-defining of the Caribbean as the ACS is a byproduct or function of the regionalization of other parts of the Western Hemisphere, as in the NAFTA and MERCOSUR formations. The free trade agreement negotiated between the United States and Canada in 1988 began a process, extended to Mexico in 1992, of rediscovering North America, making it a relevant unit of policy (Henrikson 1993). Some U.S. strategists have even imagined the North American territory to include the Caribbean, conceived of as the "fourth frontier" or southern flank of the United States. The drawing together of the elements of South America too, via trade pacts and other relationships (Brooke 1995), has made the Caribbean seem almost residual, squeezed by the massive northern and southern parts, or "quarter-spheres," of the Western Hemisphere.

There is, of course, a basis for a positive conception of the Caribbean. This is, however, largely "a rationale to be discovered" (Casimir 1992, 7). The main premise for any definite notion of a Caribbean regional identity must be, of course, its geography—the mental map as well as the physical map (Henrikson 1991). "I sang our wide country, the Caribbean Sea / who hated shoes, whose soles were cracked as a stone, / who was gentle with ropes, who had one suit alone," as the St. Lucian poet-dramatist Derek Walcott conjures the elements of the sun-filled Caribbean in the mind's eye (Walcott 1990, 320). The Caribbean sea-territory, though widely dispersed between its oceanic extremities, does form a natural unity. The Gulf of Mexico and Caribbean Sea together encompass a navigable area of 2,156,500 square kilometers: a "continent of islands" (Kurlansky 1992). At the eastern Atlantic boundaries lie the Greater and Lesser Antilles. Though separate, these are in many cases intimately interconnected. Like the vertebrae of a "fragmented" nation, they stretch in "an inclined backbone from the Florida peninsula to the slanted northern coastline of South America" (Knight 1978, 3). From Macqueripe beach near Port of Spain, Trinidad one can see the Venezuelan coast a dozen miles away. Swimmers can "nudge with their toes" the new cable that links the telephone systems of Trinidad with those of Venezuela and Brazil and carries signals northward to the United States (Never the twain shall speak 1994). Along the spine of Central America on the western, or Pacific, side of the wide Caribbean expanse, too, the proximity of states is a factor, making many of them, even though they may be politically opposed at times, feel that they almost belong to "one country." Actual physical contiguity in Central America makes it possible, for example, to establish peace parks, the first such demilitarized transnational zone already having been set up on the border between Costa Rica and Panama (Child 1992, 114).[10]

The sense of Caribbeanness, of course, also has a cultural basis. The very diversity of the Caribbean–Central American region—indigenous, European, African, North and South American, South and East Asian—makes it, in one characterization, a "cauldron of cultures" (R. F. Smith 1994, ch. 5). Its ethos is a mixture of parochialism and cosmopolitanism. "There is a tendency to identify only with one's own small island," recognizes an American reporter familiar with the area, Mark Kurlansky. Yet there is a yearning to feel a part of something larger, to be able to say, "I am a Caribbean." This impulse transcends linguistic, racial, and class divisions, as well as geographical and historical ones. Haiti, in particular, "tugs at those emotional strings," Kurlansky notes. "Haitians, as the poorest, are the lowest-status Caribbeans. But it is also remembered that they were the first and they have paid for that. They are the conscience of the Caribbean." To have stood up for Haitians, he notes, is to have

---

[10] Other peace parks are planned for border areas between Belize and Guatemala, Mexico and Guatemala, and Costa Rica and Nicaragua.

earned one's Caribbean credentials (Kurlansky 1992, 285). One can see this motive demonstrated, for example, in the current engagement of CARICOM countries in the democratization and redevelopment of Haiti.

There is also a political tradition upon which a wider Caribbean unity and the future ACS can be based. Both Central America (after 1823 for a time, and again briefly in 1921) and the West Indies, particularly from 1958 to 1962, have experienced federation. The Central American states, following the turmoil of the 1980s, are today drawing on their common past and working together more, if not within a single constitutional form. The Central American Common Market (1960) is being revived, as is the subregional habit of domestic and diplomatic concertación (Lenter 1993, 200; Torres Rivas 1993). The Caribbean states, having for the most part achieved political independence only in the late twentieth century, are striving for nineteenth-century nationhood and a twenty-first century trade bloc at the same time. Their sole experiment in formal political unification, the West Indies Federation (1958–1962), broke up when Jamaica, the Federation's largest member, opted for outright independence and the next largest, Trinidad and Tobago, followed suit. "Federation has been argued over in the English Caribbean like political status in Puerto Rico," notes Kurlansky (1992, 278). "In Barbados, a popular expression about people not getting along was, 'Oh, they fight like a federation.'" The Caribbean ideal of achieving strength and prosperity through unity endures, however. The West Indies Federation failed, it has been ironically explained by the Guyanan statesman Sir Shridath Ramphal, "partly because of the strenuous efforts of a generation of committed West Indian politicians to secure and strengthen it as the focus of West Indian aspiration" (quoted in Burrowes 1984, 226).

Caribbean-style governance and politics, whether conducted in the Westminster manner of parliamentary debate, Spanish disputation, or French discourse, is a polemical feast. The sharpness and spiciness, as well as the undeniable demagogic impact, of the oratory of prototypic Caribbean and Central American leaders—Eric Williams, Michael Manley, Omar Torrijos, Daniel Ortega, Fidel Castro, Jean-Bertrand Aristide—can be a devastating force. This can be buffered by the quasi-fraternal character of Caribbean politics, particularly in the West Indian subregional system. Considerable allowances were made by the other West Indian governments, for example, for the People's Republic of Grenada (PRG) under "errant brother" Maurice Bishop. The Caribbean sociologist Anthony Maingot calls this tolerance "a very important characteristic of politics in archipelagic areas." Despite the absence of specific reciprocal ties, "processes of interaction (no matter at what level or type) tend to create norms and mutual obligations"—a "diffuse reciprocity," he calls it, which exists above and beneath relationships based on state-to-state treaties or other rational-legal bonds. Such mutuality of regard, and tolerance for youthful rebellion and for ideological (if not ethical) waywardness, has given Caribbean politics a certain predictability (Maingot 1989, 240–245).

The external liaisons of Caribbean countries also stabilize and politically define the region. Because they derive from Spanish, French, British, Dutch, Danish, Swedish, African, Asian, and U.S. sources, the numerous Caribbean states are grouped internationally in many different ways. While these ties can cut against each other, they also form a network, a veritable tapestry of international relationships. Besides belonging to the United Nations and the Organization of American States, the governments of the region have dealt with each another and the outside world through the Commonwealth of Nations, *la Francophonie*, the Ibero-American Summit, the Africa-Caribbean-Pacific (ACP) programs of the European Union, and, in a somewhat more politicized way, through the Non-Aligned Movement and the Socialist International. The countries of the English-speaking Caribbean have sometimes segregated themselves, as, for example, during the 1982 Falklands/Malvinas conflict between the United Kingdom and Argentina, when they supported the British position (as did the United States). That crisis caused a "widening of the gap between the two areas of the OAS: Latin America and the Caribbean" as the Argentine secretary general of the OAS at that time, Alejandro Orfila, has said (Orfila 1986, 142).

The structure of Caribbean relations with external organizations and powers, it must be admitted, has been marked by a certain dependency, an infra-hierarchical reliance if not actual subordination. A large part of the difficulty, of course, is the sheer disparity in size—this is now generally termed the "asymmetry" of the parties. Whether it be the Caribbean ACP countries vis-a-vis the European Union, Puerto Rico vis-a-vis the United States, or Cuba vis-a-vis the Soviet Union/Russian Federation, the gap in the magnitude and complexity of state structures is enormous. The negotiating capacities of the small and large parties are also disparate. For the Caribbean states, the only answer would seem to be greater integration: association or concertación might not suffice. To be taken seriously as a single entity, the larger Caribbean community simply needs to take on weight. It needs solidity, and this can only be achieved through unity, probably of a formal kind. The 1994 Association of Caribbean States makes such further consolidation possible, though certainly not inevitable. The "new regional architecture" that the ACS theoretically establishes, as Anthony Bryan observes hopefully, "could eliminate the historical divisions existing within the wider Caribbean and provide a framework for closer economic, political and functional cooperation" (Bryan 1994, 41).

U.S. Policy: From the Caribbean Basin Initiative to a Free Trade Area of the Americas

To consider recent U.S. policy regarding the Caribbean, we will start with a proposal made in November 1979 by former California Governor Ronald Reagan during his presidential campaign. Reagan proposed a North American accord, a three-way understanding that would foster a "developing closeness among Canada, Mexico, and the United States." Though simply defined, his concept was the germ of the U.S.-Canada Free Trade Agreement a decade later, followed by the North American Free Trade Agreement that included Mexico (Henrikson 1993).

An offshoot of Reagan's North American idea was the Caribbean Basin Initiative (CBI), which he presented to the Organization of American States in February 1982. The Republicans' thinking along Caribbean lines had been prompted a year earlier by Jamaica's new prime minister, Edward Seaga, the first head of state invited to visit Washington in the Reagan period.[11] The president, recalling for his OAS audience his earlier expressed ambition to bring about "an accord with our two neighbors here on the North American Continent," reported with satisfaction that, in subsequent meetings with Canadian Prime Minister Pierre Elliott Trudeau and Mexican President José López Portillo, he had "established a relationship better than any our three countries have ever known before." He then proceeded to extend his circle of friendship southward. "Today I would like to talk about our other neighbors—neighbors by the sea—some two dozen countries of the Caribbean and Central America." These countries, he said, are "not unfamiliar names from some isolated corner of the world far from home." El Salvador, for example, "is nearer to Texas than Texas is to Massachusetts." The Caribbean region as a whole is "a vital strategic and commercial artery for the United States," he emphasized. "Nearly half of our trade, two-thirds of our imported oil, and over half of our imported strategic minerals pass through the Panama Canal or the Gulf of Mexico. Make no mistake: The well-being and security of our neighbors in this region are in our own vital interest" (Reagan 1982).

A remarkable feature of the CBI project, though not its express purpose, was the unprecedented joining of the Central American isthmus—the main focus owing to the current civil strife and Cuban and Soviet meddling there—

---

[11] Seaga, a businessman and political moderate, was considered, in the words of Secretary of State Alexander Haig, "a prime candidate for a creative aid program" (Haig 1984, 91). The Canadian government, under the Progressive Conservative leader Brian Mulroney, apparently had the same view. The Canadian and Commonwealth Caribbean counterpart of the CBI, called CARIBCAN, originated in a proposal made by Seaga to Mulroney, when the latter visited Jamaica in February 1985 (Basdeo 1993, 65).

and the Caribbean islands within a single span of policy. The main elements of the Caribbean Basin Initiative itself were economic aid, preferential trade access, and tax incentives to encourage U.S. business to invest in plants in the region—as in Puerto Rico, the implicit model (Bloomfield 1985). The CBI did not treat all aspects of the development problem and did not cover the entire Caribbean region (it excluded Cuba and highlighted troubled El Salvador, whose only shores are on the Pacific). Only the small countries were included. Somewhat marginalizing the middle powers of the Caribbean region (Colombia, Venezuela, and Mexico, which, along with Canada, were expected to be donors to the U.S.-led project), the Reagan CBI project defined the Caribbean in terms of "its weakest links" (Serbin 1990, 5). By association, it extended the image of crisis in Central America to the relatively tranquil area of the insular Caribbean. At the time, the Reagan administration blew hot and cold on the subject of Cuba. The nuclear carriers Eisenhower and Kennedy with their battle groups were sent on "routine" Atlantic Fleet maneuvers in the waters around Cuba. Secretary of State Haig went to Mexico to see Cuban Vice President Carlos Rafael Rodríguez, and General Vernon Walters met with Fidel Castro (Haig 1984, 130–131, 133–136). The U.S. government "made overtures to Fidel Castro to encourage him to rejoin the orbit of the Western Hemisphere," as the president put it, but Castro "wasn't interested" (Reagan 1990, 475).

The Reagan administration's focus on the "American lake," as it had been regarded since the days of Theodore Roosevelt, was mainly geostrategic. The Caribbean Basin Initiative was designed to blunt the Soviet Union's penetration deep into the Caribbean–Gulf of Mexico zone, thus entering the "strategic rear" of the United States and thereby "outflanking" NATO.[12] Military specialists recognized that the Caribbean Basin needed to be differentiated. Paul Gorman, the general who headed the mainland-oriented Southern Command (SOUTHCOM) in Panama from 1983 to 1985, favored "one unified command" for U.S. military forces throughout the entire Caribbean region, but he recognized local as well as institutional realities. Given the diversity of the Caribbean area, he argued, trying to achieve "an embracive coalition" would consume energies better spent on attainable goals. The wiser course would be "to support such sub-regional security groupings as may emerge"—notably that in the Lesser Antilles (the Regional Security System, or RSS) or even a revived

---

[12] The literature on U.S. and Soviet security doctrine regarding Central America, the Gulf of Mexico, the Caribbean Sea, and the Atlantic Ocean during the latter part of the Cold War is extensive. See, for example, the Atlantic Council study co-chaired by James R. Greene and Brent Scowcroft (1984); also, from a Canadian perspective, an examination of Soviet policy (MacFarlane 1985); and from a European perspective, a political-geographical analysis (Foucher 1987). The flanking-of-NATO theme may be found in accounts by two senior U.S. Army officers, General Paul F. Gorman (1989) and General Wallace A. Nutting (1989). The larger historical setting of the evolving U.S.-Soviet rivalry in the Western Hemisphere is given in Henrikson (1986).

Central American confederation—with "the impulse" being left largely to those foreign states. To Gorman, the "free nations" of the Greater and Lesser Antilles seemed barely capable of policing their own citizens, let alone coping with criminals and subversives coming from outside. "Their beginning moves toward collective security deserve our continuing support," he advised (Gorman 1989, 344, 349).[13] Despite the end of the Cold War, much of this American thinking about contingencies in the Caribbean, focused mainly on Cuba, continues to be influential, despite the removal of the Soviet threat itself.[14]

The CBI, the actual economic program, took on a life of its own, even while a proxy war in Central America was being fought. The Caribbean Basin Economic Recovery Act (CBERA) of 1983 codified it, so to speak. Most Caribbean goods—except for textiles, footwear, and leather products, as well as non-quota sugar—gained duty-free access to the United States market for a period of twelve years, through the end of September 1995. Special tax provisions for the tourist sector were added, as well as compensatory measures to support the economies of Puerto Rico (for which President Reagan favored statehood) and the U.S. Virgin Islands.[15] Whatever the limitations and imperfections of the CBERA, such as the inadequate provision for textiles, the fact that, as Winston Dookeran has pointed out, this was "the first time that the United States had granted preferential economic treatment to an entire geographic region," was very well appreciated among Caribbean leaders (Dookeran 1995).

The Reagan administration's Caribbean initiative of the 1980s did cause the American public, and probably many in the Caribbean, to see the region more comprehensively. Though the CBERA itself did not include all Caribbean-area countries—particularly Cuba, but also Colombia and Venezuela on the South American coast—it projected a unifying vision of the Caribbean–Central American expanse. For a century or more, the U. S. government had referred in its Pan American policies to "Latin America and the Caribbean," knit-

---

[13] Anthony Maingot (1989, 248) points out the internal subregional origins of the RSS, characterizing it as "a scaled-down version" of the so-called Adams Doctrine, named for Barbadian Prime Minister J. M. G. M. (Tom) Adams. A critical assessment of external U.S. security support, which through training and joint exercises transformed the local police "into global actors," is presented by Alma H. Young (1991, 10–11).

[14] In October 1979, the Carter administration, concerned about a Soviet combat brigade in Cuba, established a Caribbean Contingency Task Force (CCJTF) at Key West, Florida (Hudson 1987, 597).

[15] A useful summary with an early assessment of the CBI and CBERA is given by Mark Sullivan (1987). The principal authors of the CBI were Assistant Secretary of State Thomas Enders and Special Trade Representative William Brock. Their efforts were considerably assisted by House Ways and Means Committee members Sam Gibbons and Jake Pickle, and, in the end, the Committee's chairman, Dan Rostenkowski (McNeil 1988, 130–132).

ted together in one comity by the formal treaties of the Inter-American System. "Yet, in reality," as Latin American policy advisor Robert Pastor has pointed out, "there are two distinct regions—the Caribbean Basin and South America—with different problems, histories, and relationships with the United States" (Pastor 1992, 22). Reagan's Caribbean Basin Initiative, though at best schematic and two-dimensional in its business and geostrategic orientation, recognized the emerging reality of the Caribbean region as such.

The conceptual premise of U.S. policy was still continentalism, however. The CBI did not cause the United States to identify itself morally with Caribbean society or to subordinate U.S. interests to the wishes of those President Reagan was pleased to call "our other neighbors—neighbors by the sea." U.S. policy was still North American in origin, and its conduct was essentially unilateral. The Caribbean Basin Initiative's agreements under the CBERA were themselves mostly bilateral—a hub-and-spoke arrangement, rather than a network pattern. These agreements bound individual Caribbean and Central American countries to the United States nonreciprocally: the Caribbean Basin partners were clearly the recipients, and the United States was unmistakably the donor.

Sometime late in the 1980s, with the diminution of Cold War pressures, this changed, and the notion of partnership began to be taken more seriously. The scope of U.S. policy toward Latin America and the Caribbean also broadened, and maintaining special relationships with tiny neighbors close by became less diplomatically feasible. With the Bush administration came the Enterprise for the Americas Initiative (27 June 1990), aimed at establishing an economic partnership throughout the entire Western Hemisphere (Bush 1990). Part of President Bush's motivation was probably to "out-Reagan" Reagan, his Republican predecessor having summoned up the Western Hemisphere only rhetorically. A more important purpose was to demonstrate that the Bush administration's view of the world, which tended toward the military and the diplomatic, had a place for business and economics.

For the small nations of Central America and the Caribbean, there was danger in President Bush's "hemispherism"—more modified globalism than expanded regionalism. Being politically insignificant and in the immediate neighborhood, they could simply be overlooked. To be sure, at the start of Bush's term in 1989, when the Nicaraguan Contras were still receiving U.S. aid and Panama's military dictator, Manuel Noriega, was still tolerated, as least the isthmian part of the Caribbean zone commanded official attention. Even then, however, global considerations were primary. For a brief time, the Central American situation affected even the entire East-West political balance. At the Malta summit meeting with Mikhail Gorbachev in October of that year, President Bush said with regard to Central America that Soviet and Cuban adventurism in the Western Hemisphere was the "single most disruptive element" in Soviet-American relations and, more graphically, a "gigantic thorn in your shoe as you try to walk smoothly along" (Beschloss and Talbott 1993, 156). Gorbachev denied any Soviet responsibility for giving surface-to-air missiles to the Salvadoran rebels, causing Bush, in order to consolidate the Soviet abandonment of the rebels, to refer publicly to "our Soviet friends" (Pastor 1992, 84). This exchange virtually removed the Soviet Union as a factor from the Central American scene, and the message was "the Russians aren't coming" (W. S. Smith 1992). The remarkable turnabout of 1989, which almost converted the U.S.S.R. into an ally of the U.S. in the Caribbean, made the whole region less strategically interesting to the Bush administration. Noriega's removal by means of Operation Just Cause in December eliminated a lesser irritant. The continued anti-American defiance of the Castro regime in Cuba now seemed almost irrelevant. Nor did the coup d'état that expelled President Jean-Bertrand Aristide and reimposed military rule upon the people of Haiti, producing waves of boat people, cause great concern.

The Democratic administration under President Bill Clinton in 1993 inherited this mixed legacy, and gave out its own confusing signals. On the one hand, the new president appeared receptive to criticism of the Reagan-Bush CBI approach, which was said to encourage U.S. business investment in Caribbean and Central American countries at the expense of job-creating reinvestments at home (Bradsher 1993). On the other hand, Clinton seemed far more responsive to human rights abuses, as well as economic-welfare needs and environmental-resource problems in places such as Haiti. His attitude toward relations with Fidel Castro and the Cuba question were little changed from the past, partly due to the political clout of anti-Castro Cuban-Americans in Florida, an electorally critical state. Hoping to win and to retain Cuban-American votes there, he endorsed with apparent enthusiasm the 1992 Cuban Democracy Act (CDA), or Torricelli Bill, a measure that somewhat contradictorily both tightened the U.S. embargo against Cuba and opened the door to increased communication with it. The CDA was described by Congressman Robert Torricelli (D.-N.J.) as "the first comprehensive U.S. strategy" toward Cuba, more likely to prove effective because the Castro regime was no longer being economically underwritten by Moscow. "The Cuban Democracy Act defines the situation for Castro in unambiguous terms. When a free and fair election is scheduled, the embargo ends" (Torricelli 1994).

Then came a Clinton proposal. Vice President Albert Gore announced in Mexico City in December 1993 that the president would invite all countries of the Western Hemisphere, except Cuba, to a Summit of the Americas in Miami in December 1994. This plan both transcended the Cuban problem and, given the choice of venue, drew further attention to it—a predictable, though unintended result. The Americas summit was to follow the North American Free Trade Agreement, for which the Clinton administration, after some hesitation, had succeeded in winning congressional support in 1993. The summit proposal implicitly continued the work the Bush administration had started with the hemispheric Enterprise for the Americas scheme.

Mainly, however, the Miami meeting was designed to be a sequel to President Clinton's own initiatives, particularly the first Asia-Pacific Economic Cooperation (APEC) summit held in Seattle in November 1993, to be followed by another gathering of APEC leaders a year later in Bogor, Indonesia. Further, the Americas summit would continue the momentum established by Clinton's success in bringing about U.S. ratification of the results of the GATT Uruguay Round, including the World Trade Organization. Despite the president's earlier characterization of the United States as being more than ever a Caribbean nation, the Miami Summit of the Americas initiative did not, to all appearances, hinge on any particular U.S. government relationship, either with hostile Cuba or with any other Caribbean-area country (Watson 1994).

The Caribbean governments that were welcomed to Miami had to be content with seeking NAFTA parity. Accession to the North American Free Trade Agreement itself was clearly a long-range and perhaps even unachievable goal. Rather than the equivalent of the NAFTA privileges that Mexico enjoyed, they were to be offered a limited Interim Trade Program for Caribbean Basin Initiative (CBI) Beneficiaries, which included duty-free access for certain items of apparel manufactured with U.S. fabric. This did not meet Caribbean countries' requests. "There has been no response on leather goods, petroleum products, and tuna," said Prime Minister P. J. Patterson of Jamaica. In return for accepting the Interim Trade Program, Patterson objected, "We are being asked to sign bilateral investment treaties and intellectual property rights agreements and to waive deferments to developing countries which are allowed under sections of the Uruguay Round." Thus, even the benefits already derived from the global trading regime could be jeopardized.

The Clinton administration, though it recognized the difficulties caused for the Caribbean countries by the inferiority of the CBI to NAFTA, did not give even these interim measures priority. Bowing to protectionist winds in Congress, the administration withdrew the proposed legislation to extend the further benefits to the fifteen Caribbean-area countries. It even withdrew its crucial request to renew the fast-track authority to negotiate trade agreements. Moreover, no rules were drawn up on how the Caribbean Basin countries, or any others, could join the North American club. "It's up to the United States to set the rules for NAFTA accession," lamented Peter Hakim, president of the Inter-American Dialogue in Washington (Brooke 1994b). This was not being done.

The U.S. government at the Miami summit (9–11 December 1994) did, however, pursue the larger objective of achieving among the hemisphere's thirty-four "democratic" leaders (minus Castro) agreement to move toward an eventual Western Hemisphere free trade area. The Clinton proposal was received by the Caribbean and Latin American visitors with, if anything, more enthusiasm than it found in the United States, where some labor union interests and textile companies, with their congressional allies, were outspokenly opposed to it. The hemisphere-wide trade project nonetheless finally emerged as the Free Trade Area of the Americas (FTAA), to be formed by the year 2005 (Sanger 1994b). Encompassing some 850 million people and with approximately $13 trillion in purchasing power, the FTAA would indeed be, as President Clinton said, "the world's largest market" (Brooke 1994c; Cooper and de Córdoba 1994).

The most that smaller Caribbean countries henceforth could expect, it seemed, was to become "building blocks" of a larger hemispheric trading system. The foundation of this would be NAFTA itself, with which all other pieces presumably would have to be aligned. The tiny Commonwealth Caribbean trading community, CARICOM, or a possible larger ACS trading arrangement, obviously would have to conform to this North America–based, or continental, structure. Indeed, in his statement of 1993 in which he averred that the United States was becoming more and more a Caribbean nation, President Clinton used the term "building block" to describe the place of Caribbean countries in "a hemispheric community of democracies linked by growing economic ties and common political beliefs" (Clinton 1993).

Only free-market Chile gained at Miami what many Caribbean countries dreamed of: an offer by the United States, with its Canadian and Mexican partners, to accede directly to the North American Free Trade Agreement. "For one year now, we've been the three amigos," commented Canada's Prime Minister Jean Chrétien. "Starting today, we will become the four amigos" (Cooper and de Córdoba 1994). The implicit "Latin American" emphasis of the American-Canadian-Mexican partners in thinking about trade expansion elsewhere in the hemisphere was clear. That some of the most highly developed, strongly market-oriented island countries in the English-speaking Caribbean—especially Trinidad and Tobago, and perhaps also Barbados—might also be able to meet the "readiness criteria" for direct NAFTA membership evidently did not command attention at Miami. It should have. In one study, those two Caribbean nations received virtually the same high evaluation as Chile (Hufbauer and Schott 1994).[16] All three countries, as Anthony Bryan points out, "apparently were better prepared than Mexico was when it applied for NAFTA membership." Recognizing that the countries of the Caribbean, like those of Latin America, are "not at the same stages of development," and also that the new

---

[16] The Hufbauer-Schott method of analysis gives Trinidad and Tobago an overall performance score of 4.4 and Barbados a score of 4.1. Chile is scored 4.4. The United States, Canada, and Mexico, for comparison, are scored at 4.7, 4.6, and 3.9, respectively (see Hufbauer and Schott 1994, 102).

ACS was not yet fully formed or ready to negotiate, Bryan posed the policy issue for the U.S. government: "The administration must decide soon whether to negotiate free-trade agreements on a bilateral basis with individual countries or begin, in consultation with Mexico and Canada, to enlarge the accession to NAFTA of subregional groupings on a comprehensive basis" (Bryan 1994, 41).

World Politics: From the New World Order to Substantive Symmetry

The wider geographical orientation of the United States toward the Western Hemisphere, though it long antedated the Cold War and thus has some historical legitimacy behind it, is today intellectually suspect. The basic principles of United States foreign policy regarding trade, human rights, and many other issues have become and, assuming that the rest of the world cooperates, will henceforth remain essentially universalist-multilateralist. This is basically the internationalist Wilsonian tradition, further developed by Cordell Hull in his Reciprocal Trade Agreements Program, by Franklin D. Roosevelt in his wartime alliance and plans for the United Nations, and, more recently, by President George Bush in his sketchy but clearly structured New World Order design (Henrikson 1991). Both in its commitment to liberalized world trade and its faith in collective security, the tradition is globalist. Such notions are not geographically confined, or even definable, by regions. In this respect, the latter-day hemispherism of the Reagan, Bush, and Clinton administrations, especially insofar as one-way regional preferences are implied by it, is unorthodox and probably not sustainable, unless it should be necessary to counter large, exclusive, and closed regional blocs in other parts of the world.

A large part of the purpose of the Reagan-Bush-Clinton plan to foster Western Hemisphere trade, even on a fully reciprocal basis, is in fact strategic, aimed at re-establishing the American position in the world at large. Some of the objectives are defensive. They would seem to include slowing the formation, around Brazil, of a semi-exclusive South American trade bloc based on MERCOSUR (Vilches 1994; Brooke 1995). Blunting the urgent drive by the European Union to form a free trade zone with the MERCOSUR countries (Gardner and Fidler 1994; Nash 1994) would also appear to be a goal. "If we don't do it, the Europeans will," as National Security Adviser Anthony Lake frankly stated in response to a question about the Clinton administration's hemispherism (Lake 1994). Secretary of the Treasury Lloyd Bentsen indicated a competitive concern about the role of Japan as well as Europe in the hemisphere. If the United States did not take the lead on trade with the South Americans, he remarked, "we're going to find that the Japanese and the Europeans are going to work to be their partners, and they will be the ones that will be creating jobs back home, instead of this country" (Sanger 1994d). Europe and Asia were also viewed offensively, with an eye toward entering their markets and reforming their trade policies. "The Europeans will be encouraged, to use a delicate word, to be more open in a number of areas we have been concerned about," commented U.S. Trade Representative Mickey Kantor. "And the Asians will also be encouraged to go in this direction, or they too will be left behind" (Sanger 1994a). The timing as well as the sequence of moves being made in U.S. hemispheric trade diplomacy, it therefore seemed, might affect the world's overall economic and perhaps even political balance.

A question arises about such global strategizing: What is its local basis, its grounding in social, economic, and physical reality? The "new geopolitics," as Deputy Secretary of State Strobe Talbott has called the imperatives of realism in the post–Cold War era, is to some degree necessarily regional. It concentrates, in a more comprehensive way than before, on the problems of particular areas. The agenda items of today's world politics, as distinct from traditional international relations, are likely to be concrete and practical, rather than ideological or grandly strategic. Some of these have arisen with systemic changes that have occurred at the end of the East-West confrontation: for example, the reduction of military tension, the opening up of new areas for travel, and the globalization of business activity. Others, however, are inherently rooted in geographic proximity, as President Clinton noted of American concerns regarding the Caribbean in 1993. It is in large part the sheer physical closeness of the United States and the Caribbean that explains why their relations, as he said, "demonstrate the absolute inseparability of foreign and domestic issues" (Clinton 1993).

In explaining the current U.S. official approach to relations with the neighboring Caribbean, Richard Feinberg, a special assistant to the president and the National Security Council's senior director for Inter-American Affairs, implicitly recognizes this interconnection of the systemic and the local. His widely cited observation is that we are now in "the era of substantive symmetry" (Feinberg 1994a). By this formulation he means that the countries of the Western Hemisphere (and, by extension, those of other closely knit regions) have "a shared agenda based on synchronous domestic concerns that can best be addressed cooperatively" (Feinberg 1994b).[17] Such common concerns include political reconciliation and democratic deepening; improving economic competitiveness; and reforming health, welfare, and educational systems. To some degree, the similar agendas of the American nations are "rooted in our common participation in the one-world economy," he observes. "A traveler encoun-

---

[17] Subsequent Feinberg quotations are from this March 1994 text. Some of his earlier ideas regarding the Caribbean–Central American area, and about Third World development issues generally, are expressed in his book *The Intemperate Zone* (Feinberg 1983).

ters common conversations in Santiago, Sao Paulo, and San Francisco." This is partly because, as he declares: "Today, all politics, like economics, is global." The similar issues that are discussed globally arise, however, at one's geographic place—a specifically inhabited "piece of the earth."

President Clinton's decision to host the Summit of the Americas in "the regional center of Miami," Feinberg told the Inter-American Dialogue, illustrates the theme of the administration that, "in a world of integrated markets, domestic interests and foreign policy are tightly intertwined." The daily lives of U.S. citizens are affected by the activities of the neighborhood surrounding them. The processes of job creation via trade and investment, population growth and immigration, as well as drug trafficking and money laundering are all, Feinberg perhaps over-generalized, "regional phenomena." They "link the welfare" of all inhabitants of the Western Hemisphere. Of this, Miami is a regional hub—a city physically closer to sixteen Caribbean and Latin American capitals than it is to Washington, D.C.[18] "Although Latin American leaders have often been seen as distant neighbors in the past, most of those who came here this weekend," as a New York Times reporter commented during the Americas summit, "knew Miami better than the American president" (Brooke 1994a).[19]

One aspect of the growing substantive symmetry of concerns throughout the larger inter-American sphere has been a "conceptual convergence," which makes coordination of policy much easier. In their preparations for the summit, Feinberg noted, the participating hemisphere leaders reached agreement to take action under three broad headings reflecting a new common outlook: democratic governance, prosperity sharing, and sustainable development. As the State Department retitled these, they were: "Making Democracy Work," or reinventing government; "Making Democracy Prosper," or integrating national economies; and "Making Democracy Endure," or safeguarding development by alleviating poverty, raising health and educational standards, and protecting and renewing natural resources (Fact sheet 1994).

The leaders at the Miami meeting did discuss these several matters. While some of them resisted the more intrusive measures of cooperation on grounds that agreement might compromise their national sovereignty, they all consented to push for legislation in their home countries that would, for example, freeze and confiscate the proceeds of drug-related money laundering. Cooperation in extraditing criminal offenders was also collectively pledged. A subsequent meeting of hemispheric justice ministers would be held to discuss the implementation of these promises. Thus democracy, the overarching concept of the summit, could be assisted and made to work in practice.

---

[18] *Washington Post* writer Joel Garreau imaginatively conceived of Miami as situated within a vernacular nation, "The Islands," including the southern part of Florida (Garreau 1981).

[19] U.S. trade with Latin America through Miami rose from $2.4 billion in 1971 to $40 billion in 1993 (Brooke 1994a). It is also a major Caribbean regional shopping center.

The Miami leaders also began consideration of some of the technicalities of greater economic integration among their countries. Besides the summit's centerpiece of agreement on an FTAA by the year 2005, new understandings were reached on an Americas-wide liberalization of capital markets and on the need for a hemispheric investment code. In this context, labor organizations as well as business interests were important. The idea of explicit linkage of future U.S. trade concessions to other hemispheric countries' respect for workers' rights and wage increases was a particular labor-business issue. An unprecedented effort was made, especially by U.S. government participants, to involve elements of civil society in the pre-summit planning and also in the follow-through efforts. Thereby, democracy, a process of social sharing as well as consensus-building, could be enabled to spread.

Environmental and resource matters, too, were taken up at Miami. Vice President Gore and the Costa Rican president, José María Figueres, continued their advocacy of sustainable development efforts in Central America and, by example, throughout the wider Caribbean region. Of all the civic groups engaged in the Miami summit-related discussions, the environmental community was perhaps the most effective.[20] The condition of Haiti, to which access was again possible following the restoration to office of President Aristide, was a special concern. "The Haitian countryside has been stripped of its natural resources and transformed into an ecological wasteland," as Richard Feinberg said to the participants in the Inter-American Dialogue. It was a test case for the summit. "We must invest in the Haitian people by helping to provide primary education and health care," he urged. "We will also help to repair the land, reforest the hills, and purify the waters." Thereby democracy, an intergenerational process as well as an inter-societal one, could be permitted to endure.

Although not the primary issues on the agenda at Miami, problems of peace and security were also on many minds. In particular, the future stability of Cuba, orphaned by the Russian Federation and refused (while Castro remained) the unlimited sale of even food and medicine from the United States, was a deep preoccupation within Caribbean and U.S. government circles (Robbins 1993; Watson 1994). It was also a profound issue within the Cuban-American community, mostly opposed to Castro but divided over the wisdom of delaying dialogue. Without a "soft landing," it was feared, a post-Castro, economically collapsed Cuba might become America's East Germany. The thought of using military force, in addition to the embargo, to bring about change in Cuba was ruled out. During the Miami summit meeting, President Clinton sent a message to *Unidad Cubana*, a coalition of Cuban-American groups which

---

[20] See, for example, the report of the 1994 workshop on the environment and sustainable development sponsored by the University of Miami's North-South Center and the University of the West Indies.

organized an anti-Castro rally in the Orange Bowl, reiterating his desire to see (only) "peaceful, democratic change in Cuba" (Navarro 1994). Moreover, the long noninterventionist tradition of the hemisphere, embodied in articles 18 and 19 of the OAS Charter, still exercised a constraint. Even after the successful, virtually unresisted Haitian operation led by American forces, U.S. officials realized that it would be politically impossible to obtain a consensus at Miami on collective military action (Sanger 1994c). They did not even try.

They did, however, point out some of the newer challenges to security that might have to be addressed together. In the Caribbean area there are sharp evidences of substantive symmetry, or domestic parallelism, in the security field. Because of the small size of many of the states, the problem of local law and order can become a question of a nation's political stability and sovereign independence. The need for an intra-Caribbean dialogue, including the United States, is increasingly recognized. At the Ninth Caribbean Island Nations Security Conference, held in Port of Spain in March 1993, Major General Raymund O'Mara, chief of staff of the U.S. Atlantic Command (LANTCOM), stated the case for "greater regional defense cooperation" so as to deal with "our emerging threats," including narcotics trafficking, racial polarizing, and gang warfare. Protection of coastal waters, widened by the 1982 United Nations Law of the Sea Convention to include 200-mile exclusive economic zones (EEZs), is another area of shared, if not identical, concern. Hurricanes and other natural disasters can simultaneously damage more than one country: the need for a coordinated response warrants discussion on a regional basis. Finally, there is the inescapable topic of regional peacekeeping, extending even to possible military intervention (García Muñiz and Rodríguez Beruff 1994, 121). These are divisive issues.

A recurrent Caribbean temptation has been to try to opt out of the power struggle altogether, an impulse reflected somewhat in the Mexican-sponsored 1967 Treaty of Tlatelolco on hemispheric denuclearization. In 1963 the Trinidadian historian and political leader Eric Williams famously proposed making the Caribbean Sea region a formal zone of peace. "If there is any justice in heaven," as Williams argued, "the area which has the just claim to being declared a zone of peace is the Caribbean area, which has for so long been afflicted by the machinations and maneuvers, the hot wars and the cold wars, of the great powers and superpowers" (quoted in Serbin 1990, 98).[21] The end of the Cold War surely makes the Williams proposal—to define the Caribbean internationally as a Sea of Peace—worthy of sympathetic reconsideration. In

---

[21] The Caribbean zone-of-peace idea was later taken up by the Guyanan diplomat, Lloyd Searwar (1991, 229–230). The similar idea of Central America as a zone of peace, emphasizing confidence-building measures, was floated by the former U.S. Army officer and Latin American political-geography specialist, Jack Child (1992, 154–156).

the Central American part of the zone, examples already have been set by Costa Rica, whose 1949 constitution prohibits the establishment of an army, and by Panama, whose Congress in 1991 passed a constitutional amendment to do the same.[22]

Yet the idea seems unrealistic, an internally necessary fantasy—the obverse of the superpowers' image of the Caribbean Basin in the 1980s as an arena of crisis. In truth, the Caribbean can be exemplary, for despite the incommensurability of some of that region's states with the majority of countries in other regions of the world, the problems it faces are much the same. The logic of substantive symmetry extends worldwide. Secretary of State Warren Christopher, outlining the goals of the Clinton administration's foreign policy in a speech in Boston on 20 January 1995, added to previous major aims (promoting free trade, developing a new security structure for Europe, pushing for a comprehensive peace in the Middle East, combating the spread of nuclear weapons) the new goal of fighting drugs and terrorism (Greenhouse 1995). Christopher's inclusion of this objective as one of the top five priorities, a State Department official explained, represents "a dramatic statement about the importance of transnational criminal activity, literally all over the world" (Ryan 1995). The Caribbean is one area where the battle against international crime must be fought cooperatively, in order to be fought effectively.

Precedents that are set in that region can be used to help establish a more positive pattern of behavior in other regions. An example is the way in which the 1994 multinational peace operation in Haiti was internationalized in order to try to oblige the Russian Federation to accept multilateral handling of comparable problems in the Caucasus, Nagorno-Karabakh in particular being mentioned (Lake 1994). In a striking departure from the exclusionary tradition of the Monroe Doctrine, the U.S. government virtually "invited the world" into Haiti. Not only did CARICOM countries participate, but so too did the United Kingdom and The Netherlands from Europe, as did Israel, India, and Bangladesh. By this rough analogical-political reasoning, peacekeeping units from the Western Hemisphere—most likely Caribbean, Latin American, and Canadian forces, rather than U.S. units—could, conceivably, be introduced into the post-imperial Russian sphere in Eurasia. At a minimum, the theoretical possibility of such extrahemispheric involvement might serve as a deterrent and a restraint.

The imperatives of substantive symmetry, as acted upon in the Carib-

---

[22] It is generally recognized that the Panama Canal needs somehow to be defended after the year 2000, when the Canal Zone is transferred to Panama under the terms of its 1977 basic treaty with the United States. A companion Treaty on the Permanent Neutrality of the Canal grants to Panama and the United States rights to defend the "neutral" Canal beyond the year 2000. An alternative that has been suggested is that the Canal be defended "with a small inter-American force composed of elements of the armed forces of the countries that use the Canal the most" (Pastor 1992, 46, 279–280).

bean region, thus can be productive of a new international order, succeeding the imposed stability of the Cold War bipolar world framework. The Miami Summit of the Americas, as one Latin American participant, President Gonzalo Sánchez de Lozada of Bolivia, said, "marked the first time we haven't come to resist, or to receive instructions" (Cooper and de Córdoba 1994). Intraregional equality and interregional equivalence, rather than spheres-of-influence divisions, must prevail. In the new international political conditions of the post-Cold War world, an order of enlightened reciprocity needs to be developed, involving increased mutual regard and consideration within and across the various regions of the globe. Comparability, interchange, and mutuality are its mechanisms—not the most potent forces, admittedly, but real ones nonetheless.

The "Miami process," as the increased consultations about domestic and foreign affairs in the Western Hemisphere may be called, promises to engender a new international comity, reminiscent of the days of the Good Neighbor Policy and the Alliance for Progress. Already, relations within the Americas are becoming less formal, unfrozen by the end of the Cold War and its attendant political and social democratization. Latin American heads of state are becoming much better acquainted and thus able to work together on a personal basis. Enrique Iglesias, president of the Inter-American Development Bank and foreign minister of Uruguay in the mid-1980s, reflects, "Now they use the familiar tú with each other," and adds, "Their wives know each other" (Brooke 1994a).

The new intimacy expressed in and through the Miami process is no doubt greatest within the neighborhood of the Caribbean, a region to which the United States—"a Caribbean nation," as President Clinton says—today more than ever belongs. The North American and Caribbean spheres are not yet integrated, however, and may never be. Gaps of knowledge and understanding still exist. During the Miami summit meeting, for instance, the Barbadian Prime Minister Owen Arthur, who was worried that "a rising tide" of liberalized trade could "overturn small boats," lectured "a surprised-looking Mr. Clinton about American policy on trade in bananas" (Sanger 1994a). Naturally more interested in the cheaper and (arguably) tastier dollar bananas grown in Central and South America, the United States has not confronted the difficulties of forming a single agricultural market in the larger Caribbean region. Nor, indeed, has the new ACS yet done so. The example, seemingly trivial, reflects different interests and outlooks.

The greatest obstacle to U.S.-Caribbean cooperation of a more systematic kind remains the dilemma of Cuba. Without Cuba (regardless of its leadership), the Caribbean cannot be regionally integrated; yet, with Cuba still under Fidel Castro's leadership, the Caribbean countries cannot acceptably negotiate as a region with the United States. The reason lies not only in the residue of

Cold War thinking in the United States but also in the new "absolute inseparability" of domestic politics and foreign policy, a doctrine upon which President Clinton has insisted (Clinton 1993). The fact that the United States is now a Caribbean nation makes it impossible to ignore internal conditions in the Caribbean region. The very intertwining of domestic and foreign affairs, of course, opens up new paths of contact and channels of communication beyond those of the U.S. and Cuban diplomatic Interest Sections in Havana and Washington, respectively.

Exploratory talk is possible, such as the interview that President Castro gave The New York Times during the Miami summit, which was "no meeting for rebels," he said (Golden and Rohter 1994). Castro then proudly stuck to his guns: "We are not going to negotiate the normalization of our relations on the basis of concessions." Yet he was personally conciliatory. Clearly worried about the consequences for U.S. policy toward Cuba of the sweeping Republican victory in the November 8 congressional elections, he said, of President Clinton's own political future, "We hope he will be successful."[23] In closing the exchange, he asked his American visitors to convey his best wishes to the new Speaker of the House of Representatives, Newt Gingrich, and to the Republican leader in the Senate, Robert Dole. Then, remembering who the new Republican chairman of the Senate Foreign Relations Committee would be, he said: "And also to Jesse Helms. Why not?"

---

[23] One of the persons at Castro's side was the Colombian novelist, Gabriel García Márquez, who had been with President Clinton "talking politics, Faulkner and Cuba" on Martha's Vineyard during the Cuban refugee crisis late in the summer of 1994 (Golden and Rohter 1994).

Bibliography

Allison, Graham T. 1971. *Essence of Decision: Explaining the Cuban Missile Crisis.* Boston: Little, Brown and Company.

Basdeo, Sahadeo. 1993. "CARIBCAN: A Continuum in Canada-Commonwealth Economic Relations." *Canadian Foreign Policy/La politique étrangère du Canada* 1(2): 55–79.

Beschloss, Michael R., and Strobe Talbott. 1993. *At the Highest Levels: The Inside Story of the End of the Cold War.* Boston: Little, Brown and Company.

Blasier, Cole. 1983. The Giant's Rival: *The USSR and Latin America.* Pittsburgh: Univ. of Pittsburgh Press.

Bloomfield, Richard J., ed. 1985. *Puerto Rico: The Search for a National Policy.* Boulder, CO: Westview Press.

Bloomfield, Richard J. and Gregory F. Treverton, eds. 1990. *Alternative to Intervention: A New U.S.-Latin American Security Relationship.* Boulder, CO: Lynne Rienner.

Bradsher, Keith. 1993. "Commerce Dept. in '91 Urged Moves to Caribbean for Low Wages." *The New York Times*, 10 November.

Brooke, James. 1995. "Brazil's Horizons Widening With New Common Market." *The New York Times*, 1 January 1995.

———. 1994. "The Hemisphere Summit Talks: Strictly Business." *The New York Times*, 12 December.

———. 1994. "On Eve of Miami Summit Talks, U.S. Comes Under Fire." *The New York Times*, 9 December.

———. 1994. "U.S. and 33 Hemisphere Nations Agree to Create Free-Trade Zone." *The New York Times*, 11 December.

Bryan, Anthony T. 1994. "The Caribbean and the U.S. Enter the 21st Century." *North-South, the Magazine of the Americas* 4(3): 39–41.

Burrowes, Reynold A. 1984. *The Wild Coast: An Account of Politics in Guyana.* Cambridge, MA: Schenkman Publishing Company.

Bush, George. 1990. Remarks announcing the Enterprise for the Americas Initiative, 27 June. In *Public Papers of the Presidents of the United States: George Bush, 1990*, Book I, 873–877. Washington, DC: U.S. Government Printing Office.

Calderón Fournier, Rafael Angel. 1994. "The Century of the Americas." *North-South, the Magazine of the Americas* 4(3): 5–6.

Casimir, Jean. 1992. *The Caribbean: One and Indivisible*. Santiago, Chile: ECLAC.

Child, Jack. 1992. *The Central American Peace Process, 1983–1991: Sheathing Swords, Building Confidence*. Boulder, CO: Lynne Rienner.

Clinton, William J. 1993. U.S. Interests in the Caribbean: Building a Hemispheric Community of Democracies. Opening statement at news conference with Caribbean leaders, Washington, D.C., 30 August. *U.S. Department of State Dispatch* 4(36): 609.

Cooper, Helene, and José de Córdoba. 1994. "Chile Is Invited to Join Nafta as U.S. Pledges Free-Trade Zone for Americas." *The Wall Street Journal*, 12 December.

de Madariaga, Salvador. 1962. *Latin America Between the Eagle and the Bear*. New York: Praeger.

Dookeran, Winston. 1994. "Caribbean Integration: An Agenda for Open Regionalism." *The Round Table: The Commonwealth Journal of International Affairs* 330: 205–211.

———. 1995. "Preferential Trade Arrangements in the Caribbean: Issues and Approaches." In *Trade Liberalization in the Western Hemisphere*, 437-470. Washington, D.C.: Inter-American Development Bank and ECLAC.

Downes, Richard. 1994. "In Defense of Democracy in the Hemisphere." *North-South, the Magazine of the Americas* 4(3): 20–22, 24–25.

The Environment and Sustainable Development. 1994. Pre-Summit of the Americas Workshop, Kingston, Jamaica, 23–25 October. Coral Gables: North-South Center, Univ. of Miami.

Fact Sheet: The Summit of the Americas. 1994. *U.S. Department of State Dispatch* 5 (39): 647.

Feinberg, Richard E. 1983. *The Intemperate Zone: The Third World Challenge to U.S. Foreign Policy*. New York: W. W. Norton & Company.

———. 1994. Substantive Symmetry in Hemispheric Relations. Address to the Latin American Studies Association, Atlanta, Georgia, 10 March. *U.S. Department of State Dispatch* 5(11): 158–162.

———. 1994. The Summit of the Americas: Creating an Architecture for Inter-American Relations. Address before the Inter-American Dialogue, Washington, D.C., 20 September. *U.S. Department of State Dispatch* 5(39): 644–646.

Foucher, Michel. 1987. "Geopolitical Approaches to the 'Mediterranean Basin' of America." In *International Geopolitical Analysis: A Selection from Hérodote*, ed. and trans. by Pascal Girot and Eleonore Kofman. London: Croom Helm.

García Muñiz, Humberto and Jorge Rodríguez Beruff. 1994. "U.S. Military Policy Toward the Caribbean in the 1990s." In *Trends in U.S.-Caribbean Relations*, Annals of The American Academy of Political and Social Science 533, ed. Anthony P. Maingot. Thousand Oaks, CA: SAGE Periodical Press.

Gardner, David and Stephen Fidler. 1994. "EU Plans Trade Zone With S Americans." *Financial Times*, 25 November.

Garreau, Joel. 1981. *The Nine Nations of North America*. Boston: Houghton Mifflin Company.

Golden, Tim and Larry Rohter. 1994. "An Evening With Castro: 36 Years and No Regrets." *The New York Times*, 13 December.

Gorman, Paul F. 1989. "Defining a Long-Term US Strategy for the Caribbean Region." In *Security in the Americas*, ed. Georges Fauriol. Washington, D.C.: National Defense Univ. Press.

Greene, James R., and Brent Scowcroft. 1984. *Western Interests and U.S. Policy Options in the Caribbean Basin*. Boston: Oelgeschlager, Gunn & Hain, Inc.

Greenhouse, Steven. 1995. "Christopher Outlines Foreign Policy Goals for the U.S." *The New York Times*, 21 January.

Haig, Alexander M., Jr. 1984. *Caveat: Realism, Reagan, and Foreign Policy*. New York: Macmillan.

Henrikson, Alan K. 1991. *Defining a New World Order: Toward a Practical Vision of Collective Action for International Peace and Security*. Medford, MA: The Fletcher School of Law and Diplomacy, Tufts University.

———. 1991. "Mental Maps." In *Explaining the History of American Foreign Relations*, ed. Michael J. Hogan and Thomas G. Paterson. Cambridge: Cambridge Univ. Press.

———. 1986. "East-West Rivalry in Latin America: 'Between the Eagle and the Bear.'" In *East-West Rivalry in the Third World: Security Issues and Regional Perspectives*, ed. Robert W. Clawson. Wilmington, Delaware: Scholarly Resources, Inc.

———. 1993. "A North American Community: 'From the Yukon to the Yucatan.'" In *The Diplomatic Record*, 1991–1992, ed. Hans Binnendijk and Mary Locke. Boulder, CO: Westview Press.

Hudson, Rex. 1987. "Strategic and Regional Security Perspectives." In *Islands of the Caribbean: A Regional Study*, ed. Sandra W. Meditz and Dennis M. Hanratty. Washington, D.C.: Federal Research Division, Library of Congress.

Hufbauer, Gary Clyde, and Jeffrey J. Schott, assisted by Diana Clark. 1994. *Western Hemisphere Economic Integration*. Washington, D.C.: Institute for International Economics.

Judge, Joseph, and James L. Stanfield. 1986. "The Island of Landfall." *National Geographic* 170 (5): 566–599, with accompanying map, "Where Did Columbus Discover America? New Evidence Marks Landfall at Samana Cay."

Kaysen, Carl, Robert A. Pastor and Laura Reed, eds. 1994. *Collective Responses to Regional Problems: The Case of Latin America and the Caribbean*. Cambridge, MA: Committee on International Security Studies, American Academy of Arts and Sciences.

Knight, Franklin W. 1978. *The Caribbean: The Genesis of a Fragmented Nationalism*. New York: Oxford Univ. Press.

Kurlansky, Mark. 1992. *A Continent of Islands: Searching for the Caribbean Destiny*. Reading, MA: Addison-Wesley.

Lake, Anthony. 1994. Discussion following address, American Power and American Diplomacy, at Harvard University, Cambridge, MA, October 21.

———. 1989. *Somoza Falling*. Boston: Houghton Mifflin Company.

Lentner, Howard H. 1993. *State Formation in Central America: The Struggle for Autonomy, Development, and Democracy*. Westport, CT: Greenwood Press.

MacFarlane, S. N. 1985. *Superpower Rivalry and Soviet Policy in the Caribbean Basin*, Occasional Paper No. 1. Ottawa: Canadian Institute for International Peace and Security.

McNeil, Frank. 1988. *War and Peace in Central America*. New York: Charles Scribner's Sons.

Maingot, Anthony P. 1989. "The English-Speaking Caribbean and Hemispheric Security Policy: The Lessons of Grenada." In *Security in the Americas*, ed. Georges Fauriol. Washington, D.C.: National Defense Univ. Press.

May, Ernest R. 1961. *Imperial Democracy: The Emergence of the United States as a Great Power*. New York: Harcourt Brace Jovanovich, Inc.

Nash, Nathaniel C. 1994. "Europe Seeks Latin Free-Trade Ties." *The New York Times*, 7 December.

Navarro, Mireya. 1994. "Miami's Cubans Rally for Solidarity Against Castro." *The New York Times*, 11 December.

Never the twain shall speak. 1994. *The Economist* 33 (7884): 44.

Nutting, Wallace H. 1989. "Coalition-Building in United States Security Policy." In *Security in the Americas*, ed. Georges Fauriol. Washington, D.C.: National Defense Univ. Press.

Orfila, Alejandro. 1986. "The Organization of American States and International Order in the Western Hemisphere." In *Negotiating World Order: The Artisanship and Architecture of Global Diplomacy*, ed. Alan K. Henrikson. Wilmington, Delaware: Scholarly Resources, Inc.

Pastor, Robert A. 1992. *Whirlpool: U.S. Foreign Policy Toward Latin America and the Caribbean*. Princeton, New Jersey: Princeton Univ. Press.

Putnam, Robert D. 1988. "Diplomacy and Domestic Politics: The Logic of Two-level Games." *International Organization* 42 (3): 427–460.

Reagan, Ronald. 1982. "Caribbean Basin Initiative," address before the Organization of American States, 27 February. *Department of State Bulletin* 82 (2061): 1–7.

———. 1983. "Peace and National Security," address to the nation, 23 March. *Department of State Bulletin* 83 (2073): 8–14.

Rippy, J. Fred. 1940. *The Caribbean Danger Zone*. New York: G. P. Putnam.

Robbins, Carla Anne. 1993. "CIA Tells Clinton He Could Face a Crisis in Cuba if 'Serious Instability' Develops." *The Wall Street Journal*, 22 November.

Rusk, Dean, as told to Richard Rusk. 1990. *As I Saw It*, ed. Daniel S. Papp. New York: Penguin Books.

Ryan, Randolph. 1995. "In Speech, Christopher Turns to Crime-fighting." *The Boston Globe*, 21 January.

Sanger, David E. 1994. "Chile Is Admitted as North American Free Partner." *The New York Times*, 12 December.

———. 1994. "An Epidemic Averted: Foot-in-Mouth Disease; For Insalubrious AFTA, Read F.T.A.A." *The New York Times*, 11 December.

———. 1994. "Hemisphere Trade Talks Open; U.S. Hedges Its Hopes." *The New York Times*, 10 December.

———. 1994. "U.S. Envisions an Expansion of Free Trade in Hemisphere." *The New York Times*, 8 December.

Savelle, Max, with the assistance of Margaret Anne Fisher. 1967. *The Origins of American Diplomacy: The International History of Angloamerica, 1492–1763*. New York: Macmillan.

Schmitt, Eric. 1994. "U.S. Gets Caribbean Backing For Possible Invasion Force." *The New York Times*, 31 August.

Searwar, Lloyd. 1991. "The Small State in the Caribbean: Policy Options for Survival." In *Conflict, Peace and Development in the Caribbean*, ed. Jorge Rodríguez Beruff, J. Peter Figueroa, and J. Edward Greene. New York: St. Martin's Press.

Serbin, Andrés. 1990. *Caribbean Geopolitics: Toward Security Through Peace?*, trans. by Sabeth Ramirez. Boulder, CO: Lynne Rienner.

Shultz, George P. 1993. *Turmoil and Triumph: My Years as Secretary of State*. New York: Charles Scribner's Sons.

Smith, Robert Freeman. 1994. *The Caribbean World and the United States: Mixing Rum and Coca-Cola*. New York: Twayne Publishers.

Smith, Wayne S., ed. 1992. *The Russians Aren't Coming: New Soviet Policy in Latin America*. Boulder, CO: Lynne Rienner.

Solís, Luis G. 1994. "Collective Mediations in the Caribbean Basin." In *Collective Responses to Regional Problems: The Case of Latin America and the Caribbean*, ed. Carl Kaysen, Robert A. Pastor and Laura Reed. Cambridge, MA: Committee on International Studies, American Academy of Arts and Sciences.

Stuart, Reginald C. 1994. "Continentalism Revisited: Recent Narratives on the History of Canadian-American Relations." *Diplomatic History* 18 (3): 405–414.

Sullivan, Mark P. 1987. "Caribbean Basin Initiative." Appendix D, in *Islands of the Caribbean: A Regional Study*, ed. Sandra W. Meditz and Dennis M. Hanratty. Washington, D.C.: Federal Research Division, Library of Congress.

Talbott, Strobe. 1994. "The New Geopolitics: Defending Democracy in the Post–Cold War Era." Address at Oxford University, 20 October. *U.S. Department of State Dispatch* 5 (46): 761–763.

———. 1994. "U.S.-CARICOM Efforts to Support UN Security Council Resolution 940." Remarks at Department of State press briefing, Washington, D.C., 31 August. *U.S. Department of State Dispatch* 5 (36): 589.

Torres Rivas, Edelberto. 1993. *History and Society in Central America*, trans. by Douglass Sullivan-González. Austin: Univ. of Texas Press.

Torricelli, Robert G. 1994. "To Keep U.S. Pressure on Castro, Resist Efforts to Lift Economic Embargo." *Sun-Sentinel* (Fort Lauderdale), 14 September.

Vilches, Jorge A. 1994. "Latin Trade Agreements Could Shut Out Nafta Members." *The Wall Street Journal*, 25 November.

Walcott, Derek. 1990. *Omeros*. New York: The Noonday Press/Farrar Straus and Giroux.

Watson, Alexander. 1994. "Update on U.S. Policy Toward Cuba," address before the *Wall Street Journal* Conference on the Americas, New York City, 28 October. *U.S. Department of State Dispatch* 5 (45): 751–753.

Weintraub, Sidney. 1994. "Trade as the Centerpiece." *North-South, The Magazine of the Americas* 4 (3): 30–34.

Young, Alma H. 1991. "Peace, Democracy and Security in the Caribbean." In *Conflict, Peace and Development in the Caribbean*, ed. Jorge Rodríguez Beruff, J. Peter Figueroa, and J. Edward Greene. New York: St. Martin's Press.

Contributors

NANCY BIRDSALL is currently the executive vice-president of the Inter-American Development Bank. She previously held various policy and management positions at the World Bank, most recently as director of the Policy Research Department. Between 1987 and 1991, she was chief of the World Bank's Environment Division for the Latin American region. Ms. Birdsall has also served as chief of the World Bank's Policy and Research Division for the Population, Health and Nutrition Department; senior adviser to the Rockefeller Foundation; and adviser for *Finance and Development*, the World Bank and IMF magazine.

RICHARD J. BLOOMFIELD is a senior visiting fellow at the Thomas J. Watson Institute for International Studies at Brown University, where he is engaged in teaching, research, and writing on foreign affairs. As a career U.S. foreign service officer from 1952 to 1982, he served mainly in Latin America and Washington. He was U.S. ambassador to Ecuador (1976–78) and ambassador to Portugal (1978–82). From 1982 to 1992 he was the executive director of the World Peace Foundation in Boston.

RAMESH DEOSARAN is senior lecturer and head of the Department of Sociology and the ANSA McAL Psychological Research Centre at the University of the West Indies, St. Augustine campus, in Trinidad and Tobago. He is a founder and executive director of CARIBCARE (the Caribbean Institute for Human Rights), and has been a visiting professor at Stanford University, the University of California at Los Angeles, the University of Hawaii, the University of Madras, and the City University of New York. He served a term as an Independent senator in the Parliament of Trinidad and Tobago.

WINSTON C. DOOKERAN, a former fellow at the Center for International Affairs at Harvard University, was the minister of planning of Trinidad and Tobago and on several occasions served as prime minister. Mr. Dookeran also served as a member of the Executive Board of the Inter-American Development Bank and as a governor of the Caribbean Development Bank. He has published several articles in academic journals on issues of Caribbean development and political economy. Mr. Dookeran was a lecturer in economics at the University of the West Indies, and has been a consultant to Caribbean governments and international organizations. In 1991 the University of Manitoba awarded him an honorary doctorate in recognition of distinguished public service.

ALAN K. HENRIKSON is director of The Fletcher Roundtable on a New World Order. The Roundtable is part of an international discussion and research group, formed in 1991 in cooperation with the United Nations Association of the United States of America and The Hitachi Foundation. Professor Henrikson teaches American diplomatic history, contemporary U.S.-European relations, and international relations at The Fletcher School of Law and Diplomacy at Tufts University. He is an associate of the Center for International Affairs at Harvard University, where he has served as counselor on Canadian affairs.

DAVID E. LEWIS is the chief of party of the Caribbean Policy Project in Antigua, West Indies, which focuses on trade and investment policy for the countries of the Eastern Caribbean. The former assistant secretary of state for Caribbean development in the Commonwealth of Puerto Rico, Mr. Lewis has been a trade and business consultant for The Colorado Group in San Juan and for Manchester Trade Ltd. in Washington, D.C. He has held fellowships at the Woodrow Wilson International Center for Scholars, The Ford Foundation, and the Organization of American States, and has lectured on Puerto Rico and the Caribbean Basin at New York University, American University, and Princeton University.

BERTUS J. MEINS, a citizen of the Netherlands, is currently regional economic advisor for Central American and Caribbean countries at the Inter-American Development Bank. He was formerly principal economist in the IDB's Department of Economic and Social Development, in charge of macroeconomic studies of the Bank's Caribbean member countries, and also served as the IDB's representative in Jamaica. Prior to joining the IDB, he served in the Ministry of Finance and the Ministry of Foreign Affairs and Development Cooperation of the Netherlands, and was executive director for the Netherlands, Belgium, Luxembourg, Switzerland, and Ireland in the International Fund for Agricultural Development (IFAD) in Rome.

SARATH RAJAPATIRANA has been with the World Bank since 1975, serving in many different departments and in various assignments, from country and senior economist in the East Asia and Pacific Region, to division chief for trade, industry and finance in the Latin America and Caribbean region. He was director of the 1987 World Development Report, a member of the World Bank Economic Review editorial board, and directed the World Bank comparative study, *Macroeconomic Experience of Developing Countries*. He has published on trade, finance, and macroeconomics. Before joining the World Bank, he was chief of money and banking research in the Central Bank of Sri Lanka.

HAVELOCK R.H. ROSS-BREWSTER, a national of Guyana, is an Alternate Executive Director of the Inter-American Development Bank. He was formerly professor of economics at the University of the West Indies. He served as deputy director of economic affairs at the Commonwealth Secretariat, London, and special research adviser and officer-in-charge of the commodities division, United Nations Conference on Trade and Development, and has been a consultant to governments and regional economic communities in Africa, Asia, and Latin America.

ANDRÉS SERBIN is director of the Instituto Venezolana de Estudios Sociales y Politicos, Caracas. He is former president of the Caribbean Studies Association and former adviser to the Venezuelan Ministry of Foreign Affairs, and has been a consultant to the Latin American Economic System (SELA), UNESCO, the Corporación Andina de Fomento, and a member of the South American Peace Commission. Mr. Serbin is currently vice-president of the Ibero-American Political Science Association and professor of sociology and international relations at the Universidad Central de Venezuela.

CHARLES A.T. SKEETE was formerly Barbados' ambassador to the United States and to the Organization for American States. He now serves as the senior advisor in the Strategic Planning and Operational Policy Department of the Inter-American Development Bank. Mr. Skeete was formerly principal policy specialist for the Department of Plans and Programs at the IDB, where he has worked since 1983. He has served as a member of the Board of Executive Directors of the IDB, representing the English-speaking Caribbean; as permanent secretary of the Ministry of Finance and Planning of the Barbados government; and permanent secretary of the Ministry of Trade.

ELENA M. SUÁREZ is currently the special programs coordinator in the External Affairs Department of the Inter-American Development Bank. After graduating from The Fletcher School of Diplomacy at Tufts University, she joined Caribbean/Latin-American Action, a nonprofit organization founded to promote private sector–generated economic development, as director of program development for the organization's annual Miami Conference on the Caribbean. There Ms. Suárez was also responsible for specific sector programs, including financial services, Section 936 Caribbean Basin Affairs, and Cuba. Throughout her public career, Ms. Suárez has prepared congressional testimony and economic and trade-related papers on Caribbean Basin matters.

AMOS TINCANI is head of the Sustainable Development and Natural Resources Unit of the European Commission in Brussels. He was formerly counselor for development affairs at the Delegation of the European Commission in Washington, D.C. From 1972 to 1979 he was parliamentary secretary to the Consultative Assembly at the Council of Europe in Strasbourg. A native of Italy, he joined the European Commission in 1979, working mainly in the Directorate General for Development (DG VIII) in various operational, negotiating, and policy functions.

KAREN S. WALCH is assistant professor in the department of international studies at the American Graduate School of Management, also known as the Thunderbird School. She teaches graduate courses in negotiation and in the political economy of the Caribbean Basin. She has worked in Honduras and Puerto Rico, and has researched the relationships between the United States and the Caribbean Basin throughout the Caribbean Basin Initiative and NAFTA parity processes in Washington.